# History of Mesoamerica Trivia

Test Your Knowledge with 500 Questions & 1,000 Facts on Ancient Mesoamerican Civilizations and Mexico

# Welcome Aboard, Check Out This Limited-Time Free Bonus!

Ahoy, reader! Welcome to the Ahoy Publications family, and thanks for snagging a copy of this book! Since you've chosen to join us on this journey, we'd like to offer you something special.

Check out the link below for a FREE e-book filled with delightful facts about American History.

But that's not all - you'll also have access to our exclusive email list with even more free e-books and insider knowledge. Well, what are ye waiting for? Click the link below to join and set sail toward exciting adventures in American History.

Access your bonus here: https://ahoypublications.com/

Or, Scan the QR code!

# Table of Contents

# Part 1: Mesoamerican History Trivia

Uncover the Secrets of Mesoamerica with 500+ Questions and Answers About Ancient Civilizations, Sacred Rituals, and Architectural Marvels

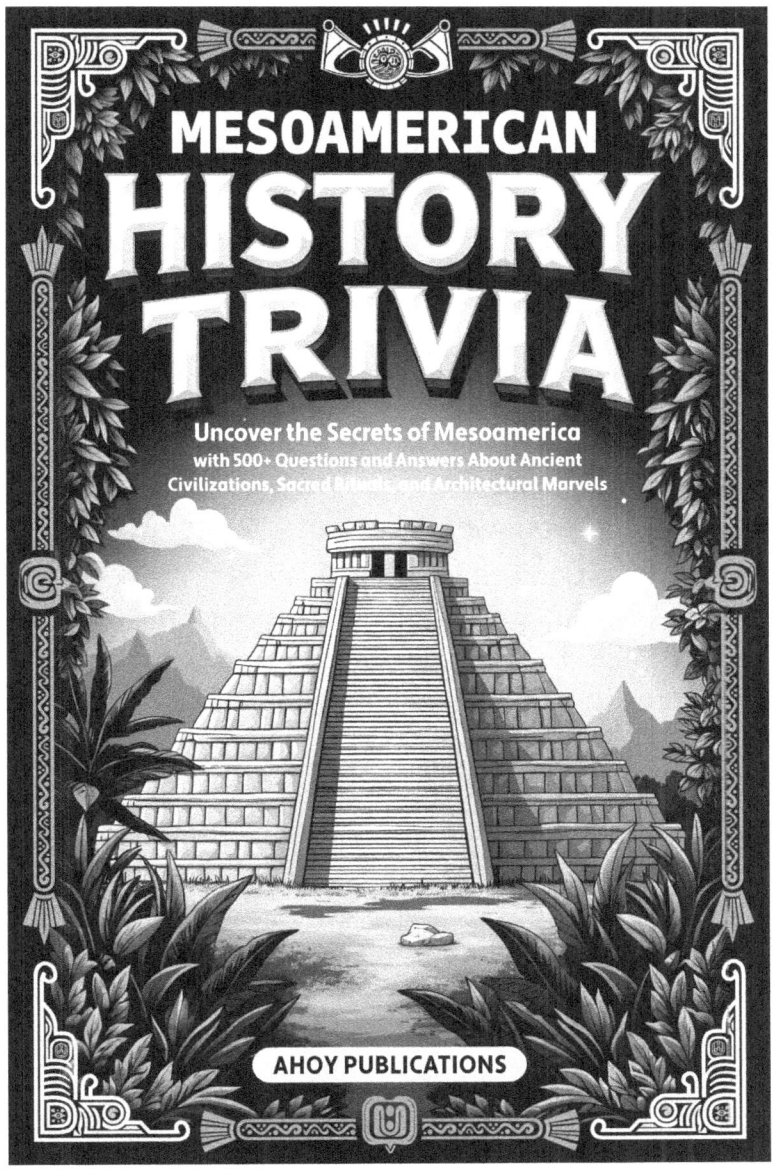

# Introduction

Mesoamerica was a place of thriving civilizations, inventions still in use today, and a source of cultural heritage for the people of modern-day Central America and North America. Its rich historical map contains the adventures and accomplishments of Olmec, Aztec, and Maya civilizations and other notable groups like the Zapotecs, Mictecs, and Toltecs.

This book will discuss how these groups built their cities, kingdoms, and empires, what they believed in, how they lived, and much more. It talks about the significance of their tools and buildings like pyramids and offers plenty of pictures to show how these looked and were used.

However, this isn't just any history book!

It's full of fun facts (some of which may surprise you) and trivia questions that'll help you learn much more about the history of ancient Mesopotamia. It's like taking a journey through a faraway land and having fun while traveling.

The best part? You can take others on this journey, too.

How? You can read the book with them or share the interesting facts you learned. This trivia book is excellent for learning about ancient cultures and can be used for fun activities like playing trivia with your friends and family. Everyone can guess their answer and then check the answer keys. The answers are provided at the end of each chapter, so it will be easy to find out who was right.

Want to know how else you can use this book?

Do you love to research historical facts you read about? If so, you can use the book as a reference to learn more about Mesoamerican civilizations. Any time you want to look up some information, you can see what the book says and then go and research more about the topic.

Keep in mind that this book is about ancient civilizations. Any dates you find on your journey are approximate. While there are some written records of Mesoamerican civilizations, very few contain exact dates, so historians can only guess or estimate when specific events might have happened.

The goal of this book is to give you a fun learning experience – and one for whoever you might share it with. This book shows how much Mesoamericans accomplished in a world very different from the one you live in now. The stories and traditions are incredibly inspiring to modern generations, and hopefully, they will inspire you, too.

If you are ready to start your journey across the colorful Mesoamerican history, please continue reading.

The fun and a treasure trove worth of information await!

# Chapter 1: The Dawn of Mesoamerica: Olmecs, the First Builders

The Olmec Civilization, also known as the first major Mexican civilization, is believed to have lived in Southern Mexico. Based on their findings, archeologists believe that the Olmec society lasted about 1,000 years.

The year 1400 BCE marks the rise of the Olmecs. During this time, the Olmecs had come up with innovative farming methods. Their agricultural practices mainly focused on cultivating beans, corn, and squash.

They cultivated various minerals and volcanic rocks to make their statues, art, weapons, and utensils. The tropical region that the Olmecs lived in also provided them with many natural elements, enriching their trade.

The Olmecs devised an intelligent trading system, which gave them access to many regions to trade with. After a long time of fine-tuning their politics, culture, and religion, the Olmec society began to decline and gradually disappear by 400 BCE.

## Multiple Choice

1. What are the Olmecs mainly known for?
    a. Figurines
    b. Pottery
    c. Colossal Heads
    d. Ancient temples
2. The Olmecs were:
    a. Monotheistic
    b. Polytheistic
    c. Agnostics
    d. Atheists
3. Where was the Olmec civilization located?
    a. Central Mexico
    b. The North Pacific Coast
    c. The Bajio
    d. The Gulf Coast of Mexico

4. Where is the Olmec Pyramid located?
   a. Laguna de los Cerros
   b. La Venta
   c. San Lorenzo
   d. Trez Zapotes
5. What material was used to build the colossal heads?
   a. Marble
   b. Limestone
   c. Jade
   d. Basalt
6. What did the Olmecs use as currency?
   a. Polished ground stone celts
   b. Maize
   c. Chocolate
   d. Salt
7. What did the Olmecs trade?
   a. Figurines
   b. Pottery
   c. Jade
   d. All of the above
8. What sport did the Olmecs play?
   a. Ballgame
   b. Archery
   c. Wrestling
   d. Swimming
9. Who did the colossal heads represent?
   a. The maize god
   b. Were-jaguar
   c. Chief/ruler
   d. The rain god
10. Which archeological site is a major Olmec site?
   a. Tikal
   b. San Lorenzo
   c. La Venta
   d. Chichen Itza

# True or False

1. The Olmec script is deciphered.

   - True
   - False

2. The Olmec civilization influenced other civilizations like the Maya and Aztecs.

   - True
   - False

3. The Olmec civilization predates the Maya and Aztec civilizations.

   - True
   - False

4. The word 'Olmec' was NOT invented by scholars.

   - True
   - False

5. The Olmecs traded polished mirrors.

   - True
   - False

6. The Olmecs were long-distance traders.

   - True
   - False

7. The Olmecs did NOT practice human sacrifice to the gods.

   - True
   - False

8. The Olmec gods' statues had animal and human features.

   - True
   - False

9. The Olmecs did NOT wear ceremonial clothes during their rituals.

   - True
   - False

10. The Olmecs consumed chocolate.

    - True
    - False

# Did You Know?

Did you know that the Olmecs are nicknamed the "rubber people" because they are believed to be the first to produce rubber heavily?

The Olmecs cleverly figured out how to naturally produce rubber. First, they extracted latex from the Castilla elastica tree, also known as the Panama rubber tree, and then they mixed the latex with the moonflower plant's juice to create rubber.

The Olmecs used rubber to waterproof their clothes, make durable balls for their sport, and make elastic rubber bands.

# Fill in the Blanks

You may use any of the following words to fill in the blanks:

| | |
|---|---|
| obsidian | body |
| woven fibers | stelae of note |
| human sacrifice | slings |
| Mesoamerican ball game | serpentine stones |
| clubs | mother civilization |
| basalt | rubber |
| blades | face |
| rubber people | basalt |
| Aztecs | knives |
| colossal heads | iron ores |
| state of Tabasco | fertility |
| Mayas | three |

1. The _____ is a sport that the Olmecs practiced for entertainment and social activity.

2. The ball the Olmecs played with was made of _____.

3. The Aztecs gave their predecessors their name, "The Olmecs," which means "_____." Linguistics later deciphered this name since they understood the language spoken by the Aztecs.

4. These individuals hold high rankings in society, such as warriors or leaders. However, when the gods choose them, they are stripped of rankings and clothes. They become _____ and are presented as offerings to the gods and deities.

5. The Olmecs built _____from_____. It is speculated that these statues represent Olmec leaders. Because these statues are still able to be viewed, they successfully give these rulers immortality.

6. The Olmec civilization is considered to be the _____ of the _____ and the _____. These two civilizations built their cultures off their predecessors. Archeologists can trace the influence of the Olmecs on these two civilizations.

7. One of the most interesting Olmec locations is Complex A, which is located in the _____, which used to be known as La Venta. Archeologists unearthed many offerings, like figurines, mosaics, _____, masks, _____, and jewelry. These offerings were given to the gods as a sign of worship and servitude. The complex is guarded by _____ colossal heads, many sculptures, and _____.

8. The Olmecs crafted their own weapons such as _____, spears, _____, _____, axes, and _____.

9. The blades and knives were made from _____; the Olmecs chose this material for its sharpness. The slings were made from _____, while the axes and clubs were made from _____.

10. ____ and _____ paint was used to decorate the skin for religious and social events. The colors were used symbolically. For instance, red was used to symbolize blood, life, and _____.

# Identify the Pictures

1. What is this mask?

**Image 1**

Response:

_____

_____

_____

## 2. Identify the object.

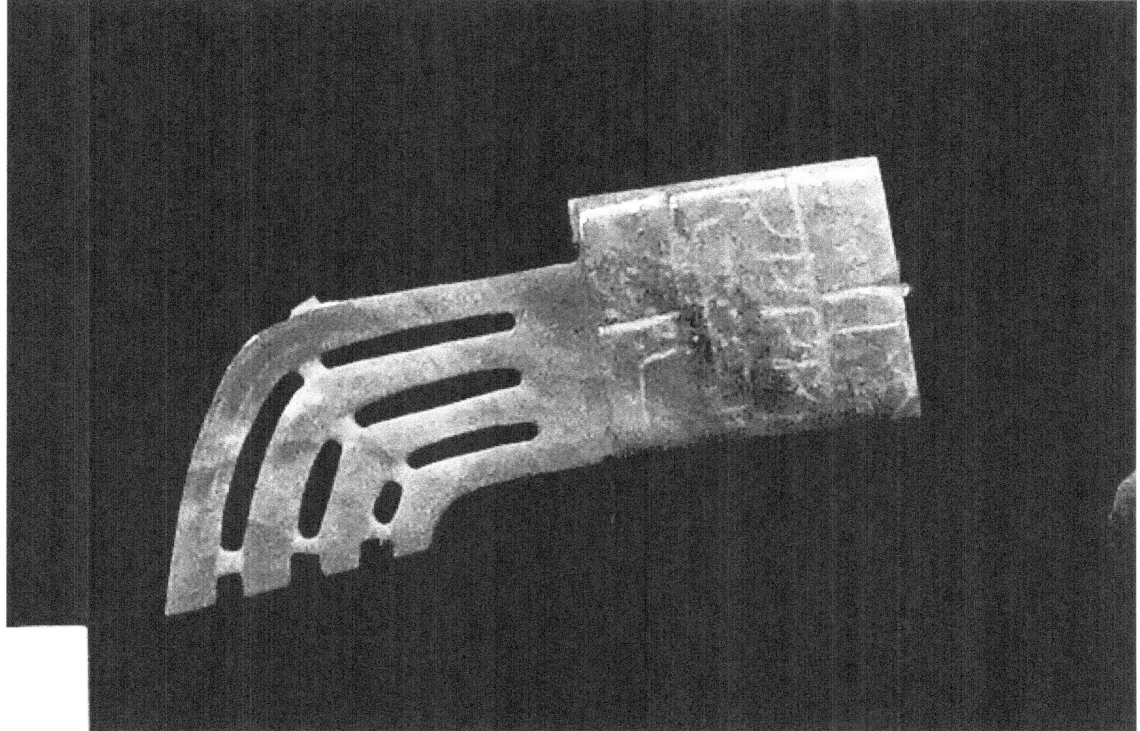

**Image 2**

Response:

_____

_____

_____

## 3. What are these?

**Image 3**

Response:

_____

_____

_____

## 4. What is this?

**Image 4**

Response:

_____

_____

_____

## 5. What is this figurine?

**Image 5**

Response:

_____

_____

_____

6. What does this statue represent?

**Image 6**

Response:

_____

_____

_____

## 7. What are these artifacts?

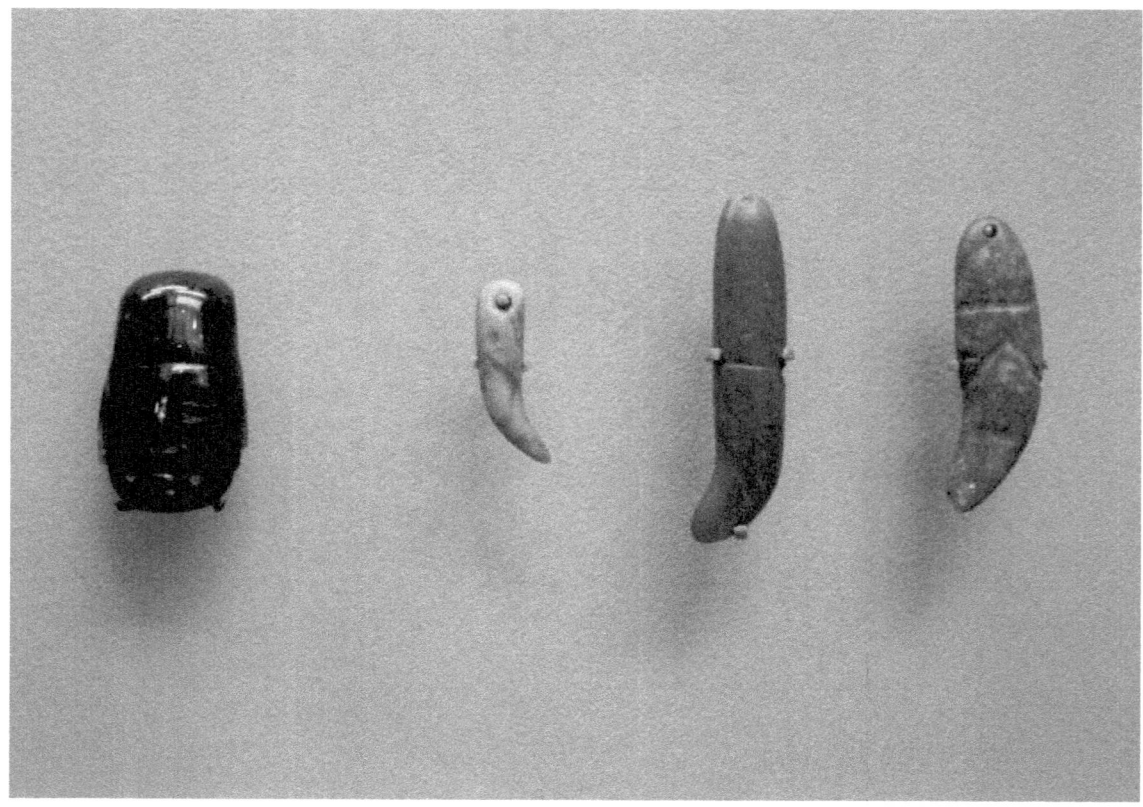

**Image 7**

Response:

_____

_____

_____

8. What does this statue represent?

Image 8

Response:

_____

_____

_____

9. What is this tool and what was it used for?

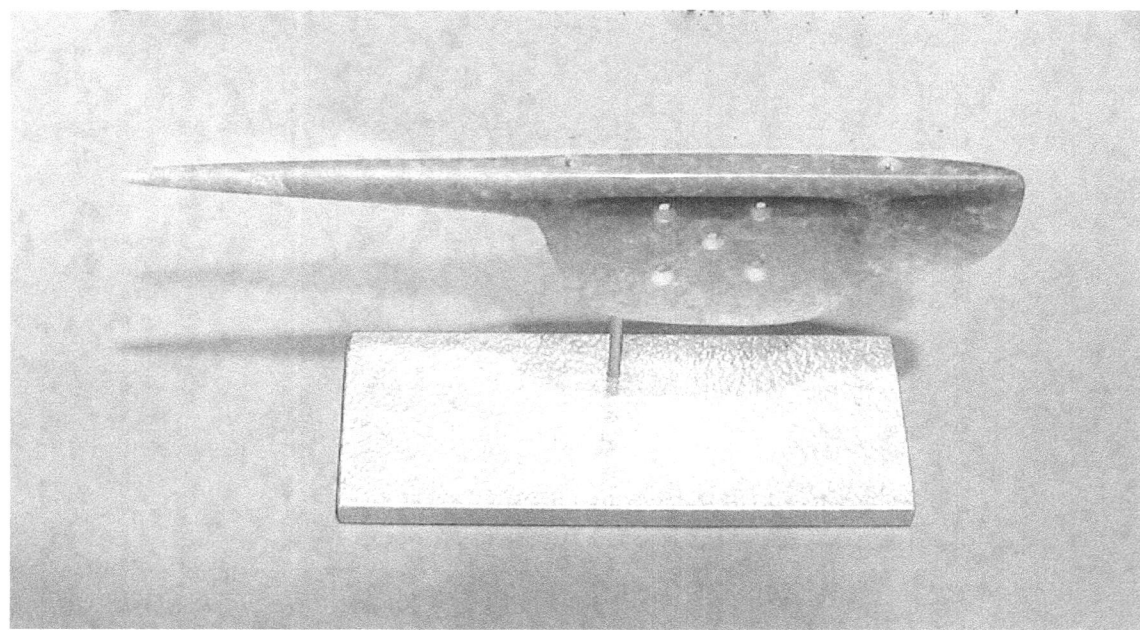

**Image 9**

Response:

_____

_____

_____

## 10. What does this sculpture represent?

**Image 10**

Response:

_____

_____

_____

# Who Am I?

1. I am a supernatural deity known for my transformation and shapeshifting abilities. I am an androgynous entity. I am often depicted as a woman, man, or child with jaguar features. I am believed to bring upon rain that blesses the land. I have rituals and sacrifices dedicated to me so I can bless the Olmecs with my power and blessings.

   _____

2. I am an androgynous deity associated with maize, vegetation, and springtime. I look more human in comparison to other gods. I have almond-shaped eyes, a cleft head, downturned lips, and a band attached to my face. The Olmecs regarded me as their provider and believed in my renewal abilities.

   _____

3. I am believed to have a special connection with the gods and supernatural beings; I hold religious ceremonial gatherings for my people. I offer advice and practice human and animal sacrifice when necessary. I am highly regarded in my society and seen as someone who can provide spiritual remedies.

   _____

4. I was the first Olmec city among the thriving settlements. Around me, political systems have been formed, and I was once known as the great Olmec capital. I was destroyed, abandoned, and replaced as the center of the Olmec civilization. However, I still have many monuments and archaeological sites. Who am I?

   _____

5. My people chose me to hold a great title and perform various duties. The title they have chosen for me is believed to grant me powers. I am seen as a spirit guardian and have the power to morph into different animals. I am capable of evil as I am capable of good. I hold a high rank in society, and my powers are exercised during rituals. I can take on many shapes and deliver messages from the beyond.

   _____

6. I am a space where ceremonies and rituals are performed. Everyone gathers in the place to receive messages from the gods and other powerful entities. Shamans and spiritual guardians are present as well. I am seen as the only sacred space for the chosen ones to receive visions and perform their duties before the Olmecs. I am also a place where different gods are worshipped. This is where Olmecs of various classes give their offerings to the gods.

   _____

# Did You Know?

Did you know that studies show that Olmecs may have practiced cannibalism?

This shocking insight rose to the surface when archeologists uncovered a monument depicting a human sacrifice being devoured by the deity's alter ego. Here is where this discovery gets darker.

The creature that represented the powerful entity's alter ego was, in fact, human. The human assigned this role is known as a "nagual." This means that after the victim was sacrificed to the deities, per the discovered monument, the nagual devoured it as a sign of acceptance of the sacrifice.

# Timeline Questions

1. Arrange these periods of the Olmec civilization in chronological order:

   - Early Formative Period
   - Late Formative Period
   - Initial Formative Period
   - Middle Formative Period

2. Which came first, the Olmec civilization developing its thriving agriculture or the formation of their hunter-gatherer society?

3. Arrange the following Olmec events in chronological order:

   - Building pyramids
   - Establishing a political system
   - Egalitarian society
   - Developing the writing system

4. Arrange these Olmec events in chronological order:

   - La Venta became the capital of the Olmec civilization.
   - San Lorenzo became the largest Olmec ceremonial center.
   - La Venta was destroyed.
   - The Olmec civilization started to thrive, rising from a group of small settlements near the Gulf of Mexico.

# Answer Key

## Multiple Choice Answers

1. **C. Colossal Heads.** (*The Olmecs are primarily known for their giant colossal heads. They also made ceremonial masks, jade figurines, thrones, ceramics, obsidian tools, statues, pottery art, celts, and remarkable jewelry.*)

2. **B. Polytheistic.** (*The Olmecs were polytheistic. They worshipped eight gods, like the giant fish, the feathered snake, the jaguar sun god, the Maize deity, Itzam-Yeh or the Celestial Bird deity, and Ix Chel or The Rainbow lady, among many others.*)

3. **D. The Gulf of Mexico.** (*Archeologists' findings prove that the Olmecs were primarily located in the Gulf of Mexico which is in Tabasco and Veracruz in modern-day Mexico. At the time, the Gulf of Mexico was rich in resources, meaning the Olmecs had fertile soil, forests, and rivers. This helped the Olmecs create their artifacts, construct tools, and trade.*)

4. **B. La Venta.** (*La Venta was the best city to be in for the Olmecs. The community thrived in this city, and in turn, the city was at the apex of culture at the time. The Olmecs built the Great Pyramid there, performed rituals, and built their statues. Leaders instructed workers to bring different materials, like humongous blocks of stone, to the city. This city is also where the Shamans decided to communicate with gods to bring forth fertility and rain for the land for the Olmec people, wherever they may be.*)

5. **D. Basalt.** (*The Olmecs mined basalt from Cerro Cintepec in the Sierra de los Tuxtlas mountains of Veracruz. They transported these massive boulders by using local rivers. These Basalt boulders covered 150km each time they traveled. Basalt was mainly used for building giant colossal heads, but it was also used to build altars, stelae, columns, stone slabs, and figurines.*)

6. **A. Polished Ground stone celts.** (*The Olmecs used polished ground stone to buy maize, squash, beans, and other regional goods. It is suggested that they only use polished stones to purchase local items. However, when they bought foreign goods, they traded stones, figurines, pottery, and other items with other civilizations near them.*)

7. **D. All the above.** (*The Olmecs had an active economic life; they traded with the Nahua groups, Tlaticli, and Chalcatzingo cultures. They traded stones, figurines, polished mirrors, jade, rubber, mica, and serpentine. In return, they received crocodile skin, cocoa, feathers, salt, jaguar skins, jadeite, and other foreign goods.*)

8. **A. Ballgame.** (*The Mesoamerican ballgame was a huge part of the Olmec culture. Not only was it their source of entertainment, but it was also a spiritual practice. Based on their findings, archeologists explain that the ball's movement across*

*the field mirrors the movement in the heavenly cosmos. This insight gives the sport a spiritual layer that enriches this activity. The Olmecs also believed that the parallelism between the ball movement and the celestial bodies ensured the turning of the seasons and heavy rainfall that nourished their fields.)*

9. **C. The Chief/ Ruler.** *(The Colossal heads were built as a representation of Olmec rulers. They date back to 900BC and their height ranges between 1.17 to 3.4 meters tall. Even though these stone heads represented different rulers, they often portrayed the same features. For instance, they all had flat noses, fleshy cheeks, and crossed eyes. However, each colossal head is adorned with a unique headdress. These tall structures were often built around sacred locations as a form of protection since these heads were viewed as guardians for the people and their spiritual practices.)*

10. **C. La Venta.** *(La Venta served as a capital for the Olmec civilization. It is located in Huimanguillo, Tabasco, Mexico. This archeological site contains more than 30 mounds, 4 colossal heads, tombs, 5 altars, and the Great Pyramid. The site is divided into various complexes. Each Complex contains various Olmec structures. For instance, Complex A has royal tombs and ceremonial locations, while Complex C has the Great Pyramid. There are also other Complexes, like Complex B, D, G, and H.)*

## True or False Answers

1. **False.** *(The Olmecs have not left enough script for modern linguistics to decipher their language. While some stones and sculptures have Olmec scripture on them, it is still not enough for linguistics to break apart and understand.)*

2. **True.** *(Seeing as the Olmec civilization is the first Mesoamerican civilization, it is considered to be the mother of all Mexican civilizations to come. Naturally, the Olmecs' successors were heavily influenced by the mother civilization.)*

3. **True.** *(According to historians, the Olmec civilization flourished in 1400 BCE, while the Maya civilization began in 1500 BCE, and the Aztec empire approximately started in 1325 AD.)*

4. **False.** *(The Olmec language wasn't decipherable, so historians didn't have enough data to know what the Olmecs called themselves. This led historians to other Mesoamerican cultures to learn more about the Olmecs. They found that the word "Olmec" was derived from the word "Olmecatl," which is Aztec for "inhabitant of the rubber country." Based on this information, historians dubbed the mother civilization as the Olmec people, inhabitants of the rubber land.)*

5. **True.** *(The Olmecs made mirrors from iron ore, like ilmenite, magnetite, or hematite. They gathered these materials and polished them until they became reflective. They most likely traded mirrors with the Zapotecs and Mayas.)*

6. **True.** *(Recent findings have shown Olmec goods in states like Oaxaca and Guerrero. Archeologists also found Olmec green stones in Guatemala, which proves that the Olmecs were long-distance traders.)*

7. **False.** *(This group practiced various forms of human sacrifice, such as bloodletting and decapitation. The Olmec burials reveal corpses positioned in a unique way that suggests that this corpse was a sacrifice, along with severed skulls.)*

8. **True.** *(Some of the Olmec gods are a hybrid between a spiritual being and an animal, like the feathered serpent, Olmec dragon, were-jaguar, and fish god. Even their physical manifestations are a hybrid between a human body and an animal head, as seen in the Olmec statues of the gods.)*

9. **False.** *(Religious ceremonies were an important part of the Olmec culture. Naturally, the Olmecs had specific attire, tools, and preparations for such events. This included body paint, accessories, and clothing.)*

10. **True.** *(The Olmecs were one of the first Mesoamerican civilizations to produce chocolate from the cacao plant. It was used for medicinal and spiritual purposes.)*

**Fill in the Blanks Answers**

1. Mesoamerican ball game.
2. Rubber.
3. Rubber people.
4. Human sacrifice.
5. Colossal heads, basalt.
6. Mother civilization, Aztecs, Mayas.
7. State of Tabasco, iron ores, serpentine stones, three, and stelae of note
8. Blades, knives, clubs, and slings
9. Obsidian, woven fibers, and basalt.
10. Face, body, and fertility.

**Identify the Pictures Answers:**

1. **Olmec ceramic mask.** *(This jade mask probably belonged to an elite in the society; it is also believed that only the anointed individuals wore masks during religious ceremonies and rituals. This mask has slight feline features, indicating that it might have been associated with the were-jaguar and served as a representation of the clawed idol.)*

2. **This is a winged Olmec jadeite pendant with a severed claw of the jaguar.** The claw represents a more humanized version of the jaguar. *(The Jaguar was viewed as a deity and a symbol of power and authority.)*

3. **Small figurines with symbolic art.** *(While it is unclear whether these figurines were the ones that were traded with other cultures or ones that decorated Olmec*

*houses, they still give people insight into how other figurines may have looked like)*

4. **Stelae.** *(This Olmec stela depicts a woman emerging from the jaguar's mouth; it is located in La Venta. It is unclear whether this stela depicts a goddess or a woman under the jaguar's protection.)*

5. **The Olmec Wrestler.** *(This figurine is made from Basalt. It shows the Olmec wrestler who likely belonged to the political-religious community. This assumption is made based on the figure's facial features. For instance, the mustache and goatee are associated with highly regarded ranks in the Olmec civilization, while the shaved head and physical structure indicate that this man is a wrestler.)*

6. **The were-jaguar.** *(This is a statue of the were-jaguar. As seen in the picture it has both man and jaguar features. It is nude and has almond-shaped eyes and down-turned lips.)*

7. **Pendants.** *(On the far left is a mask pendant worn to merge the wearer's identity with the spiritual entity. It is also believed that the face mask pendant could either offer the wearer a new identity or connect them to one of their ancestors. The other pendants are most likely parts of the jaguar god.)*

8. **The feathered serpent.** *(The feathered snake, also known as Quetzalcóatl, rules the wind and rain. It is one of the most important gods in the Olmec civilization. There is a lot of speculation regarding the serpent god's role in creating the universe and humanity per Olmec beliefs.)*

9. **Bloodletting spoon.** *(Bloodletting is a sacrificial ritual practiced by the Olmecs. The bloodletting spoon's edge was possibly used to pierce part of the body, and the spoon collects the blood. The blood was supposedly used to communicate with the gods)*

10. **The bird god sculpture.** *(The bird god is associated with the heavens, mind-altering substances, maize, and fertility)*

**Who Am I Answers:**

1. Were-jaguar.
2. Banded eye god.
3. Shaman.
4. *San Lorenzo.*
5. Nagual.
6. Sacred temple.

**Timeline Answers:**

1.

- Initial Formative Period: It lasted from 1775 to 1500 B.C.E., Encompassing the time when the Olmecs formed their first settlements until they began to thrive.
- Early Formative Period: Lasting from 1450 to 1005 B.C.E., this period marked the formation of the first larger cities across the Olmec land.
- Middle Formative Period: Encompassing the years from 1005 to 400 B.C.E., this period marks the centralization from one Olmec capital to another.
- Late Formative: The last Olmec period began around 400 B.C.E. and ended with the decline of the civilization.

2. Before developing their thriving agriculture and settling finally, the Olmecs were hunter-gatherers who moved around looking for better territories to find food.

3.

- Egalitarian society: In the early days, the Olmecs weren't divided into ranks. Everyone was equal regardless of wealth, gender, etc.
- Establishing a political system: Once they settled and developed their agriculture, they also established a complex political system.
- Building public buildings: With the rise of the political scene, public speaking and ceremonies became common, so the Olmecs built many buildings, including massive pyramids and religious sites.
- Developing the writing system: As their society developed, the Olmecs needed a more efficient way to communicate and created a unique writing system.

4.

- Around 1200 B.C.E., the Olmec civilization started to thrive, rising from a group of small settlements near the Gulf of Mexico.
- In 1200 B.C.E., San Lorenzo became the largest Olmec ceremonial center.
- After 900 B.C.E., La Venta became the capital of the Olmec civilization.
- Between 300 B.C.E. and 400 B.C.E., La Venta was destroyed, marking the end of the Olmec civilization.

# Chapter 2: Zapotec Zenith: Life in the Clouds of Monte Albán

The Zapotec civilization flourished in the Oaxaca Valley from 700 BCE until 1500 AD. This society heavily influenced the Mesoamerican civilization; they were nothing short of advanced.

Not only did they invent an exceptional writing system, but they also had remarkable city planning, an efficient trading system, and high artistic skills.

The Zapotecs are also known as "the cloud people." This name was attributed to them because the Zapotec people believed that they descended from the clouds to the earth and, upon their death, would return to the clouds again. The name "cloud people" is also interesting since some of the Zapotec society lived on top of the tallest mountain, meaning they were a bit closer to the clouds than most.

This civilization lasted around 2000 years. During this time, they had perfected their trading systems, established their customs, traditions and beliefs, and built their temples.

During their peak, the Zapotec population is estimated to have reached around 35,000 people, just in the capital city.

## Multiple Choice

1. What was the main archeological site that served as the center of the Zapotec civilization?
    a. Chichén Itzá
    b. Monte Albán
    c. San José Mogote
    d. Palenque
2. Who did the Zapotec trade with?
    a. Teotihuacan people
    b. Olmecs
    c. Mayas
    d. All of the above

3. Which of the following crops was the primary food source in the Zapotec civilization?
    a. Maize
    b. Coconuts
    c. Wheat
    d. Berries

4. Which religious system did the Zapotecs follow?
    a. Animistic
    b. Monotheism
    c. A and D
    d. Polytheistic

5. What kind of government did the Zapotecs have?
    a. Theocracy
    b. Anarchy
    c. Monarchy
    d. Oligarchy

6. The Zapotec rulers were believed to have direct contact with which of the following?
    a. Spirits of the dead
    b. Trees
    c. gods
    d. The sun

7. Which of the following primarily supported the Zapotec economy?
    a. Woodworking
    b. Agriculture and trade
    c. Metalworking
    d. Pottery production

8. Which of the following mediums were the Zapotec artisans known for?
    a. Pottery
    b. Metal statues
    c. Mosaic art
    d. Ceramics and stone

9. Which present-day country represents the center of the Zapotec civilization?
    a. Peru
    b. Mexico
    c. Brazil

10. Which of the following people conquered the Zapotecs?
    a. The Spaniards
    b. The Aztecs
    c. The Olmecs
    d. The Mayas

# True or False

1. The Zapotecs developed an alphabetic writing system.

    - True
    - False

2. Burial at sea was the traditional way to send mummies into the afterlife.

    - True
    - False

3. The Zapotecs are direct descendants of the Aztecs.

    - True
    - False

4. Like the Olmecs, the Zapotecs had a ball court to practice their sport.

    - True
    - False

5. Rainforests were the most vital feature of the Zapotec agriculture.

    - True
    - False

6. The Zapotecs worshipped female goddesses alongside male ones.

    - True
    - False

7. During their religious ceremonies, the Zapotecs often offered human and animal sacrifices to the gods.

    - True
    - False

8. Slavery was not practiced in the ancient Zapotec civilization.

    - True
    - False

9. Monte Albán is known for its Edificio de los Danzantes cravings.

    - True
    - False

10. The Zapotecs had instruments made from human bones.

    - True
    - False

**Did You Know?**

Did you know that the Zapotecs made jewelry beads from bones?

Like many Mesoamerican civilizations, the Zapotecs had gorgeous jewelry. They made their beads from different materials, including animal bones.

Some bone bead was made from dogs' limbs and teeth, others from turkeys' legs. The Zapotecs were refined with their bead production; they wouldn't use the bone bead in its raw form.

After they extracted the bones they needed, they filed the surface, shaped the bone into a bead, and polished it. Some bone beads were colored red; others were left with their natural color.

# Fill in the Blanks

You may use any of the following words to fill in the blanks:

| | |
|---|---|
| Public offices | animism |
| gift giving | Pitao Cozobi |
| polytheism | animal sacrifice |
| Aztecs | public service |
| dance of feathers | Otomanguean |
| Chatino | human blood |
| Guelaguetza | Mixtecs |
| maize god | Huechaana |
| Duality | |

1. The maize god known as _____ represented fertility and life longevity. Rituals such as offerings and dancing were offered to this god as a means of prayer. The Zapotecs believed consistent offerings would result in abundant crop yield, securing their food supply.

2. The Zapotec people had a rich spiritual life; it was a hybrid between _____ and _____. The average Zapotec person prayed to different gods to earn their favor and be bestowed their blessings. Still, they also believed that spirits could be in trees and take different forms in nature.

3. The Zapotecs developed their own language, which was derived from the _____ language family in Mexico. The Zapotec language is a mix between _____ and Zapotec language.

4. The goddess, _____, is seen as the mother of the Zapotec people. Some believe that she gave birth to mankind, while others think that she created man out of clay. She also rules the _____ and _____, which reflects her femininity and life-giving abilities.

5. The Zapotec people came up with a system known as _____; this system allowed people to trade or exchange services, such as farming goods, labor, public services, money, and gifts.

6. The Guelaguetza system is divided into three types of service a Zapotec can provide: _____, _____, and _____ during feasts.

7. The Zapotec people had conflicts with various groups, such as the _____ and the _____. Their civilization rapidly declined after they lost the war to the Spaniards due to their lack of advanced weapons and political naivete.

8. During rituals for Pitao Cozobi, the _____, people offered _____ and _____. While these practices may seem extreme, it was a normal tradition for the Zapotec people since they ensured that they would continue to receive blessings from the gods and avoid their wrath.

9. The _____ was one of the Zapotec traditions, where they reenacted their conquests. Their reenactment involved music, dance, and dialogue.

10. Zapotec spirituality had a binary nature to it, where the gods had a certain _____ to them. This can be seen through Zapotec beliefs, the same god who blesses their land with rich rains can also flood their homes. Their belief in this binary expression of the gods' powers validates their emphasis on sacrifice and offerings to the gods to only receive their blessings.

# Identify the Pictures

1. Who is this?

**Image 11**

Response: _____

## 2. Who does this statue represent?

Image 12

Response:

_____

_____

_____

3. Who does the statue represent?

**Image 13**

Response:

_____

_____

_____

## 4. Who does this statue represent?

**Image 14**

Response:

_____

_____

_____

## 5. What is this instrument?

**Image 15**

Response:

_____

_____

_____

## 6. What is this object?

**Image 16**

Response:

_____

_____

_____

7. What is this object?

**Image 17**

Response:

_____

_____

_____

## 8. What is this object?

**Image 18**

Response:

_____

_____

_____

9. What is this object?

**Image 19**

Response:

_____

_____

_____

10. Identify what this object is and who it is dedicated to.

**Image 20**

Response:

_____

_____

_____

# Who Am I?

1. I am one of the most revered gods in Zapotec spirituality. I am known as the god of life, fertility, and maize. Ancient Zapotecs used to hold ceremonies in my honor; they gave me abundant harvest and danced for me as part of the ritual. This was meant to appease me so that they could ensure my continued blessings on their maize harvest.

   _____

2. We travel long distances and significantly enrich our economy. We exchange goods with neighboring cities and often enter hostile environments to fulfill our duties. We are known to bring rare resources and luxurious items home. We are highly respected for our bravery and endeavors in our community. We are given privileges that are not often given to the ordinary man.

   _____

3. I am the god of the underworld. My mother is the Earth goddess, and I have 2 wives, one of whom is known as "mother death." I also represent luck and masculinity. This can be seen through the Zapotec depictions of me as a well-endowed god. I am also the god of chickens and protect crops and lands. To appease me, the people sacrificed adults, children, and animals to me.

   _____

4. I am known as the rain god. I rule the lighting, thunder, and rain. The people worshipped me to bless the crops with life-giving water. It is believed that I created humans from clay and put life into them using my godly lightning.

   _____

5. I am an innovative practice that helps grow crops and nurture animals. The Zapotecs were among the first civilizations who used me to develop their small settlements into large urban centers.

   _____

6. We are the lowest level of the Zapotec hierarchy, and we have no rights. Our daily task was transporting blocks from one place to another and carrying out jobs that the locals don't typically do. We were either war captives or criminals.

   _____

**Did You Know?**

Did you know the Zapotecs had two different calendars to navigate their days?

One calendar was used for seasonal activities and agriculture planning, while the other was for societal and religious rituals. The agriculture calendar is known as the "Yza calendar," which had 365 days divided into 18 months, each with 20 days.

The religious calendar was called the "Piye calendar", which had 280 days in it that were divided into 13 months, each with 20 days.

The Piye calendar also helped indigenous people name their newborns. The Piye calendar has names for each day during the month, each named after a certain animal.

**Timeline Questions:**

1. Arrange the following Zapotec events in chronological order:

   - Mitla became the Zapotec capital
   - Monte Albán became the capital of the Zapotecs in the Oaxaca Valley
   - San Jose Mogote was named the capital of the Zapotec civilization
   - Monte Albán grew and became an even more important center

2. When did Monte Albán reach its peak, before or after it became known as Monte Albán II?

3. Did the agricultural development of the Zapotecs lead to complex hierarchical structures and innovations like the writing systems and calendars, or did the development of these structures and practices cause agriculture to thrive?

4. Arrange the following Zapotec events in chronological order:

   - Development of the urban planning system
   - Building of the first pyramids
   - The Mixtec influence begins to show in the Zapotec culture.
   - Development of the writing system

# Answer Key

**Multiple Choice Answers:**

1. **B. Monte Albán.** *(Monte Albán served as the Zapotec capital in ancient Mesoamerican. Historians speculate that the Zapotecs made Monte Albán their capital for its remote location. This site is located in Oaxaca on top of a great mountain away from nearby valleys. This is why Monte Albán is known as the "disembodied capital")*

2. **D. All of the above.** *(The Zapotecs had a rich trading network. They traded with various people, such as the Olmecs, Mayas, and Teotihuacan people.)*

3. **A. Maize.** *(Maize was the staple crop for many Mesoamerican civilizations, including the Zapotec people. It held such great importance that the Zapotec worshipped a Maize god so that he blessed them with a rich Maize harvest every year.)*

4. **C. Animistic and Polytheistic.** *(The Zapotecs believed in many gods, which makes them polytheistic. They also believed that trees had spirits or that spirits could reside in nature around them, making them animistic.)*

5. **C. Monarchy.** *(The Zapotec were ruled by a monarchy, which meant that a king and his heir ruled them would rule after him. The king had his advisors, military, and noblemen. The Zapotec kings often had statues depicting them in their royal attire.)*

6. **C. The gods.** *(In Mesoamerican civilizations, it was a common belief that the kings were descended from the gods, which meant they had direct contact with them.)*

7. **B. Agriculture and trade.** *(The Zapotec economy was held by trade and agriculture. The merchants traded natural resources found in their land for luxurious resources brought home to their people.)*

8. **D. Ceramics and stone.** *(The Zapotec artisans mainly used stones and ceramics in their artwork. They used various stones, such as turquoise, jade, obsidian, serpentine, and basalt.)*

9. **B. Mexico.** *(The Zapotecs occupied many cities in Mexico, such as Monte Albán and Mitla.)*

10. **A. The Spaniards.** *(The Spaniards defeated many people in Ancient Mexico, including the Zapotecs. This invasion took place in the 16th century, marking the end of the Zapotec civilization.)*

**True or False Answers**

1. **False.** *(Like many ancient Mesoamerican people, the Zapotecs used hieroglyphics to express themselves and document their daily lives.)*

2. **False.** *(The dead went through the proper Zapotec funerary ritual. They were buried beneath the ground with jewelry, pottery, and artifacts. The items the dead*

were buried with were meant to be used in the afterlife and protect them as they traveled to the underworld.)

3. **False.** *(the Zapotecs came from southern Mexico and were not direct descendants of the Aztecs. The Zapotec civilization is older than the Aztec civilization.)*

4. **True.** *(The Pok-A-Tok game was a common sport in most Mesoamerican civilizations.)*

5. **False.** *(Terraces were the most important feature since they boosted agricultural productivity and fostered urban growth. They also preserved rainwater, which was later used to water crops.)*

6. **True.** *(Given that the Zapotecs were polytheistic, they worshipped many gods and goddesses.)*

7. **True.** *(The Zapotecs often sacrificed various beings to the gods. Some were animals, while others were human. The sacrifice could involve bloodletting, beheading, or both.)*

8. **False.** *(The Zapotecs had slaves who were either war captives or criminals. The slaves often had to do hard labor.)*

9. **True.** *(Monte Albán is known for its beautiful carvings depicting ancient Zapotec art.)*

10. **True.** *(The Zapotecs created everyday tools and ritual instruments from human bones.)*

**Fill in the Blanks Answers:**

1. Pitao Cozobi.
2. Animism and polytheism.
3. Otomanguean, Chatino.
4. Huechaana, moon, and water.
5. Guelaguetza.
6. Public service, public office, and gift giving.
7. Mixtecs and Aztecs.
8. Maize god, animal sacrifice, and human blood.
9. Dance of feathers.
10. Duality.

**Identify the Pictures Answers:**

1. **The Bat god.** *(This is a statue depicting the bat god of the underworld.)*
2. **Cocijo, the rain god.** *(A statue of Cocijo, the rain god, wearing his godly attire with ear flares.)*
3. **Statue of the Monte Alban Priest.** *(A statue of a Zapotec priest wearing his jewelry, headwear, and earl flares.)*
4. **Maize god.** *(A statue of the Pitao Cozobi, the maize god.)*

5. **Bat foot with claws.** *(This is an instrument shaped like a bat foot with claws. Given that bats were associated with sacrifice and death, this instrument was most likely used during sacrificial rituals.)*

6. **Funerary urn.** *(This funerary urn is most likely depicting the lightning god.)*

7. **Zapotec pendant plaque.** *(This pendant was most likely attached to a garment.)*

8. **Urn figurehead.** *(Many Zapotec urns had a figurehead like this one.)*

9. **A Snake pottery piece.** *(This snake pottery piece showcases how the Zapotecs created totems or pottery figurines.)*

10. **A funerary urn of Cocijo.** *(This is a funerary urn placed with one of the deceased nobles.)*

**Who Am I Answers:**

1. Pitao Cozobi
2. Merchants
3. Pitao Bezelao
4. Pitao Cocijo
5. Irrigation system
6. Slaves

**Timeline Answers:**

1.

- Around 500 B.C.E., San Jose Mogote was named the capital of the Zapotec civilizations.
- Between 500 B.C.E. and 450 B.C.E., Monte Albán became the capital of the Zapotecs in the Oaxaca Valley.
- Between 150 B.C.E. and 150 C.E., Monte Albán grew and became an even more important center.
- Around 900 C.E., Mitla became the Zapotec capital.

2 Monte Albán reached its peak between 200 and 800 A.D., a few centuries after it grew and became known as Monte Albán II.

3. The Zapotecs' ability to develop their initial agricultural practices led to the establishment of complex hierarchical systems and innovations like writing systems and calendars.

4.

- Urban planning started developing around 800 B.C.E. when the first larger settlements were established.
- The Zapotecs built their first pyramids around 800 B.C.E. - 600 B.C.E. at Monte Albán.
- The Zapotec writing script was developed around 900A.D
- The Mixtec influence began to show in the Zapotec culture after 900 A.D., marking the decline of the Zapotec civilization.

# Chapter 3: The Mystique of the Maya

One of the most dominant Mesoamerican civilizations is the Maya, and there is a reason for that. The Mayas had a rich culture and left behind a myriad of artifacts, complex structures, and temples.

The Maya empire flourished in 1500 BCE and lasted approximately 3500 years. The Mayas lived in many places; they covered the Yucatán Peninsula as well as Chiapas, Belize, El Salvador, Guatemala, and Honduras.

No wonder Maya temples can be found in numerous countries and cities!

The Mayas stood out in many areas, such as their complex trading and agriculture systems, mathematics, linguistics, astronomy, astrology, advanced calendars, architecture, sports, and politics.

Like many Mesoamerican cultures, the Mayas were highly spiritual. They dedicated ceremonies and offerings to the gods and had their own ideologies about how the world came to be and the afterlife.

## Multiple Choice

1. The Mayans occupied different cities and countries. Which of the following cities was their capital?
    a. Tikal
    b. La Venta
    c. Teotihuacan
    d. Monte Albán
2. The Ancient Mayas created an advanced calendar system to keep up with agricultural routines, religious rituals, and social events. How many calendars did they have?
    a. 1
    b. 2
    c. 3
    d. 4

3. Ancient Maya sites are known for their magnificent structures. Which of the following structures are they most known for?
    a. Religious temples
    b. Pyramids
    c. Altars
    d. Tombs

4. Various animals were considered sacred in Ancient Maya. Which of the following animals were highly regarded?
    a. Chaac and deer
    b. Feathered serpent, jaguar, chaac, and macaw
    c. Kukulkan, crocodile, monkey, and jaguar
    d. Macaw, deer, Feathered serpent, and crocodile

5. The Ancient Mayas believed that one of the planets was the Sun's companion and was associated with the feathered serpent god. Which of the following planets fits this description?
    a. Neptune
    b. Mercury
    c. Saturn
    d. Venus

6. Like many ancient civilizations, the Mayas had strict burial rituals. The deceased was often buried with several objects. Which of the following objects were found with the Maya mummy?
    a. Jade, face mask, mirror, and pottery
    b. Cocoa beans, emeralds, jade, and scarab
    c. Beads, pottery, jewelry, and wands
    d. Face mask, scarab, beads, and jade

7. The Mayas had important figures in society who helped them understand heavenly messages from the gods and the stars, which of these figures were assigned with that task?
    a. The queens
    b. The kings
    c. The priests
    d. The scribes

8. The Mayas made great advancements in mathematics, including developing their own numerical system. Which of the following is the system they used?
    a. Binary
    b. Vigesimal
    c. Decimal
    d. Quinary

9. Their numerical system had an important symbol for a vital number that helped the Mayas calculate large sums and distances. Which concept is that?
    a. Negative numbers
    b. Infinity
    c. Fractions
    d. Zero
10. The Mayas documented important information on stone and paper. What kind of paper did the scribes use to write on?
    a. Bark paper
    b. Papyrus
    c. Parchment
    d. Clay tablets

# True or False:

1. The Mayans developed their own language and used a hieratic writing system to document their daily lives and important discoveries.
   - True
   - False

2. Like many Mesoamerican civilizations, the ancient Maya played a ball game known as "Pok-A-Tok."
   - True
   - False

3. Known for their architecture, the Mayas built their structures and cities with bamboo sticks and wood.
   - True
   - False

4. The Mayas built their pyramids, ball courts, temples, and observatories in harmony with planetary movements and constellations.
   - True
   - False

5. The observatory at Xochicalco has a hole in the ceiling so that the sun shines through it during certain times of the year.
   - True
   - False

6. The Mayan kings were tasked with receiving messages from the gods, performing rituals, and interpreting calendars.
   - True
   - False

7. Maya kings and royalty were buried in the pyramids.
   - True
   - False

8. The Post-classic period marks the peak of the Maya civilization.
   - True
   - False

9. El Castillo, a pyramid with 91 steps on each side, was built for Kukulcan.
   - True
   - False

10. The Mayas used wheels to transport large stones from one place to another.

- True
- False

**Did You Know?**

Did you know that the Mayas practiced facial scarification?

The Mayas had their own beauty standards. To them, beauty was not just about physical appeal but also about its spiritual and social significance.

They practiced many body modifications, from ear flares to artificial cranial deformation and facial scarification. It is most likely that the elites were the ones to scar their faces with artistic patterns, although this practice was not strictly done by the nobles of society.

The Mayas believed that the more painful the body modification is, the closer they are to the gods. In other words, the more physical alterations one has, the more blessed they are by the deities.

# Fill in the Blanks

You may use any of the following words to fill in the blanks:

| | | |
|---|---|---|
| Maya zodiac | dental modification | the sky world |
| screen-fold book | 8 | rare mollusk shells |
| Catholic priests | astronomical | 4 |
| artificial cranial deformation | beekeeping | the Madrid Codex |
| rituals | 74 | pyramids |
| the Maya Codex of Mexico | Venus table | 584 |
| animals | the middle world | Kinich Ahau |
| human femur bones | Maya dentists | heads |
| the Dresden Codex | La Danta | the underworld |
| constellation | astrological | the Paris Codex |
| religious | two | agriculture |
| Venus | deities | 20 years |

1. The Maya scribes were tasked with writing the codices, which is a_____ made from bark paper. There was an ample number of codices. However, most of them were destroyed by _____ and conquistadors. The codices that survived are preserved in different museums; these codices are known as _____, _____, _____, and _____.

2. _____ scribes wrote the Dresden Codex, and it contains _____ pages with rich information on astronomy and Maya spirituality. The scribes used fine brushes to paint colorful images in the Codex; they also included various _____ and _____ tables. For instance, the Dresden Codex is famous for its _____ and conjunctions of _____, moon, and planets. Calendars and _____ references were also included.

3. The Madrid Codex is similar to the Dresden Codex in many ways, except that it contains detailed data on _____. It also includes details on deer hunts and _____.

4. Like the Dresden Codex, the Maya Codex of Mexico contains detailed astronomical data on _____ and its movements in the sky. The Venus cycle is spread out across ____ days, which are divided into _____ sections. Each section represents a certain _____. The Mayas paid close attention to Venus' movements since it had great cultural importance to them and influenced their warfare.

5. The Paris Codex contains astrological information, such as the _____, which is a bit similar to modern zodiac signs. The Codex contains a list of various _____, and each of them is linked to various constellations that move across the ecliptic. It also has information on ceremonies and _____ that take place throughout _____.

6. The Mayas built ____ types of _____. Some were strictly built for the gods, while others were built for religious ceremonies and rituals. Located in El Mirador, _____ is considered to be one of the largest ancient structures to this day.

7. The Mayas practiced _____, which was a process of filing the teeth into certain shapes. Scholars suggest that filing the teeth was used for aesthetic reasons. Furthermore, _____ drilled holes into teeth to decorate them with colorful stones. It is said that decorating the teeth with stones was done when one entered adulthood.

8. The Mayas used _____ to display their social status and enhance their physical appearance. Children were given instruments to wear on their _____ to meet Maya beauty standards.

9. According to Maya cosmology, the creator divided the world into 4 sections: _____, _____, the earth, and _____. It was believed that certain gods ruled each section. For instance, many Maya gods were associated with the underworld, while _____ is the ruler of the sun.

10. The kings were buried with _____, hieroglyphs carved into _____, and a mask with jade stones on it.

# Identify the Pictures

1. Who is this?

Image 21

Response:

_____

_____

_____

2. What is this object?

Image 22

Response:

_____

_____

_____

## 3. What is this?

**Image 23**

Response:

_____

_____

_____

4. Identify what this is.

**Image 24**

Response:

_____

_____

_____

5. What is this figurine of?

Image 25

Response:

_____

_____

_____

## 6. What is this?

**Image 26**

Response:

_____

_____

_____

7. Who is this figurine of?

**Image 27**

Response:

_____

_____

_____

## 8. What is this object?

Image 28

Response:

_____

_____

_____

9. What is this jewelry made of?

**Image 29**

Response:

_____

_____

_____

## 10. What is this mask, and what is it made of?

**Image 30**

Response:

_____

_____

_____

# Who Am I?

1. The Mayas believed me to be the son of the creator god. I am often depicted in many myths and legends as the Mayas highly regarded me. I am believed to have provided the people with vital information, such as maize harvesting and creating medicine. I am also believed to have helped with Maya hieroglyphs and creating accurate calendars. I am viewed as the god of wisdom, knowledge, and instructions. In my people's art, I am depicted as an old man with a toothless grin, and it is suggested that my name means lizard house.

   _____

2. I am celebrated among Maya women as the goddess of womanhood. I bless them with love, fertility, and childbirth. I have the power to heal and destroy. I rule over the moon and its cycles, meaning I control the tides. I am depicted as a woman with a snake on my head and a rabbit on my lap. My spouse is one of the most powerful gods in Maya beliefs, and with him, I have given birth to many gods.

   _____

3. I am a multifaceted god; I rule over many areas in the average Maya's life. For instance, I am seen as the god of traders and cacao and the god of destruction, chaos, and war. Both merchants and warriors pray to me for different reasons. In Maya art, I could be either depicted as the warrior god or the merchant god, but I am never shown as both warrior and trader. As the warrior god, I am shown to defeat enemies. As the merchant god, I am shown as an old man with a long cane carrying some goods on my back.

   _____

4. I am the sun deity, believed to have created heat, light, time, and the four directions. I am also the god of battle, and my worshippers seek my protection before war by offering sacrifices and dancing. I am depicted as an old man with crossed eyes and a large nose. My physical features influenced the Maya's beauty standards, and it was known that a child born with crossed eyes like mine was blessed by me. Oftentimes, I am depicted as an eagle, deer, or jaguar.

   _____

5. We are known to bridge the gap between the physical and the spiritual realm. In our society, we are the healers and spiritual guides. We are known to interpret dreams and receive visions and prophesies. We also medicate the people using herbs and natural remedies. We conduct ceremonies and rituals which are necessary to

appease the gods. Given our role in society, we are highly regarded, which gives us social and political power. Often, leaders and kings seek our advice and guidance.

_____

6. My name translates to "the solitary god"; I am seen as the creator of the universe. The Mayas believed my godly manifestation came from love, light, thought, sound, and energy. There are no depictions of me because the Mayas believed me to have no physical attributes or manifestation. I am the source of all things.

_____

**Did You Know?**

Did you know that the Mayas conducted human sacrifices underwater?

Human sacrifice did not just take place on top of a great pyramid; it was also done underwater.

The Mayas used to dive into underwater caves, also known as cenotes. These caves were believed to be portals to the underworld. To this day, human bones still reside within these underwater Maya caves.

Chichén Itzá was a significant urban center and a site of great political, economic, and religious influence in the Maya region. Its strategic location facilitated trade and cultural interaction between different cities and regions.

# Timeline Questions

1. Arrange the following events in chronological order:

    - The approximate date of the oldest Mayan burial sites.
    - The date when the Mayan King K'utz Chman of Retalhuleus tomb was built.
    - The Mayans started to interact with the Olmec culture.
    - The Mayans thrived in the Archaic Period of Mesoamerica.

2. Arrange these dates in chronological order:

    - The Mayans began to form larger settlements at Copan and Chalchuapa.
    - The first major Mayan city is built.
    - The Mayans built the first large buildings in the city of El Mirador.
    - Farming villages began to form across the Maya region.

3. Arrange these events in chronological order:

    - The Mayans built their first pyramids.
    - The first Mayan calendar was recorded in a stone.
    - The Mayans started relying on farming to expand their cities.
    - The Mayans developed their writing system.

4. Did the Mayans have a monarchy before the Classic Period or was this form of rule developed afterward?

# Answer Key

**Multiple Choice Answers:**

1. **A.** *(Tikal was strategically located, which eased the trading system. It was also rich in resources, making the Mayas economically wealthy. Tikal also had a strong military, which allowed the Mayas to dominate cities around them)*

2. **C.** *(They had 3 calendars, and they used them simultaneously. The first calendar is the long count, and this one identifies the years. The second calendar, called the "Tzolkin" calendar, was made for religious purposes. The third one is called "Haab," also known as the civil calendar.)*

3. **B.** *(The Mayas have built multiple pyramids, each of them unique and serving certain purposes. The Mayas are known to be the people who have built the largest pyramid known to mankind which is La Danta.)*

4. **B.** *(There were a lot of animals that represented divine qualities for the Mayas, however, there are certain animals that had the most importance. These animals served as totems for very powerful gods.)*

5. **D.** *(Venus played a great role in Maya culture. It was seen as the sun's companion, and its movements dictated spiritual ceremonies and warfare. It was so important that it had its own table in more than one Maya codex. These tables showed the planet's movements in the cosmos and its cycle.)*

6. **A.** *(Maya kings were buried with face masks made from jade to protect them through their afterlife journey. The mirrors were also placed for the same reason)*

7. **C.** *(The kings were believed to have descended from the gods, which made the Mayas believe that their rulers had communication with the gods and could, therefore, receive messages and relay them to the people.)*

8. **B.** *(The Mayas used the vigesimal system, which means it was based on the number 20. They used dots and bars to write down the number, so one dot meant one unit and a bar meant five.)*

9. **D.** *(The Mayas are considered to be one of the earliest civilizations to use the concept of zero in their calculations. At the time, this was groundbreaking because it helped make accurate calculations.)*

10. **A.** *(The Mayas used bark paper to write vital information on it and create their codices. Using bark paper made it easier for scribes to write and paint on it instead of carving the same data into stone.)*

**True or False Answers:**

1. **False.** *(The Mayans used Hieroglyphic writing. They had little drawings in the square, and each drawing or square represented a letter from the alphabet.)*

2. **True.** *(Like other Mesoamerican civilizations, the Mayas played Pok-A-Tok with a ball made from rubber. The sport held spiritual significance since it represented how planetary bodies move in the sky.)*

3. **False.** *(The Mayans mainly used stone to build their cities and structures such as pyramids and temples.)*

4. **True.** *(They believed that the movement in the cosmos influenced the movement on earth, so to achieve harmony, they built their structures based on planetary movements.)*

5. **True.** *(It is highly suggested that the Mayas put a hole in the ceiling to better track the yearly solar cycle and hold religious ceremonies when the sun shines through the temple.)*

6. **False.** *(It is a priest's duty to hold religious ceremonies, perform rituals, and receive visions and prophesies. The kings were believed to receive messages from the gods but did not hold spiritual gatherings as priests do.)*

7. **False.** *(The Maya pyramids were used for multiple purposes, either for rituals and religious ceremonies or worship.)*

8. **False.** *(During the Classic period, the Maya civilization saw great political, economic, religious, artistic, and architectural advancements.)*

9. **True.** *(Each step has 91 steps, making 364 steps when added together. Now add 364 steps to the one step on top of the pyramid, and you get 365 steps representing 365 days of the year.)*

10. **False.** *(It is suggested that they used sleds and rails instead of wheels. It is suggested that they thought the wheels would not be functional.)*

**Fill in the Blanks Answers:**

1. Screen-fold book, Catholic priests, The Madrid Codex, the Dresden Codex, the Paris Codex, and the Maya Codex of Mexico.
2. 8, 74, astronomical, astrological, Venus table, constellation, and religious.
3. Agriculture and beekeeping.
4. Venus, 584, 4, deities.
5. Maya zodiac, animals and rituals, and 20 years.
6. 2, pyramids, La Danta.
7. Dental modification, Maya dentists.
8. Artificial cranial deformation, heads.
9. The sky world, the middle world, and the underworld, **Kinich Ahau**.
10. Rare mollusk shells, human femur bones.

**Identify the Pictures Answers:**

1. **One of the paddler jaguar gods.** *(The paddler jaguar god ferries the god across the water.)*

2. **Tiny Maya figurine.** *(Judging by the headwear, ear flares, and facial scarification, this figurine is either a priest or one of the Maya nobles.)*

3. **A Maya green pendant.** *(This pendant is most likely made from jade, and it was either attached to a necklace or given to a Maya noble.)*

4. **Maya Calendar on stone.** *(This is one of the Maya calendars carved into stone.)*

5. **Figurine of a Maya woman wearing her jewelry.** *(A pottery figurine that shows a Maya woman wearing her ear flares and jewelry.)*

6. **Ear flare set.** *(A set of ear flares used by Mayas to style their ears.)*

7. **A Maya figurine of a soldier.** *(This soldier figurine showcases what Maya pottery looked like.)*

8. **Chichen Itza Disc.** *(This is a disc found on the throne in Chichen Itza.)*

9. **Maya jewelry made from jade.** *(This is a set of Maya jewelry that showcases what the ancient Mayas used to wear.)*

10. **Funerary Maya mask made from jade.** *(This mask most likely belonged to Maya kings since they were buried with jade masks covering their faces.)*

**Who Am I Answers:**

1. Itzamna
2. Ix Chel
3. Ek Chuaj
4. **Kinich Ahau**
5. Shamans
6. Hunab Ku


**Timeline Answers:**

1.

- The Mayans thrived in the Archaic Period of Mesoamerica between 7000 B.C.E. and 2000 B.C.E.
- The approximate building date of the oldest Mayan burial sites is around 2600 B.C.E.
- The Mayans started to interact with the Olmec culture around 1200 B.C.E.
- ◦ The Mayan King K'utz Chman of Retalhuleus tomb was built around 700 B.C.E.

2.

- Farming villages began to form across the Maya region around 2000 B.C.E.
- The Mayans began to form larger settlements at Copan and Chalchuapa around 1000 B.C.E.
- The Mayans built the first large buildings in the city of El Mirador around or after 600 B.C.E.
- ◦ The first major Mayan city was built around 600 B.C.E.

3.

- The Mayans developed their writing system in 700 B.C.E.
- The Mayans started relying on farming to expand their cities around 600 B.C.E.
- The first Mayan calendar was recorded in stone in 400 B.C.E.
- The Mayans build their first pyramids around 100 B.C.E.

4. The Mayans introduced monarchy (and the rule of a king) around 300 B.C.E., before the beginning of the Classic Period.

# Chapter 4: Teotihuacán: The Avenue of the Gods and the Pyramids of Mystery

Lying in the Valley of Mexico, the ancient city of Teotihuacán was once one of the largest cities in Mesoamerica. After giving home to thousands of people two centuries ago, the city was abandoned, but it continued to serve as a worship site for one of the greatest Mesoamerican empires, the Aztecs, almost until their fall in the early 16th century.

With its colorful murals, towering pyramids, numerous temples, and artifacts, Teotihuacán has rightfully become a UNESCO World Heritage Site.

In this chapter, you can test your knowledge about the history and culture of this ancient Mesoamerican center. You'll take a virtual tour of its many structures, explore its architecture and religion, and witness the rise and fall of the city.

## Multiple Choice:

1. What is the famous street in Teotihuacán that translates to "Avenue of the Dead"?
    a. Calzada de los Muertos
    b. Camino de los Dioses
    c. Paseo de la Historia
    d. Ruta de los Tesoros
2. Which cities did the people of Teotihuacán conquer during their peak?
    a. Chichén Itzá
    b. Calakmul
    c. Tikal
    d. Copán
3. What kind of influence did Teotihuacán have in Mesoamerica?
    a. Cultural and military
    b. Military and arhitectural
    c. Religious, cultural, and architectural
    d. Political
4. According to archaeologists, which civilization was the most likely builder of Teotihuacán?
    a. Zapotec

      b. Mixtec

      c. Maya

      d. All of the above

5. *Talud* and *tablero* were two terms used in what aspect of Teotihuacán life?

      a. Architecture

      b. Religion

      c. Cleaning

      d. Trading

6. What was the Pyramid of the Moon associated with?

      a. Sacrifice to gods

      b. Fertility

      c. Cleansing

      d. Beauty

7. What was the original color of many buildings and artifacts in Teotihuacán?

      a. Grey

      b. Blue

      c. Green

      d. Red

8. When was Teotihuacán the most powerful?

      a. Between 100 B.C.E. and 650 A.D.

      b. Between 200 B.C.E. and 750 A.D.

      c. Between 100 A.D. and 500 A.D.

      d. Between 200 A.D. and 350 A.D.

9. What did Teotihuacán export the most?

      a. Obsidian and ceramics

      b. Textiles and food

      c. Weapons

      d. Gold

10. Besides a place of worship, what other role did the Temple of the Feathered-Serpent have?

      a. Trading place

      b. A giant clock

      c. Public speaking post

      d. None of the above

**Did You Know?**

Many ancient buildings of Teotihuacán are decorated with colorful murals.

These were not just beautiful paintings and works of art. They give a sneak peek into the lives of the locals, including their religion and society. Many of their murals symbolized either a male or female deity, both shown from the front.

The deities are surrounded by symbols linked to them (for example, fertility symbols for the goddess and a lightning bolt for the god).

Teotihuacán artists also liked to include animals in their murals — with jaguars, owls, and coyotes appearing in many of them. Many murals were simply painted red, but others had blue, green, and even yellow colors in their palettes.

The murals were always flat, although sometimes the image of the deities was raised slightly to show their importance.

# Fill-in-the-Blank

You may use any of the following words to fill in the blanks:

| | | |
|---|---|---|
| solstices | creation | sacrifice |
| equinoxes | craftsmen | festivities |
| largest | volcanoes | rituals |
| decoration | worship | abandoned |
| Egyptian | entire | gods |
| thousands | household | defined |
| centuries | mysterious | astronomy |
| gods' | lowest | |

1. The Pyramid of the Sun in Teotihuacán is one of the _____ pyramids in the world.

2. Teotihuacán had _____ of homes, many _____, and pyramids as large as the well-known _____ pyramids.

3. The pyramids were the place of _____ and _____. Evidence of sacrifice had been found in the _____ layers, meaning it was used to gain the _____ approval for building.

4. The Aztecs named Teotihuacán the birthplace of the _____ because they believed that the city was the center of all _____.

5. The ancient city of Teotihuacán was built amid several large _____.

6. The Pyramid of the Sun and the Pyramid of the Moon are aligned with astronomical events, like _____ and _____. This shows that the city's builders had great knowledge of _____.

7. The Ciudadela was the largest _____ place in the city. Archaeologists suggest that it was large enough for the _____ population of the city to gather for _____.

8. The city had many _____ even for making similar objects. For example, some clay artists worked on creating figurines used in _____ while others made clay items for _____ and _____ purposes.

9. The fall of the city occurred several _____ before the Aztecs discovered it.

10. How Teotihuacán went from a thriving city to an _____ site is just as _____ as its rise to fame.

# What am I?

1. I am a large central Teotihuacán structure used for rituals and ceremonies. I have a round shape and a sunken interior. What am I?

   _____

2. I am a unique artifact found at the foot of the Pyramid of the Sun but was later removed for my protection. Now you can see me in a museum. What am I?

   _____

3. You can see my likeness between the feathered serpent heads of one of Teotihuacán's most beautiful pyramids. I am also a symbol of a powerful Mesoamerican deity. What am I?

   _____

4. I am a structure named after a combination of words that, in some translations, mean feather and butterfly. In other translations, my name means feather and serpent. I am also a god and a ruler. What am I?

   _____

5. I gave the city the ability to make important resources. I am very large, and I feed people and allow them to thrive and take care of their families. A powerful Mesoamerican deity governs my birth, life, and death. What am I?

   _____

6. The people of Teotihuacán found me in volcanic mines and traded me to other cultures. I was used to making weapons, decorations, and tools locally and by other civilizations. I have a striking color, but I am not vibrant. What am I?

   _____

7. I am known as the written language of Teotihuacán. I don't have words, but people have used me to express their thoughts, feelings, and traditions. What am I?

   _____

8. You can see me on the heads of priests depicted in Teotihuacán art. I have one eye of an owl, a long snout, and bird feathers. What am I?

   _____

9. I have metallic dust on my walls, golden glitter on my floors, and hundreds of clay shapes that look like stars, planets, and other elements of the cosmos. I am connected to one of the most prominent structures at Teotihuacán. What am I?

_____

10. I am a light volcanic rock that's easy to carve and carry. I was used to making sturdy buildings with intricate decorations all across Teotihuacán. What am I?

_____

# True or False

1. Teotihuacán was the capital of the Aztec Empire.

   - True
   - False

2. Teotihuacán was named by its original builders.

   - True
   - False

3. Teotihuacán had no military structures.

   - True
   - False

4. There are no written records from Teotihuacán.

   - True
   - False

5. The Pyramid of the Moon was built in the 1st century.

   - True
   - False

6. The Palace of Quetzalpapálotl is decorated with images that symbolize the earth.

   - True
   - False

7. Besides religion and architecture, trade and astronomy also played crucial roles in the success of Teotihuacán.

   - True
   - False

8. The city's grid layout was filled out with buildings randomly.

   - True
   - False

9. Some stones used for building the most important structures in Teotihuacán were much lighter than others.

   - True
   - False

10. There are only three pyramids in Teotihuacán.

    - True
    - False

# Picture-Based

1. Describe what this picture depicts.

Image 31

Response:

_____

_____

_____

## 2. What's shown in this picture?

**Image 32**

Response:

_____

_____

_____

3. What can you tell about this Teotihuacán reconstruction?

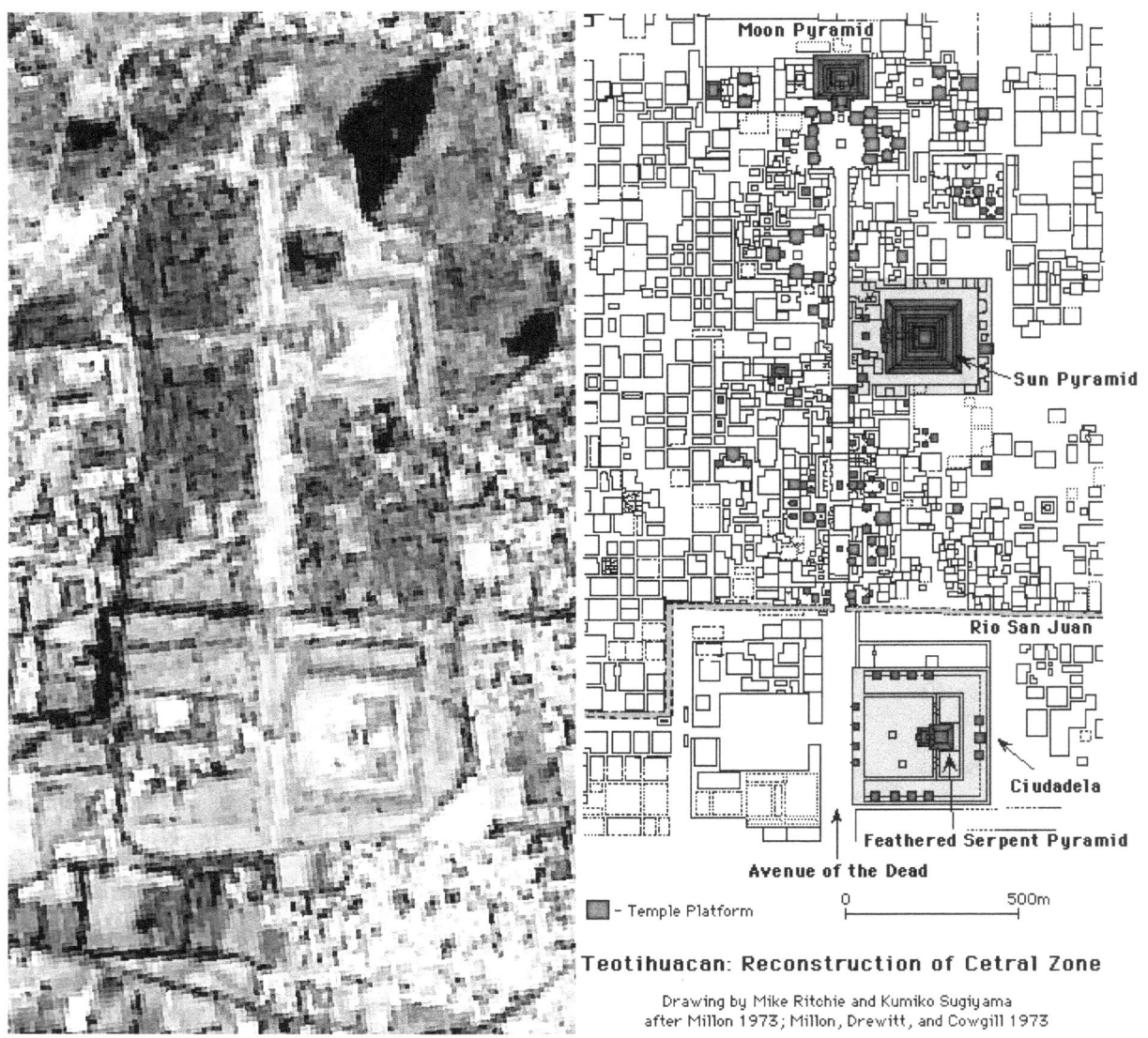

Image 33

Response:

_____

_____

_____

4. Which Teotihuacán structure is located on the far left?

**Image 34**

Response:

_____

_____

_____

## 5. Where is this sculpture located?

Image 35

Response:

_____

_____

_____

6. What's shown in this picture?

Image 36

Response:

_____

_____

_____

7. Who does this mural depict?

**Image 37**

Response:

_____

_____

_____

8. What was the purpose of this object?

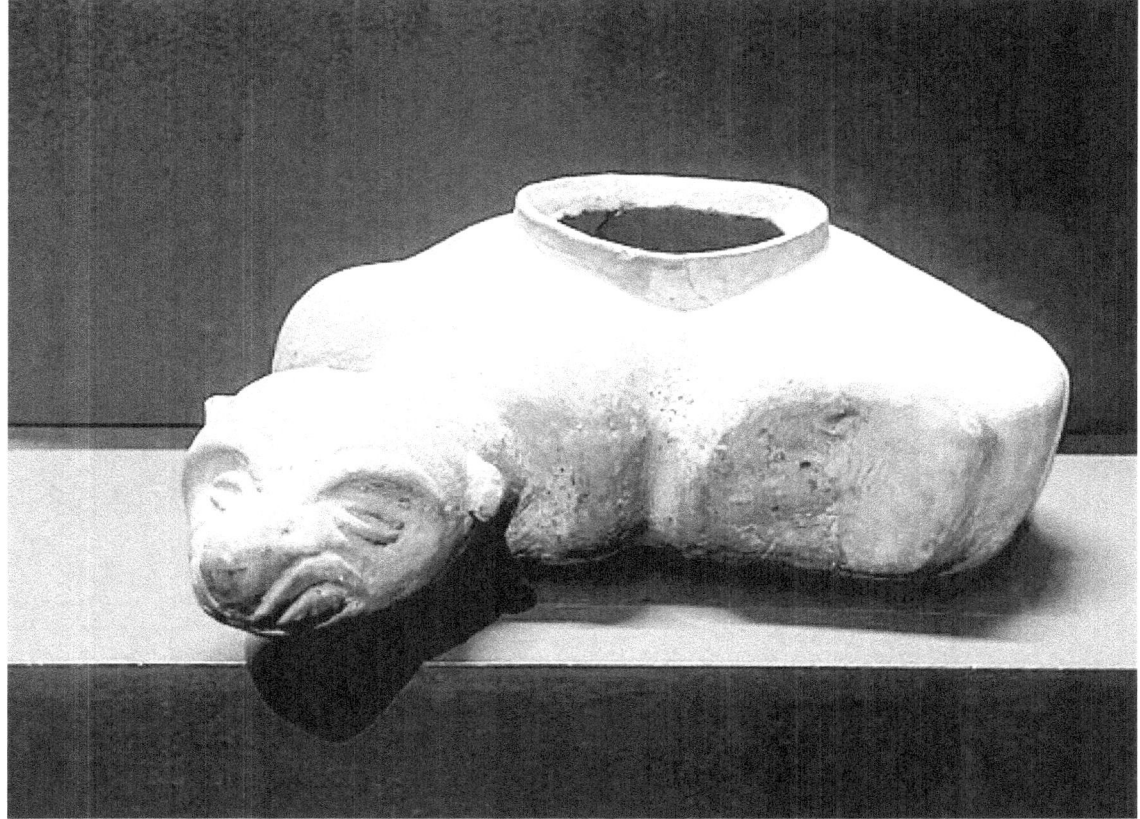

**Image 38**

Response:

_____

_____

_____

## 9. What's shown in this picture?

**Image 39**

Response:

_____

_____

_____

10. What does this picture depict?

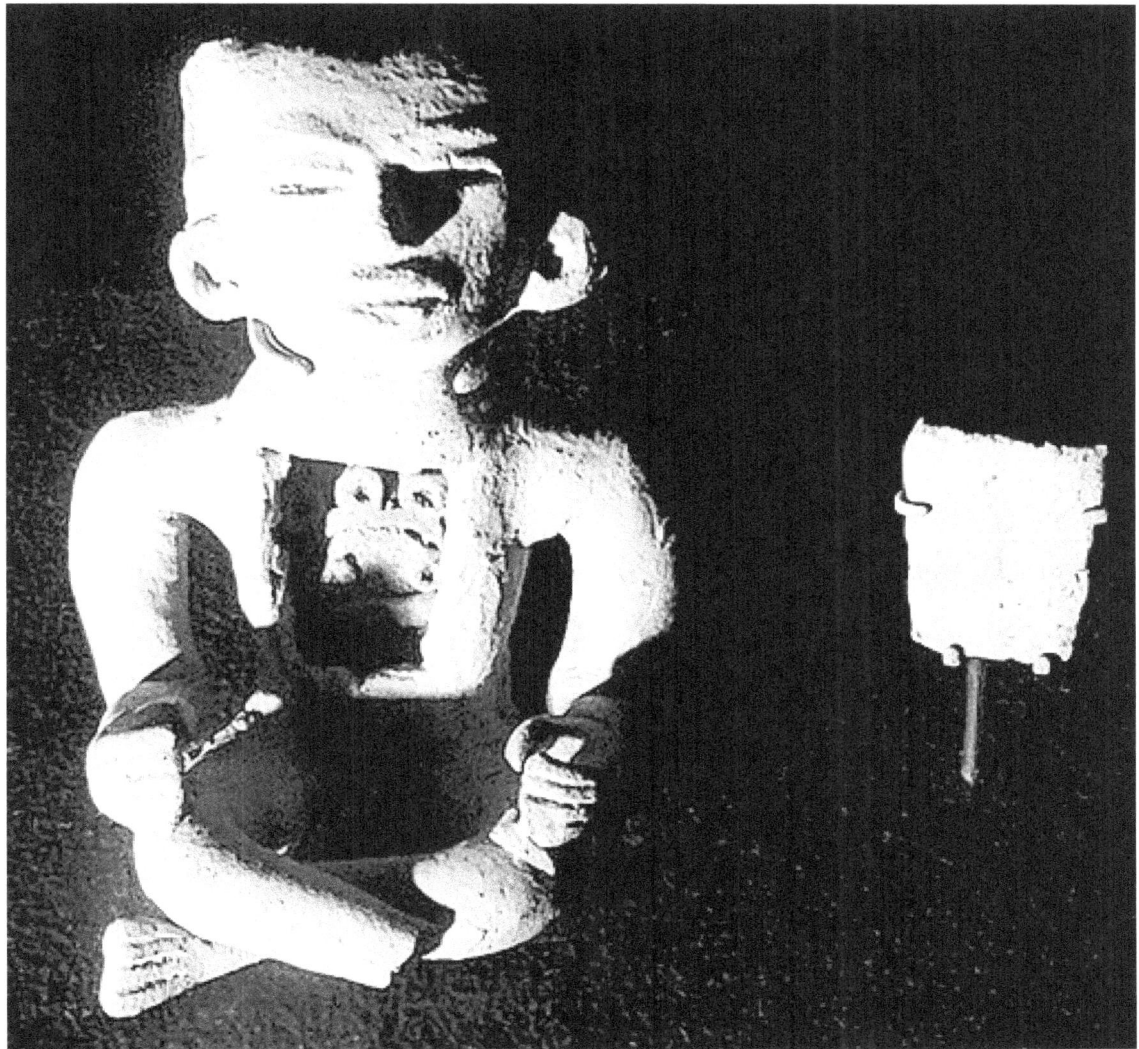

**Image 40**

Response:

_____

_____

_____

# Bonus Pictures

# Color Your Own Mural

How would you color this Teotihuacan mural? Let your creativity on the loose and use any colors you want.

**Color the mural.**

# Recreate the City Layout

Based on pictures 33 and 34 above, where do you think these places were located in the city?

**Place 1.**

**Place 2.**

Response:

1. _____

2. _____

**Did You Know?**

Despite expanding and thriving for several centuries, the great city of Teotihuacán was simply abandoned around the 8th century A.D.

Why? That's a great question! It was probably the changes in their environment – being surrounded by volcanoes, the locals probably suffered many losses when one or more of these volcanoes erupted.

This may have led to famine, extreme competition, and conflicts among the local populations. Ultimately, people decided to find a better place to live – somewhere they wouldn't have to worry about whether wars and volcanoes would threaten their harvest and lives.

# Timeline Questions

1. Arrange these events in chronological order:

- Southern cities of Mesoamerica are abandoned.
- Teotihuacán started to influence the culture of Mesoamerica.
- Teotihuacán is established in the Valley of Mexico.
- Teotihuacán started to decline and lose its function as a cultural center in Mesoamerica.

# Answer Key

## Multiple Choice Answers

1. A. Calzada de los Muertos. It is the city's longest road, running through its center — and along many impressive buildings like the Pyramid of the Sun.

2. C. and D. Tikal and Copán. Teotihuacán conquered these two powerful Mayan cities at its most powerful state, successfully expanding its influence in the region.

3. C. Religious, cultural, and architectural. Teotihuacán was so connected with all parts of Mesoamerica that it influenced the region with its culture, religious beliefs, and building styles.

4. D. All of the above. Many archaeologists speculate that the Zapotec, Mixtec, and Maya people joined forces to build Teotihuacán. This claim is supported by the fact that artifacts unique to these three civilizations have been found within the city.

5. A. Architecture. Many important buildings within the city were built the same way. They had a panel sitting perpendicularly to the ground (called *tablero*), which was supported by an inward-sloping structure (known as *talud*).

6. B. Fertility. Lunar (moon) symbols in Mesoamerica (and other cultures as well) have been known to symbolize fertility. Historians believe this was the purpose of the Pyramid of the Moon, too — it was the place of worship dedicated to the Great Fertility Goddess of Teotihuacán.

7. D. Red. Many structures, murals, and objects were painted red. Teotihuacan builders and craftsmen used a natural red color extracted from crushed pyrite to color their creations. You can still see the red tint in some structures and items.

8. A. Between 100 B.C.E. and 650 A.D. During this time, the city of Teotihuacán was the most influential settlement in the Valley of Mexico and one of the greatest ones in Mesoamerica.

9. A and B. Obsidian and ceramics and textile and food. Besides fertile lands where they could produce grain and feed animals to make food items, the locals also had several mines at their disposal.

10. B. A giant clock. The symbols in and outside the Temple of the Feathered-Serpent suggest that the place was used to measure the passing of time (days, months, seasons, etc.).

## Fill-in-the-Blank Answers

1. Largest.
2. Thousands, temples, and Egyptian.
3. Worship, sacrifice, lowest, gods'.
4. Gods, creation.

5. Volcanoes.

6. Solstices, equinoxes, astronomy.

7. Defined, entire, festivities.

8. Craftsmen, rituals, decoration, household.

9. Centuries.

10. Abandoned, mysterious.

**What am I Answers**

1. La Ciudadela.

2. Teotihuacán Ocelot.

3. The symbol of the rain god Tlaloc.

4. The Palace of Quetzalpapálotl.

5. The fertile land near Teotihuacán.

6. Obsidian.

7. Teotihuacán art.

8. The headdress of priests is depicted on Teotihuacán buildings.

9. The tunnel underneath the Pyramid of Quetzalcoatl.

10. Tezontle.

**True or False Answers**

1. False. By the time the Aztecs discovered it, Teotihuacán was long abandoned. Instead of reviving it, the Aztecs simply used Teotihuacán as a place of worship and religious gathering, making the much larger Tenochtitlan the capital of their empire.

2. False. While the exact time Teotihuacán was built is unknown, the city certainly existed for over a thousand years before the Aztecs discovered it. They, however, found it so mysterious and beautiful that they named it Teotihuacán — the city (or birthplace) of gods.

3. True. Despite being the largest city in the Western Hemisphere at the time, archeologists hadn't found any evidence that Teotihuacán had any military structures. This is particularly strange because the city was known to have a massive political and governing influence in the region — it's unclear how they kept order without military structures.

4. True. One of the reasons the history of Teotihuacán is still a great mystery is that no texts have been found in the city. Its people had access to and knowledge to create written records — but preferred to pass down their culture through oral traditions, craft, and architecture.

5. False. The Pyramid of the Moon was built in seven stages. The first stage is believed to have started in the 1st century. The last one was finished in the 3rd century. Its massive structure was built without any machinery, so it's not surprising it took two centuries to finish.

6. False. Along the Palace of Quetzalpapálotl, you can find many images and decorations symbolizing water and aquatic life. This includes shells, birds that live near water, animals with a blue background, etc.

7. True. While religion connected people in the city and to the outside world, trade and astronomy were just as crucial for making the city thrive. Over time, the city became a major regional trade hub and attracted travelers from many other civilizations.

8. False. The city's grid layout divided the buildings into several sectors. The sectors were established based on who lived in them. For example, craftsmen lived in one section (the largest), and the nobility built their homes in another part of the city.

9. True. The builders hauled different types of stones from the nearby mountains. Some were much lighter than others, so they were easier to work with. Despite this, they were just as sturdy — many still stand and are part of the ancient building remains.

10. False. The three main pyramids — the Pyramid of the Sun, the Pyramid of the Moon, and the Pyramid of Quetzalcoatl — are surrounded by 11 smaller structures that look like mini pyramids. These had similar purposes as the large ones, except smaller groups of people used them.

**Picture-Based Answers**

1. An image of a large cat. With its open mouth and large, extended claws, it's likely a puma. Found in the Teotihuacán structure called Puma Complex, the mural is surrounded by several temples and elevated platforms. The painting itself features a sharp contrast between the cat and the green, red, and white colored stripes in the background. The mural is surrounded by a panel molding embellished with green circles that likely represent gemstones.

2. The Pyramid of the Moon. It's one of the three largest structures in Teotihuacán. Like the other two, this pyramid also played a crucial role in shaping the local culture and daily life.

3. The picture shows the city's precise and incredibly well-organized grid system. Taking the Avenue of the Dead as the main axis on which the grid was founded. This avenue was lined with the largest buildings (the pyramids) and surrounded by residential homes to accommodate over 100,000 inhabitants (some estimate that at one time, up to 200,000 people lived in the city.)

4. In this picture, taken from the Pyramid of the Moon, you can see the Pyramid of the Sun on the far left. A little closer, toward the middle, is the Citadel, and even closer is the Avenue of the Dead.

5. A serpent's head. This is one of the many serpent heads decorating the outside of the Temple of the Feathered Serpent. There are some differences between the serpent heads, meaning they likely have slightly different meanings. A serpent's

body also appears between the heads in some places across the building's structure.

6. A Stone censer dedicated to a deity. Originating from around 200-750 A.D., this volcanic stone censer symbolizes the Old Man Fire God. This was a much-feared and revered deity in the Teotihuacán culture, with many festivities, rituals, and legends tied to his name.

7. The mural is dedicated to the Great Goddess of Teotihuacán (also known as the La Gran Diosa de Teotihuacán del Tlalocan de Tepantitla). She was one of the most worshiped goddesses in the city and other regions, where she was known under other names.

8. A sculpture of a curled-up dog with an opening on top. This is called an effigy vessel (containers shaped like people or animals) and was often used in religious rituals. In Teotihuacán, these vessels were made from a special orange clay only found in this region. The dog was a popular theme in vessels made for funerals, so it's possible that the locals often had dogs in their household and wanted to be buried with the symbols of these animals.

9. The replica of the inside of the Temple of Quetzalcoatl. Like many other elements of the temple and the surrounding complex, the symbols on this replica combine religious, artistic, and astronomical signs.

10. This is a hollow clay figurine. It symbolized the ancient Mesoamerican belief that all people carry another essence inside. This could be the essence of a deity, the ancestors, or the elements of nature.

## Bonus Answers

1. On the main street, between the larger buildings.
2. Around a smaller building, likely one of the smaller temples or palaces.

## Timeline Answers

1.

- Teotihuacán was established in the Valley of Mexico around 100 B.C.E.
- Teotihuacán started to influence the culture of Mesoamerica around 400 A.D.
- Teotihuacán started to decline and lose its function as a cultural center in Mesoamerica in 600 A.D.
- Southern cities of Mesoamerica, including Teotihuacán, were abandoned around 900 B.C.E.

# Chapter 5: Toltec Tales: Warriors, Artisans, and the Legend of Quetzalcoatl

Rising from the remnants of Teotihuacán and its vast influence in the Valley of Mexico, the Toltec civilization emerged between the 10th and 12 centuries. Much of what's known about the Toltec people — including their name, which means "the place of the artisan" — comes from Aztec recountings of ancient tales.

While known for their extraordinary craftsmanship, the Toltecs also cultivated a set of spiritual, social, and military practices. Some of these practices were based on tactics adopted from earlier civilizations. Others were groundbreaking and much-welcomed innovations in a changing world.

This chapter will introduce you to the world and culture of the Toltecs, the conquerors who left an immense legacy in Mesoamerica. You'll learn about their artistry, legends (like that of the feathered serpent god), and why their successors, the Aztecs, so admired them.

## Who Am I?

1. I am a legendary Toltec ruler and warrior who is believed to have founded the city of Tula. Who am I?

_____

2. I am a dark deity who tempted the ruler of Tula, causing the city to fall. Who am I?

_____

3. I was a great warrior and ruler. I lost everything and ascended to the sky. Who am I?

_____

4. I am a powerful king who conquered several Toltec cities and burned their books and artifacts to erase their culture. Who am I?

_____

5. My and my fellow companions' statues stand in the Pyramid of Quetzalcoatl. Who am I?

   _____

6. According to some legend, I rebelled against my overlords in Huehuetla Pallan. After 13 years of fighting, I left the Toltecs to found another city. Who am I?

   _____

7. I invented a fermented syrup made from the maguey plant and sent my daughter to bring the syrup to Tecpancaltzin, the leader of the Toltecs. Who am I?

   _____

8. I am a deity widely worshiped at Tula and later by the Aztecs as well. Who am I?

   _____

9. I am the last Toltec leader who led his people to settle in Chapultepec. Who am I?

   _____

10. I am the first Toltec leader and father of Cē Ācatl Topiltzin. Who am I?

    _____

# The Legend of Quetzalcoatl

The mysterious deity of Quetzalcoatl is the main character of countless Mesoamerican tales. He had many roles from a mythical being to a priest to a warrior.

According to one narrative, his name comes from the Nahuatl words Quetzal (the name of a bird with beautiful feathers) and Coatl (which means snake) — hence the name feathered serpent god. This double symbol is one of the major features of Toltec and other Mesoamerican beliefs about the origin of life.

Legend has it that life was created when forces of air, water, and earth united. After this, all deities and humans lived in harmony — well, most of them anyway. Quetzalcoatl didn't like that the humans had to serve the gods, and they had no knowledge or skill of their own. He thought that maybe if he was also part human, he could share the wisdom of deities with the other humans.

Quetzalcoatl arrived in their world to start teaching people and traveled through it until he reached Tula. Here, he saw humans offer sacrifice to Tezcatlipoca, another god. Quetzalcoatl wanted to stop them, but the priests performing the ritual became very angry and started yelling. Dark clouds gathered in the sky, but Quetzalcoatl blew them away, assuring the locals that their city would thrive.

Seeing his power, people wanted to honor Quetzalcoatl, but he told them that they could do this by listening to his lessons and not by offering him sacrifices and other items. He taught them astronomy, agriculture, mining, writing, and worship without sacrifice. As people learned from the gods, Tula grew and developed into a beautiful city.

However, Tezcatlipoca wasn't happy that he wasn't honored anymore through sacrifice, and he made the plan to destroy Tula and its people. Disguising himself as an old man, he brought a gift to Quetzalcoatl, who accepted it. He believed the old man brought him a drink with healing properties — but this was not true. As he drank the liquid, Quetzalcoatl became so intoxicated that he started to sing and act unruly toward others.

Realizing what he had done, Quetzalcoatl decided that he was no longer worthy of the leadership of Tula and abandoned the city. Reaching the sea, he sailed toward the sunset, but as he traveled, he promised the Toltecs that he would return later.

Design Your Own Feathered Serpent

What do you imagine a feathered serpent would look like? Would it look like a dragon? Or a snake with bird-like feathers? When you think of a feathered serpent, draw whatever picture pops into your head. You can use any colors you want and design the serpent to your liking.

# True or False

1. Quetzalcoatl was a real historical figure, not a mythical god.

   - True
   - False

2. The predecessors of the Toltecs, the Tolteca-Chichimeca people, came to the Valley of Mexico from the northwestern deserts.

   - True
   - False

3. Over time, Tula became the largest city in Mesoamerica.

   - True
   - False

4. The gifted craftsman of Tula played a crucial role in making the city thrive.

   - True
   - False

5. The Toltec capital, Tula, continued flourishing until the end of the 13th century.

   - True
   - False

6. The fall of the Toltec civilization occurred due to both outside and inside factors.

   - True
   - False

7. The Toltecs were greatly influenced by another famous Mesoamerican city and its civilization.

   - True
   - False

8. Besides passing down cultural traditions and beliefs to other civilizations, the Toltecs also created an intellectual legacy.

   - True
   - False

9. The ball game Toltecs played in the Tula ball court had religious purposes.

   - True
   - False

10. The feathered serpent god appearing in many Toltec legends was unique to the Toltec culture.

    - True
    - False

# Picture-Based

1. What does this artifact signify?

**Image 41**

Response:

_____

_____

_____

## 2. What does this picture depict?

**Image 42**

Response:

_____

_____

_____

3. What does this artifact show?

**Image 43**

Response:

_____

_____

_____

4. What do you think this object was used for?

**Image 44**

Response:

_____

_____

_____

## 5. What's the significance of these artifacts?

**Image 45**

Response:

_____

_____

_____

6. What was the purpose of this object?

**Image 46**

Response:

_____

_____

_____

7. What's shown in this map?

**Image 47**

Response:

_____

_____

_____

## 8. What's shown in this picture?

**Image 48**

Response:

_____

_____

_____

## 9. Which deity is shown in this picture?

**Image 49**

Response:

_____

_____

_____

## 10. What's the significance of this picture?

**Image 50**

Response:

_____

_____

_____

# Toltec Artistry Unveiled

As the power of Toltecs rose, they started creating a monumental legacy, complete with innovative architecture, intricate designs, and the emerging artisan culture that soon took over Mesoamerica.

The Toltecs were skilled sculptors, mural painters, and pottery workers. Their sculptures (some still standing) could be seen in palaces, across city landscapes, temples, and other religious sites and places of gathering. Some sculptures, like the warrior figures in Tula, are very similar, indicating that the Toltecs could mass-produce sculptures.

Many Toltec sculptures symbolized authority, whether political or religious. In pottery, Toltecs liked to use geometric shapes, symbols inspired by nature, and figures resembling humans or animals. Showcasing a duality in the Toltec worldview, these symbols tied the human world to the spiritual realm. This had cultural and religious meanings as the artistic connections between the two realms were often made through a symbol of a deity, social status, or tale.

Art and crafts were forms of expression for the Toltecs, but they also acted as historical records. Their colorful murals show how they viewed historical events, religious rituals, daily life in their community, values, and more.

Toltec arts are amazing narratives that tell countless stories taught many lessons to the next generations. For example, their successors watched in awe how the Toltecs were able to create murals and decorations that showed carved pieces in different depths. This required skills and techniques that weren't very well known before that time — but became very popular later across Mesoamerica.

Create Your Own Toltec-Style Art

You can get inspired to create Toltec-style art in many ways. For example, if you love drawing, you can draw a colorful picture of something related to nature.

**Instructions:**

1. Imagine sitting in a garden with a cup of hot chocolate in your hand. It's fall, and the leaves are falling around you.
2. Now, draw this. Start with a cup of hot chocolate. You can draw yourself or just a cup.
3. Draw colorful leaves around the cup, as if falling from a tree (or you can draw a tree, too). Use vibrant yellow, orange, green, and red colors. Add some blue or green, too — for example, for the cup.
4. You can add tree roots, birds, etc.
5. Finish the drawing as you like.

# Fill-in-the-Blank

You may use any of the following words to fill in the blanks:

| | | |
|---|---|---|
| Maya | political | Mesoamerican |
| Tula | pyramids | irrigation |
| social | grid | large |
| priests | gods | Aztec |
| pottery | decline | ball courts |
| walkway | democracy | cities. |

1. Toltec artisans were known for their intricate _____ work.

2. The name Tula is translated as the "place of reeds," which was often used to describe _____ settlements in _____ languages.

3. Like many other Mesoamerican cities, Tula also had a _____ layout at its center.

4. Besides the lavishly decorated palaces, Tula also had two _____ and two _____. These were surrounded by houses and connected through a large _____.

5. The legendary stories of battles between the _____ Quetzalcoatl and Tezcatlipoca show that a power struggle may have led to the _____ of the Toltec civilization.

6. The Aztecs have destroyed what was left of the remains of _____ and other great Toltec _____.

7. The Toltec culture had a massive influence on later civilizations, including the _____ and _____ people.

8. The Toltecs have developed a complex and well-working _____ and _____ system, which was ruled by warriors and _____.

9. The Toltecs supported their growing population by creating a very effective _____ system, which helped them grow more crops for people and animals.

10. With the rule of Mimixcoamazatzin, the Toltec people established _____, which allowed them to start extending their influence.

# Multiple Choice

1. One of the greatest Toltec warriors, Ce Acatl Topiltzin, was known as...

    a. One Flint Cloud Serpent

    b. The Milky Way

    c. One Reed Sacrificer

    d. None of the above

2. Where did the Toltecs first settle?

    a. Culhuacan

    b. Tula

    c. Tollan

    d. Kukulcan

3. According to mythology, what were the palaces of Tula (Tollan) made of?

    a. Gold

    b. Jade and turquoise

    c. Quetzal feathers

    d. All of the above

4. Besides pottery and metalwork, what did the Toltecs produce the most?

    a. Obsidian

    b. Colorful cotton

    c. Gold

    d. Food items

5. What did each group of regular Tula houses have in its center?

    a. Walkway

    b. Courtyard

    c. Altar

    d. Small pyramid-like structures

6. What did the pyramids of Tula have on top?

    a. Altars

    b. A semi-closed structure

    c. Burial places

    d. Monuments decorated with Toltec signs and symbols

7. What are friezes?

    a. Walls

    b. Slanted roofs

    c. Horizontal bands

    d. Toltec sings

8. What were the roles of the Toltec tribulation states?

    a. Political influence

    b. Economic and regulatory control

    c. Religious influence

    d. Social and cultural exchange

9. How did the Toltecs expand their influence in Mesoamerica?

    a. Through battles and conquests

    b. Through trading

    c. Through art

    d. All of the above

10. Toltec writing and iconography were influenced by which previously established civilization?

    a. Maya

    b. Olmec

    c. Aztec

    d. None of the above

## Timeline Questions

1. Arrange these events in chronological order:

- Ce Acatl Topiltzin, the legendary leader of the Toltecs, was born.
- Huemac lead the Toltecs to Chapultepec.
- The Toltec civilization began to thrive in Mesoamerica.
- The Toltec capital of Tollan (Tula) was destroyed.

# Answer Key

## Who am I Answers

1. Cē Ācatl Topiltzin.
2. Tezcatlipoca.
3. Venus.
4. Izcoatl.
5. Toltec warrior.
6. Chalcatzingo.
7. Papantzin.
8. Xochiquetzal.
9. Huemac.
10. Ce Técpatl Mixcoatl.

## True or False Answers

1. False. The great god Quetzalcoatl was a mythical figure in many tales across Mesoamerica and even modern-day Central America. However, according to some legends, the title of Quetzalcoatl was also linked to a real Toltec ruler, Ce Acatl Topiltzin.

2. True. The Toltecs originated from settlers who came from a desert northwest of the Valley of Mexico. They were the Tolteca-Chichimeca people, who settled in the valley and started conquering nearby regions.

3. False. While highly influential as the Toltec capital, Tula was never as large as the formerly abandoned Teotihuacán or the majestic Chichen Itzá. At its largest, Tula had around 40,000 inhabitants.

4. True. The craftsmen and artists of Tula were so talented that their work was known and wanted in lands far away. This allowed them to expand trading and their influence to the nearby regions in Mesoamerica.

5. False. Around the middle of the 12th century, Tula was destroyed either by natural forces or due to invasion (there are many diverse myths surrounding the city's decline).

6. True. Besides natural forces and attacks from nomadic groups in the region, the Toltecs also became threatened by local rebellions against the rulers. The combination of uprisings where many people fought against each other (or left the cities) and not being able to sustain themselves could have led to the fall of this great civilization.

7. True. While Teotihuacán had long been abandoned before the Toltecs came to rise, its influence was very notable in Toltec culture, architecture, religious practices, and mythology.

8. True. The Toltecs were not only talented in art and architecture, but they were also very intelligent. They passed the knowledge they gathered about the world to the new civilizations in most parts of Mesoamerica.

9. True. Like many other Mesoamerican civilizations, most Toltec social gatherings had religious purposes. This included the ball game they enjoyed on Tula ball courts.

10. False. The feathered serpent deity appears in many other Mesoamerican cultures. Some are older, while others are younger than the Toltec civilization — this makes it unclear where the myths of this deity originated from.

**Picture-Based Answers**

1. Glyphs. This artifact contains glyphs, the unique symbols Toltecs used in their writing system. The Toltecs expressed their culture and beliefs through art, so they developed a way to show even more. Through symbols like these, historians could learn more about the social practices, religious ideas, and historical events that shaped the Toltec civilization.

2. Priest. The picture shows a Toltec stone head symbolizing a priest who served the great god Quetzalcoatl. Items like these were often used in religious ceremonies and rituals performed by Toltec priests in smaller and bigger communities.

3. This is a relief of a Toltec warrior. Their fierce warriors were often depicted with darts and spear throwers. This relief was originally painted red and white, which meant it was highly important for its creators.

4. A drum. Besides everyday objects, reliefs, building decorations, and religious objects, Toltec artists were also skilled in creating musical instruments. This drum-shaped pottery has holes around its rim, which allows its user to make sounds with it. It was likely used for celebrations and rituals.

5. Gold ornaments. These are beautiful gold decorations featuring feathered serpents. For example, in the third piece, you can clearly see the serpent's head in the bottom right quarter. Decorations like these were very popular in the 11th and 12th centuries.

6. A throne made of stone. Many religious sites and gathering places had specific places for rulers and priests to stand or sit. Like other permanent parts of these areas, the thrones were also made of durable materials like stone.

7. Toltec expansion. The map shows the massive influence of the Toltec civilization in the mid-10th century. At this time, a large portion of Mesoamerica was under Toltec control, extending to the Yucatan Peninsula.

8. Wheeled objects. These are unique figurines that originally had wheels for moving around. Wheeled figurines were invented by the Toltecs, who always looked to add something unique to their creations.

9. Quetzalcoatl — the winged serpent god whose name is linked to the founder of Tula and many other great achievements of the Toltecs.

10. This picture shows two distinct forms of Quetzalcoatl as described in different legends. Some tales claim he was an all-mightly deity (pictured as the feathered serpent on the left). Others describe him as the god of wind (shown with a beard, black skin, and a red mask on the right).

## Fill-in-the-Blank Answers

1. Pottery.

2. Large, Mesoamerican.

3. Grid

4. Pyramids, ball courts, walkway.

5. Gods, decline.

6. Tula, cities.

7. Maya, Aztec.

8. Political, social, priests.

9. Irrigation.

10. Democracy.

## Multiple Choice Answers

1. C. One Reed Sacrificer. Born between 935 and 947, Ce Acatl Topiltzin's native name was One Reed Sacrificer. He was the son of One Flint Cloud Serpent, who was also called the Milky Way, or Ce Técpatl Mixcoatl.

2. A. Culhuacan. When they first arrived in the Valley of Mexico, the Toltecs settled at Culhuacan, their first capital. Later, they moved to the capital by founding a bigger city, Tula (Tollan).

3. D. All of the above. According to Mesoamerican mythology, the great palaces of Tula were made of gold. They were adorned with turquoise, jade, and quetzal feathers.

4. B. Colorful cotton. Besides their intricate metalwork and amazing pottery skills, the Toltecs were known for producing cotton in many natural colors, including blue, green, yellow, and red.

5. B. and C. Courtyard and Altar. People in Tula lived in houses built in small groups. Each house group was connected with its own courtyard in the middle, and in each courtyard was an altar where people from these homes gathered for ceremonies and rituals.

6. B. A semi-closed structure. The pyramids of Tula were originally topped with a structure with a roof held by massive pillars. These pillars, shaped like Toltec warriors, still stand on top of one pyramid in the archaeological site of ancient Tula. The structure also had a doorway, which only exists today partially.

7. C. Horizontal bands. Invented by the Toltecs, *friezes* (or *coatepantli*) were decorative horizontal bands that ran along the outside of pyramids and other

monuments. They were often adorned with images of rituals, sacrifice, animals, and war symbols.

8. A. and B. Political influence and Economic and regulatory control. By establishing the tribulation states, the Toltec rulers had better control over their territories. This included political and financial regulation, establishing laws, and overseeing trading.

9. D. All of the above. Their craftsmen's talents allowed the Toltecs to expand through trading, but their true influence came from the many battles they won and territories they conquered. The Toltecs were true warriors, capable of heroic deeds and overcoming any enemy they encountered.

10. A. and B. Maya and Olmec. Toltec writing and iconography were influenced by Maya and Olmec symbols, which were developed to represent concepts people wanted to understand and communicate to others. The Toltecs adopted symbols for deities, historical and natural events, and astronomical observations. They expanded these with their own symbols, creating a glyph system that allowed them to express social, political, cultural, and religious beliefs and pass these to the next generations.

**Timeline Answers**

1.

- The Toltec civilization began to thrive in Mesoamerica after 900 A.D.
- Ce Acatl Topiltzin, the legendary leader of the Toltecs, was born somewhere between 935 A.D. and 947 A.D.
- The Toltec capital of Tollan (Tule) was destroyed in several attacks between 1156 A.D. and 1168 A.D.
- After the capital's destruction, Huemac led the surviving Toltecs to Chapultepec.

# Chapter 6: The Mixtec World: Goldsmiths and Codex Crafters

Known for their mastery of metalworking, pottery, jewelry making, and decoration, the Mixtecs were a highly skilled Mesoamerican civilization. After settling in the 8th century, the Mixtecs evolved into one of the most thriving cultures in the region, reaching their peak during the 11th century.

They continued to thrive through craft and trade until the 16th century, leaving a significant mark in Mesoamerican history. This chapter will introduce you to their intriguing work, including their way of recording their history and traditions for the next generations.

Among other interesting facts, you'll learn about the Mixtec goldsmiths and codice crafters, who played a crucial role in growing the Mixtec influence.

## Mixtec Goldsmithing Brilliance

Imagine seeing the most exquisite pieces of gold jewelry laid out on a table at the market, many of them decorated with precious stones like jade, turquoise, or obsidian. This scene was fairly common in Mixtec markets where local artisans and those from other regions displayed their latest works.

This jewelry was the result of extraordinary skills that allowed the Mixtects to develop innovative metallurgical techniques and craft unique pieces that conquered the market. Besides making intricate stone settings, goldsmiths also used graduation and embossing methods to create designs with cultural and personal significance.

Among the people who sought the Mixtec jewelry were local nobility, rulers, priests, and foreign traders who wanted to acquire these unique items. For the former, wearing gold jewelry was often a symbol of power — jewelry was one of the ways Mixtecs showed social standing.

Given that most gold jewelry was worn by the wealthiest, the pieces were often imbued with symbols of nature, animals, and other extravagant motifs tied to traditions and elite status. Many of these were considered sacred in the Mixtec culture and even in the entire Mesoamerica.

Besides making wearable jewelry, Mixtec goldsmiths crafted pieces for ceremonies and rituals. Religious leaders wore this jewelry during their work. These pieces showed the connection to the spiritual world and the ancestors, whose wisdom was often evoked during rites.

Other ceremonial jewelry was tied to deities or family lines. Like codes, Mixtec jewelry was another way to preserve the colorful history and rich heritage of the Mixtec people. In many families, the making or ownership of gold jewelry was passed down for many centuries.

Over time, the craft of Mixtec goldsmiths became known in the entire region, attracting collectors and faraway traders who wanted to introduce something unique to their own culture.

## Multiple Choice Questions

1. What was the primary material used by Mixtec goldsmiths to create exquisite jewelry?

    a. Silver

    b. Jade

    c. Gold

    d. Copper

2. How were the Mixtec territories governed?

    a. By one ruler

    b. By different rulers in each kingdom

    c. By three rulers

    d. By a religious and military ruler

3. How was the Mixtec society divided?

    a. Nobility in the majority and few classes of traders and farmers

    b. Nobility, farmers, classes, and artisans in the same numbers

    c. Nobility in the minority, and several classes of traders, farmers, artisans, and slaves

    d. Nobility in the majority, then traders, and slaves fewest in numbers

4. When were the Mixtec regions united?

    a. 10th century

    b. 12th century

    c. 9th century

    d. 11th century

5. Besides geography, what else made life challenging for the Mixtecs?

    a. Weather

    b. Enemy attacks

    c. Competition with neighboring civilizations

    d. Rivalries among the kingdoms

6. Who could become a codex writer?

    a. Only those with the highest status

    b. Enslaved people working for the nobility

    c. Artisans and merchants

    d. None of the above

7. Besides dominating historical events and cultural and religious practices, what other purpose did the Mixtec codices have?

    a. Passing down information through generations

    b. Talking about achievements

    c. Making a statement to the enemies

    d. All of the above

8. How many calendars did the Mixtecs have?

    a. One

    b. Tree

    c. Two

    d. None

9. How did the Mixtecs record dates in codices?

    a. With a star

    b. Signs resembling modern numbers

    c. Signs resembling the letters O and A

    d. With lines

10. What were Mixtec jewelry pieces linked to?

    a. The sun and the moon

    b. Ancestors

    c. Families connections between regions

    d. The earth

# Fill-in-the-Blank

You may use any of the following words to fill in the blanks:

| | | |
|---|---|---|
| animals | insects | pottery |
| deerskin | same | resources |
| gatherers | readings | metals |
| jewelry | sacred | precious |
| gemstones | greens | storytelling |
| rivers | agriculture | close |
| elderly | sun. | |

1. Mixtec codices were made from _____ and were used to record important events and histories.

2. The Mixtecs in different regions have limited _____, so they traded these among each other. For example, those living in lower areas traded _____ for _____ produced in the higher regions.

3. Besides being excellent gold-workers and blacksmiths, the Mixtecs were also handy at _____ and carving _____.

4. Before becoming skilled artisans, the Mixtec people lived in small settlements near the _____. Until 600 B.C.E., they sustained themselves through _____.

5. To sustain themselves through the year, the Mixecs were also regular _____. They collected anything from wild _____ to _____.

6. The Mixtecs had a _____ family structure, where not only did the parents and children live together but also other relatives, especially the _____ or orphans.

7. While they could only be read by a few, Mixtec codices were available to more people through _____ readings and _____.

8. Mixtec calendars would overlap every 52 years, which was considered a _____ event. According to Mixtec legends, every 52 years, the _____ was reborn, which caused the reset in one of the calendars.

9. If a codex page doesn't have a date, this means that the events depicted happened on the _____ day than the events from a _____ page with a date.

10. The nobles wore more and large pieces of _____ than those in the lower classes.

# What Am I?

1. I am a valuable Mixtec artifact, often made of jade or gold and worn as a status symbol. What am I?

_____

2. If you follow me, I make Mixtec codices easier to read. What am I?

_____

3. My pages contain tales about the Mictec beliefs, religion, culture, and the universe. What am I?

_____

4. I'm not as famous as Mixtec metalwork or codices, but I am a popular artisan craft, too. What am I?

_____

5. I am the only Mixtec codex finished after the decline of my civilization. What am I?

_____

6. I hold a family tree of 26 generations of Mixtecs that lived between 970 A.D. and 1490 A.D. What am I?

_____

7. My signs are very similar to and often inspired by Mixtec codices. What am I?

_____

8. I am a mushroom-shaped sign in Mixtec codices. What am I?

_____

9. I am the symbol of the cycle of life and agriculture in Mixtec jewelry. What am I?

_____

10. My symbolism in jewelry comes from the complex pantheon of Miztec mythology. What am I?

_____

# True or False

1. Mixtec codices are easy to read and understand, similar to modern books.
    - True
    - False

2. The Mixtecs all spoke the same language and kept in contact with each other.
    - True
    - False

3. Codex Bodley and the Zouche-Nuttall are both Mixtec history books.
    - True
    - False

4. The known heroic actions of Lord Eight Deer "Jaguar Claw," were all based on historical records.
    - True
    - False

5. Many artisans took to arts and crafts out of necessity.
    - True
    - False

6. The Mixtecs also used clothes to express their culture and status.
    - True
    - False

7. Everyone knew how to read codices in Mesoamerica.
    - True
    - False

8. All Mixtec codices were crafted in the same style.
    - True
    - False

9. Symbols represented the names of figures in Mixtec codices.
    - True
    - False

10. The art of jewelry making was passed down through generations.
    - True
    - False

# Deciphering Mixtec Codices

The Mixtec codices are unique in content and structure. Some talk about the alliances and conquests of kingdoms (typically, each kingdom would have a codex of its own) or the family ties to the ancestors and people living in other kingdoms and regions. Even while the kingdoms were governed separately, they were also united through marriages, trade, and migration — the codices allowed them to record all of this.

Other codices simply enlist the rulers, their wives, and children. Some describe the roles of the main deities and priests entrusted to serve them through rituals and ceremonies. Some codices have detailed family trees of the main kingdoms' families. Others show the family lines in each of the three main regions under Mixtec rule separately.

The Mixtecs have also recorded in codices the effects of early colonialism on their society and culture. Records of major events like these make Mixtec codices a significant part of history. They help modern generations learn about the events that shaped one of the greatest Mesoamerican civilizations.

However, to read Mixtec codices, a person must learn to decipher the glyphs and symbols they contain. The symbols are divided into groups, and the groups depict events in chronological order. To follow the group events, you must look at the characters, symbols, and signs representing the dates.

# Picture-Based

1. This is an image of a Mixtec codex page. What do you think it depicts?

**Image 51**

Response:

_____

_____

_____

2. What material is this figure made of?

**Image 52**

Response:

_____

_____

_____

3. What does this mask symbolize?

**Image 53**

Response:

_____

_____

_____

4. What was this object used for?

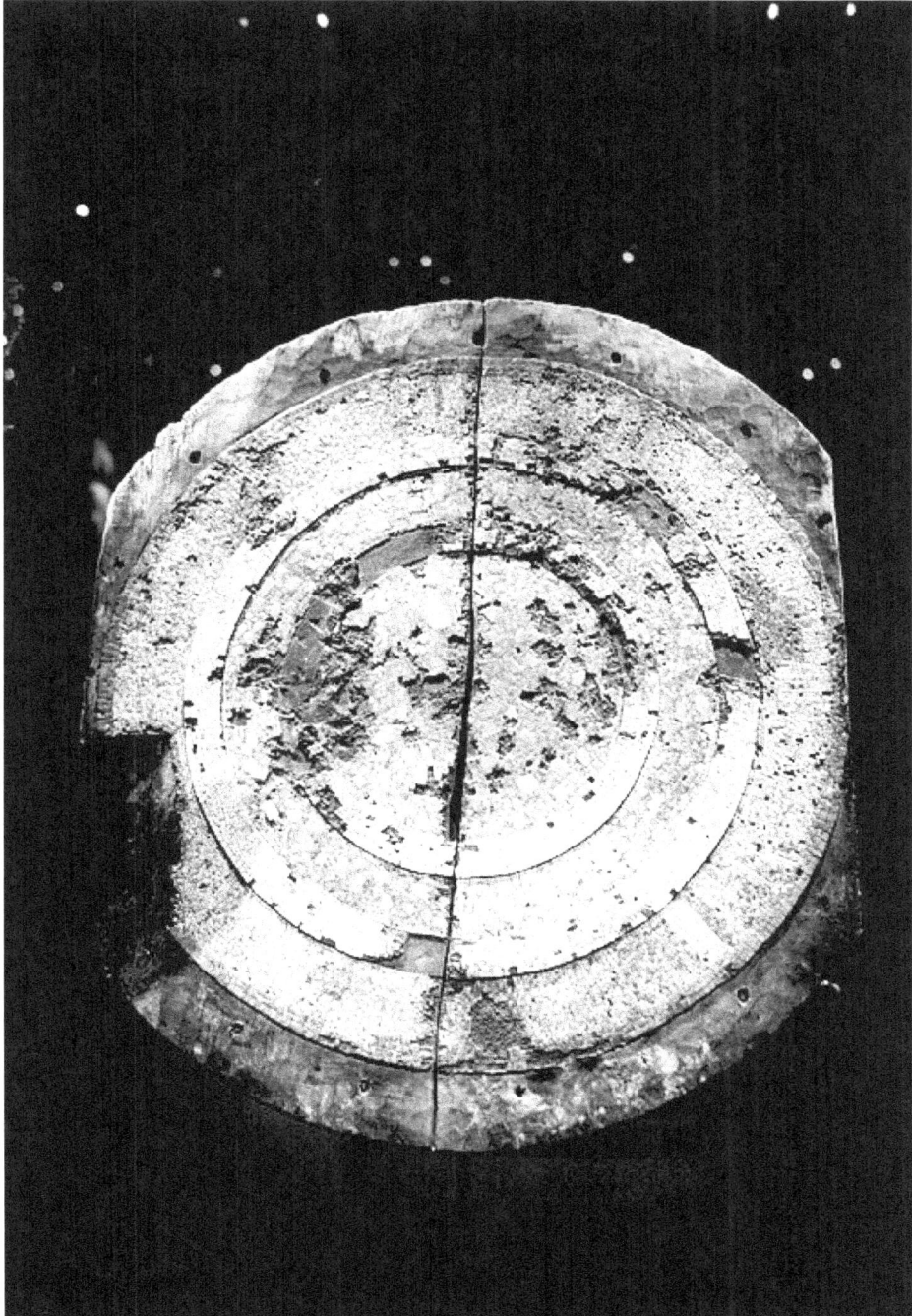

Image 54

Response:

_____

_____

_____

5. Identify the object.

**Image 55**

Response:

_____

_____

_____

6. What was this object used for in the Mixtec world?

**Image 56**

Response:

_____

_____

_____

7. Which deity was this figure dedicated to?

**Image 57**

Response:

_____

_____

_____

8. Identify the object.

**Image 58**

Response:

_____

_____

_____

9. What's the significance of this plate?

**Image 59**

Response:

_____

_____

_____

## 10. What's shown in this picture?

**Image 60**

Response:

_____

_____

_____

# Timeline Questions

1. Arrange these events in chronological order:

- The Mixtecs became known for their metalwork, fine pottery, and codices.
- Mixtec regions were conquered by Spanish colonizers.
- Tilantongo became the most important Mixtec city for government, business, and culture.
- The Mixtecs migrated from Northern Mexico to Oaxaca.

# Answer Key

**Multiple Choice Answers**

1. C. Gold. While Mixtec jewelry makers used many other materials like jade, silver, or obsidian, their favorite medium was gold. Many Mixtec jewelry was often made of solid gold, whether used for ornaments, as a status symbol, or in religious and cultural events.

2. B. By a different ruler in each kingdom. The Mixtec society was organized into kingdoms, and all of these had their rulers. With the help of nobles and military leaders, each ruler governed the society and the army in their kingdom.

3. C. Nobility in the minority and several classes of workers, farmers, artisans, and slaves. Besides the king and his noble advisors, very few people belonged to the uppermost class. The majority of the population was made of traders, farmers, artisans, and slaves.

4. D. 11th century. The Mixtec regions were united under the same rule in the 11th century, under the reign of Lord Eight Deer "Jaguar Claw."

5. A. Weather. Not only was the weather slightly different among the regions (mild to hot and humid on the coasts and cooler and dry on the mountains), but it was also unpredictable in all territories. Rainfall was inconsistent and becoming less and less frequent, and the extreme temperature changes made life very challenging in all Mixtec territories.

6. A. Only those with the highest status. Many codices talk about religious practices and historical events known only to rulers and other people with a higher status. Moreover, lower classes could not afford to take the time to learn the craft of codex writing. All these show that only people of the upper classes could have written Mixtec codices.

7. D. All of the above. Many rulers paid for codices to be written about their achievements. Through these books, they could show their superiority and higher status and subtly warn the enemies. They also gave accounts to the next generations who wanted to learn more about their ancestors' lives.

8. C. Two. The Mixtecs had two calendars — one had 260 days, the other 365 days. The latter was inspired by the solar cycle. The 260-day version was considered the most sacred. Many historical events were recorded based on this calendar.

9. A. and C. With a star and signs resembling the letters O and A. These letters were often intertwined, which could have indicated different dates in the Mixtec calendar.

10. B. and D. Ancestors and the earth. The Mixtecs held much respect for the wisdom of their ancestors, as well as for the earth that fed them. They used jewelry to honor both by displaying symbols representing ancestors and elements of nature or using natural materials.

## Fill-in-the-Blank Answers

1. Deerskin.
2. Resources, animals, metals.
3. Pottery, gemstones.
4. Rivers, agriculture.
5. Gatherers, greens, insects.
6. Close, elderly.
7. Public storytelling.
8. Sacred, sun.
9. Same previous.
10. Jewelry.

## What am I Answers

1. Mixtec jewelry.
2. A vertical red line in Mixtec codices.
3. Codex Vindobonensis (Codex Vienna).
4. Mixtec woven art (textiles, baskets, etc.).
5. Codex Selden.
6. Codex Waecker-Gotter.
7. Sacred Mixtec calendar.
8. The symbol for a place (usually a city).
9. Sun.
10. Animal representation.

## True or False Answers

1. False. Containing images, glyphs (symbols), separated sections, borders, and other separators, Mixtec codices aren't the easiest to read. It's a unique form of communication that requires practice to conquer!

2. False. The Mixtecs lived in an area divided into three different geographical regions. They didn't communicate frequently because of certain natural barriers like mountains, streams, valleys, etc. One of the reasons the Mixtec culture became so diverse was because the Mixtec people in Mesoamerica developed different languages, skills, beliefs, and traditions.

3. True. Codex Bodley and the Zouche-Nuttall are similar to modern history books because they tell the events of the Mixtecs' lives. They talk about battles, victories, losses, conquests, moves from one place to another, kings, and more.

4. False. While Lord Eight Deer "Jaguar Claw" was often described as a mighty hero in Mixtec written records, some of his actions only existed in legends. As the ruler of Tilantongo (one of the most powerful Mixtec kingdoms), this king was highly respected and served as an inspiration for many tales and myths.

5. True. In areas with more unpredictable weather, the soil wasn't of good quality. In this soil, the families couldn't produce enough to sustain themselves, so they had to find other ways to earn money. Some worked for others, while others decided to put their skills to good use and became artisans. Once they started earning a living from their craft, some abandoned their farms and dedicated their time to creating and trading the gods they were making.

6. True. While jewelry was one of the main ways of cultural and status expression for the Mixtecs, they also used clothes to differentiate themselves. For example, people in one region would wear clothes in different colors that people wore in other regions.

7. False. To read and craft codices, Mixtecs underwent many years of training. Experts read codices as history or religious books, but they could only do this if they practiced for a long time. Not everyone could do this, meaning only a few people could read or write codices in Mesoamerican times.

8. False. Mixtec codices have slight differences in their styles. For example, some read right to left, then left to right, then back to right to left, and so on, alternating directions whenever they reach the end of a line. Others go up and down the same way. A third kind will go left to right for two or more pages, right to left for one or two pages, then again left to right for two or more pages, and so on.

9. True. Symbols represented the names of the people described in the codices. These were usually the symbols associated with or included in their traditional name.

10. True. The skills of making exquisite jewelry were often passed down from one line to another in a family. Besides continuing the tradition, each line added a little twist to it to make unique pieces that became more and more popular in Mesoamerica.

**Picture-Based Answers**

1. A Lord. This is a depiction of a lord who attended a gathering in 1098. Lord 12 Rain 'Coyote' (you can recognize him by the 12 circles aligned next to him) was one of the 112 lords invited by Lord Eight Deer 'Jaguar Claw,' the king who united the Mixtec kingdoms. The picture shows how the Mixtecs represented people and their names in codices.

2. The figure was made from polychrome, an innovative material Mixtecs started working with as their artisanry evolved. The material was easily available and represented a connection to nature — just like many deities in the Mixtec pantheon. Besides expanding their traditions, new technologies like this allowed the Mixtecs to grow and leave a mark on history.

3. A traditional Mixtec mask. This carved basalt mask of Tlaloc (the rain god) was a popular way Mixtecs represented their deities.

4. A traditional wood shield decorated with metals and gemstones. Not only did decorating their shields allow the Mixtecs to distinguish between the statuses of the owners, but made the shields more effective in battle.

5. A Ceramic ritual object. This is a ceramic censer used in rituals. Its intricate design shows how skilled the MMixtecartisans were at pottery and carving. From the shape and work put into it, it also likely belonged to an institution or person with a higher status.

6. A ceremonial knife. Originating from the height of the Mixtec civilization, this ceremonial knife is made from obsidian, reson, spondylus shells, and turquoise. It was likely used for sacrifice in religious ceremonies or rituals.

7. This object is dedicated to two deities, Xiuhtecuhtli and Xochipilli. It wasn't uncommon for the Mixtecs to combine the aspects of several deities in myths, rituals, and ceremonies. They often represented two gods or goddesses with a joined symbol or ceremonial vessels like this one.

8. Greenstone. Originating from between the end of the 12th and the mid-14th centuries, this ornament is made of greenstone. While most Mixtec jewelry was made from metals and gemstones, some artists used other mediums, including clay and greenstone.

9. Glyph use. Dating to 1555, this plaque is an example of how important glyphs were in the Mixtec writing system. It was displayed at a monastery, which shows that the Mixctecs used writing to signal and memorialize prominent buildings and individuals.

10. The top of the tree of life as imagined by Mixtec artists. The tree life is a powerful symbol in many Mesoamerican beliefs and cultures, connected to stories about the origin of the universe, ancestors, practices, and more.

**Timeline Answers**

1.

- The Mixtecs migrated from Northern Mexico to Oaxaca around 1500 B.C.E.
- Tilantongo became the most important Mixtec city for government, business, and culture between 1000 B.C.E. and 200 A.D.
- The Mixtecs became known for their metal work, fine pottery, and codices around 1000 A.D.
- Mixtec regions were conquered by Spanish colonizers between 1521 A.D. and 1527 A.D.

# Chapter 7: The Zapotec and Mixtec Rivalry

Living alongside each other wasn't always easy for the Mixtecs and the Zapotecs — but the two civilizations still thrived until the Aztec conquests. Still, as you'll learn from this trivia-punctuated chapter, both had to overcome many conflicts and differences along the way. The chapter highlights how they used common heritage and shared beliefs to grow their influence despite their heavy rivalry.

## Zapotec-Mixtec Clashes and Collaborations

After arriving in the early Mesoamerican region around the 5th century B.C.E., the Zapotecs lived in peace — until their new neighbors, the Mixtecs, popped up. While they didn't mind a little competition, and the two groups even found common ground culturally, the aggressive Mixtec strategy to expand eventually became too much for the Zapotecs to tolerate.

A series of conflicts over securing the best lands ensued from then on, and the Zapotecs did their best to withstand the Mixtec assault. However, over time, the Mixtec strategy became much stronger, and the Zapotecs had to give up the majority of their territories.

The Mixtec strategy wasn't only based on military advancement. It also included influencing the Zapotecs (and others in the region) through trade and culture — and it worked. Fortunately, this influence also empowered the shared heritage of the two civilizations, allowing both to inspire each other and collaborate to create architecture, agricultural, and even military strategies that benefited everyone.

## The Legends of Zapotec and Mixtec Heroes

At the core of Zapotec mythology are powerful gods like Pitao Cozobi, who created the universe and people, shaping them from clay. Being created from the soil gave the Zapotecs a connection to nature. Similarly, honoring Xipe Totec, the goddess of fertility and agriculture, was a way to express interconnectedness with the natural environment and how people experienced it.

Mictlantecuhtli, the god of the underworld, reigned over the afterlife and the souls of people who passed away. The Zapotec believed that when someone died, they went into another realm, where they had to face challenges to prove the worthiness of their soul.

In Mixtec mythology, the most prominent deity was the Dzahui rain god, who gave life to everything on the earth. Along with Cihuacoatl, the Mixtec goddess of fertility, the rain god was deeply honored for his ability to provide fertile lands and make crops and animals grow.

The Mixtec sun god, Tonatiuh, was associated with warmth and enlightenment. He could provide wisdom, sometimes leading to conflicts, so he was also said to govern wars.

The prolific Mixtec literature also talks about Yacatecuhtli, the god of trade, a hero who embarked on a treasure quest. At the end of his journey, he got the treasure he sought, bringing wealth to the people who honored him.

# Myth or History?

1. In Mixtec legend, a hero known as "Eight Deer" is believed to have ruled over multiple cities. Is this legend based on historical facts or purely a myth?

_____

_____

_____

_____

2. The rain god was a highly honored deity in the Zapotec pantheon. However, according to some stories, he could have originated from the Mixtec pantheon. Is this a myth or historical fact?

_____

_____

_____

_____

3. According to some of their tales, the Zapotec had a close connection to ferocious animals like jaguars. Is this a myth?

_____

_____

_____

_____

4. Some of their stories claim that the Zapotec abandoned Monte Albán as their capital after being guided to another place. Is this a myth or historical fact?

_____

_____

_____

_____

5. According to some Mixtec tales, the deities associated with war and the underworld also kept them connected to their ancestors and other civilizations. Is this a myth?

_____

_____

_____

_____

6. The Mixtecs (and later the Zapotecs, too) were inspired to create art because they believed it would connect them to their ancestors. Is this a myth?

_____

_____

_____

_____

7. The Mixtec and Zapotecs believed that burying people with their possessions would help them prosper in the afterlife. Is this a historical fact or a myth?

_____

_____

_____

_____

8. According to Zapotec stories, the deities are all linked to some aspect of human life. Is this a myth or history?

_____

_____

_____

_____

9. The Mixtecs affirmed that the universe was created from a primordial void. Is this a myth?

_____

_____

_____

_____

_____

10. The Zapotecs claimed that every force on this earth has two sides, one good and one bad. Is this a myth?

_____

_____

_____

_____

_____

# Picture-Based

1. Who was this Mixtec leader and what is this leader known for?

Image 61

Response:

_____

_____

_____

2. Who is the king on the left?

Image 62

Response:

_____

_____

_____

3. This ruler was one of the most famous ones in Mixtec history. Who is he?

Image 63

Response:

_____

_____

_____

## 4. Who was this ruler?

**Image 64**

Response:

_____

_____

_____

5. Name this ruler and their role.

**Image 65**

Response:

_____

_____

_____

6. Who is this Zapotec ruler?

Image 66

Response:

_____

_____

_____

7. A Spanish artist made this picture of a Zapotec ruler. Who was this ruler?

**Image 67**

Response:

_____

_____

_____

8. Name this ruler and his role in Zapotec history.

**Image 68**

Response:

_____

_____

_____

9. What does this map depict?

**Image 69**

Response:

_____

_____

_____

10. What does this picture show?

**Image 70**

Response:

_____

_____

_____

## Multiple Choice Questions

1. What was one of the key factors that led to conflicts between the Zapotec and Mixtec civilizations?

    a. Competition for the best agricultural land

    b. Religious differences

    c. Disagreements over trade routes

    d. A friendly rivalry

2. How were the Mixtecs and Zapotecs connected?

    a. Trough marriages

    b. Trough trade

    c. By living next to each other

    d. All of the above

3. What did the Mixtecs and Zapotecs share with each other?

    a. Technologies and new ideas

    b. Deities

    c. A common origin story

    d. Languages

4. What was one of the main lessons that can be learned from the interactions of the Zapotec and Mixtec?

    a. Conquest is the best way to secure fertile land

    b. Mutual respect can help everyone thrive

    c. Familiar relationships weaken political powers

    d. Military control is stronger than respect for shared heritage

5. What are some of the main differences between the Mixtec and Zapotec civilizations?

    a. Social organization

    b. View of nature

    c. Religious practices

    d. Political views

6. What shows the blending of two religions the most?

    a. Architecture

    b. Rituals

    c. Icons

    d. All of the above

7. How did the two civilizations form political alliances?

    a. Trough conquests

    b. Through migration

    c. Through trade

    d. Though marriage and inheritance

8. What did the Mixtecs adopt from the Zapotecs?

    a. Agricultural practices

    b. Military strategies

    c. Nature worship

    d. Gemstone work

9. What kind of political system did the Zapotecs have?

    a. Decentralized

    b. Centralized

    c. Mixed

    d. Status-based

10. When did the power shift permanently from the earlier settler Zapotecs to the newly developed Mixtec civilization?

    a. 13-15th century

    b. 11th century

    c. 13th century

    d. 10-13th century

# Fill-in-the-Blank

You may use any of the following words to fill in the blanks:

| | | |
|---|---|---|
| writing | competition | adaptation |
| ceramics | houses | alliances |
| gold | diversity | cooperation |
| northwest | observatories | mathematics |
| evolution | mythology | history |
| astronomy | blending. | |

1. The Zapotec and Mixtec civilizations often formed _____ to strengthen their positions against other Mesoamerican groups.

2. The Mixtecs often traded _____ jewelry (crafted by their own skilled artisans) for intricately designed _____ made by the Zapotecs.

3. Seeing its use for recording _____ and _____, the Zapotecs adopted the Mixtec _____ system.

4. The interactions between the Zapotec and Mixtec people show how two cultures _____ to each other and _____ depending on their relationship.

5. _____ and _____ were both important for forming a mutually beneficial relationship between the Zapotec and the Mixtec.

6. The Mixtecs were fascinated by the Zapotec skills in _____ hand _____ and started incorporating these skills into their knowledge base, too.

7. A unique feature the Zapotec adopted from Mixtec art was the seamless _____ style.

8. Mixtec ruler Eight Deer "Tiger Claw" played a crucial role in creating greater _____ among all the cities he conquered and ruled.

9. Until the Mixtec started to pressure them, the Zapotec built very few buildings — they only created some _____ and _____ in their early settlements.

10. When invading the Zapotec capital, the Mixtecs initially came from the _____.

# True or False

1. The Zapotec and Mixtec civilizations never collaborated on cultural or artistic endeavors.

   - True
   - False

2. The cultural and technological exchanges helped both civilizations thrive.

   - True
   - False

3. Even where wars were fought over territories, the shared culture often helped create peace and alliance between the Mixtecs and the Zapotecs.

   - True
   - False

4. Monte Albán was one of the earliest urban centers in Mesoamerica.

   - True
   - False

5. The Mixtec never used former Zapotec sacred sites at Monte Albán.

   - True
   - False

6. The Mixtecs and the Zapotecs had no common elements in their languages.

   - True
   - False

7. The Mixtec art had a larger influence on Zapotec culture than the Zapotec art on Mixtec arts and crafts.

   - True
   - False

8. Some Mixtec codices feature Zapotec influence, too.

   - True
   - False

9. When a Mixtec or Zapotec territory was conquered by the other, the conquerors' culture replaced the existing one.

   - True
   - False

10. The Zapotec had a more aggressive approach to conquering fertile lands.

   - True
   - False

# Timeline Questions

1. When did the Mixtecs start to marry into Zapotec tribes, right after their arrival or a few centuries later?

2. When did the Zapotecs abandon their capital: after they started a cultural exchange with the Mayans or after the Mixtecs' arrival?

# Answer Key

**Myth or History Answers**

1. History. Eight Deer, better known as Lord Eight Deer Jaguar Claw, was a real-life ruler of multiple cities and kingdoms. He founded a new royal line, and his fame surpassed him after his death, converting his heroic actions into myths.

2. History. Archeological evidence shows that the Mixtecs also had deities with roles and properties similar to the Zapotec rain god. They also had rituals which were performed almost the exact way as were the ones honoring the rain god.

3. Myth. The connection to animals like jaguars likely comes from religious beliefs. Many Zapotec deities were associated with large and imposing animals, so it's not surprising that in legends, people ascribed a closer connection to these creatures. By claiming they are related to animals the gods were also linked to, they felt a closer connection to the deities.

4. Myth. Monte Albán, their initial capital, had very little natural resources. As the Zapotec civilization grew, they needed to find another place to center around, so they relocated the capital to Zaachila, which had much better resources and trade routes.

5. History. Records show that Mixtec deities associated with the underworld and war are very similar to similar deities from other Mesoamerican cultures, including the Zapotec.

6. A little bit of both. The skills and talents were passed down through many generations in both cultures, which allowed newer generations to feel connected to their ancestors. It was also a way to honor the ancestors' wisdom, knowledge, and culture.

7. History. Both groups buried their dead with as many possessions as they could. Kings and the nobility were buried with gold, silver, amber, turquoise, and animal bones (usually jaguar or other large animal).

8. History. Their writings and artistry show that the Zapotecs had gods and goddesses for everything. These deities were honored based on their associations.

9. Myth. The Mixtecs' legends about the primordial void have likely come from their belief that the heavenly bodies governed what happened on the earth. This belief was partially adopted from the Zapotec astronomical observations — but the Mixtecs saw it as a great way to explain events they didn't understand.

10. Myth. While some beliefs of the dual powers were represented in their artistry, it was likely that the Zapotecs used this to understand why some natural forces can be nurturing one moment and turn destructive the next.

## Picture-Based Answers

1. Lady Six Monkey, the queen of Jaltepec. Ruling from 1090 to 1101, she was one of the most formidable Mixtec rulers. She even went into war (and won several battles) against Lord Eight Deer, a powerful king of another Mixtec kingdom.

2. **Lord Eight Grass**, king of Tlaxiaco, the last Mixtec ruler. While he fought valiantly against the Aztecs, in 1503, they still emerged victorious and have overtaken Tlaxiaco.

3. Lord Eight Deer Jaguar Claw, the king who united several Mixtec kingdoms. To do this, he had to fight many vicious battles, overthrow the rulers of Acatepec, Tututepec, and Manialtepec, and usurp their thrones.

4. Lord Nine Lizard Fire Face, the king of Jaltepec from 1381. During his reign, his kingdom was attacked by the Toltec kingdom of Zaachila. In this attack, he lost all but one son. The surviving son, Lord 2 Jaguar, succeeded his father and continued fighting against the Zapotec.

5. Lady 12 Flower Broken Mountain Butterfly. She was the first queen of Tilantongo after the kingdom was separated from the united kingdoms in 1341. She was also part of a mixed Zaachila-Teozacoalco dynasty, created through the unification of families (marriages) between the Zapotec and the Mixtec.

6. Lord Eight Deer Fire Serpent, the ruler of Zaachila from 1487. He fought several battles against the Mixtec, including one led by his own twin sister, Lady Eight Deer, the queen of Tlaxiaco.

7. Cosijopii II, the last king of Zaachila. His reign ended in 1504. Ruling jointly with his sister Pinopija, he tried to prevent the Aztecs from taking over, but like the Tlaxiaco ruler, he was unsuccessful.

8. He attempted to recover Monte Albán from the Mixtecs, but the Mixtecs had much stronger allies. He founded a new Zapotec capital at Zaachila, established by his great-uncle, Zaachila I. After his rule, the Zapotec started to fall into decline.

9. The massive influence of the Zapotec civilization in Mesoamerica — more specifically, in what is known today as the state of Oaxaca in Mexico.

10. Zapotec ceramic vessel. Its form shows the Mixtec influence of Zapotec artistry — including the use of sacred motifs (in this case, jaguar) in pottery.

## Multiple Choice Answers

1. A. Competition for the best agricultural land. Since the Zapotecs lived in their settlements for much longer than the Mixtecs, they felt they had more rights to fertile agricultural lands. Conversely, the Mixtecs wanted to secure more land as they expanded in their new settlements in Mesoamerica.

2. D. All of the above. Not only were the Mixtecs and Zapotecs living next to each other in neighboring settlements, but they also traded goods among each other. There were also many marriages between the two groups, which further deepened their connection.

3. A. and B. Technologies and new ideas and deities. Despite the rivalry, the Mixtecs were happy to share their innovations with the Zapotecs. The Zaptotecs, in turn, inspired the Mixtecs with their own ideas. Some of these innovations and cultural exchanges happened because the two groups shared deities among their pantheons.

4. B. Mutual respect can help everyone thrive. If there is something everyone can learn from the way the Mixtecs and the Zapotecs interacted with each other despite their rivalries and the need to secure fertile land, it is that you can gain far more with mutual respect than through conflict and forceful control.

5. A. and C. Social organization and religious practices. While both groups had some similar deities in their pantheons, they worshiped them differently. Moreover, Mixtec society was far more organized and controlled than the Zapotec — this allowed the Mixtecs to advance more rapidly and take over the Zapotec territories.

6. D. All of the above. Archeological findings show that the Mixtecs and Zapotecs shared elements of their religions through similarly performed rituals and crafted religious iconography. Some of their religious monuments and sacred worship sites are also built and decorated similarly.

7. D. Through marriage and inheritance. It wasn't uncommon for Zapotec or Mixtec leaders to marry into the other group. They gained an ally, and their children gained a new territory. Sometimes, siblings would rule in two different cities or even civilizations, as they inherited both thrones from their parents.

8. A. Agricultural practices. Given that the Zapotecs settled earlier in the region, they knew how to work with the land and unpredictable weather. In the beginning, when the Mixtecs arrived and settled next to them, they saw Zapotecs use efficient agricultural practices and adopted them.

9. B. Centralized. This system was where the main political powers were centered in bigger cities. These controlled the smaller regions as well. This was the opposite of the Mixtecs' decentralized system, yet that one was more powerful because it used more effective strategies.

10. A. 13-15th century. While the Mixtec civilization began thriving in the 10th century, the major shift of power in their region happened between the end of the 13th and the middle of the 15th century. It was when they overtook many Zapotec territories and established dominance in the region.

**Fill-in-the-Blank Answers**

1. Alliances.
2. Gold, ceramics.
3. Mythology, history, writing.
4. Adapt, evolve.
5. Competition, cooperation.

6. Mathematics, astronomy.

7. Blending.

8. Diversity.

9. Houses, observatories.

10. Northwest.

**True or False Answers**

1. False. Due to their many familial links, the Mixtecs and the Zapotecs exchanged cultural and artistic influences regularly. They also worked together to create items representing both cultures and their joint beliefs and traditions.

2. True. Trading was beneficial for both the Mixtec and Zapotec economies. Merchants on both sides could always find buyers on the other side and earn money to sustain their families and settlements. This was particularly good for the elite members. Still, everyone benefited from having access to a wider range of ways to express their cultural beliefs and traditions.

3. True. Due to the frequent marriages and cultural exchanges, the Mixtecs forged alliances with the Zapotecs in joint communities. Sometimes, these communities were forged in places where the leaders of each group fought over political and military control of the region. The shared connection was more powerful than any order and prevailed against any issue that brought the leaders to conflict.

4. True. As the capital of the early Zapotec civilization, Monte Albán quickly became a growing hub of farmers, workers, and traders. It started as a small settlement, but by 750 A.D., the city had approximately 25,000 citizens.

5. False. When the Mixtec arrived at Monte Albán, the Zapotec abandoned the local sacred sites. While they didn't use many religious worship sites, the Mixtecs did open some of the Zapotec burial sites to bury their own dead. They also held burial ceremonies at these sites.

6. False. While the Mixtec and Zapotec languages have always differed, they have some common elements. After all, the two groups began their interactions by living next to and trading with each other in ancient Mesoamerica. To trade, they needed to have a way to understand each other, hence why they have common elements in their languages.

7. True. While the Zapotec had many skilled craftsmen, the Mixtec were more determined to spread their products through trade. It allowed them to show their power and influence in the region just as much as victories and conquests.

8. True. While Mixtec codices mentioning the Zapotec typically talk about conquests of familial relationships between the two groups, some also feature Zapotec's influence in the images themselves. For example, the Codex Zouche-Nuttall has symbols and motifs representing the beliefs and ideas of both cultures.

9. False. Instead of replacing or erasing the original culture, the conquerors simply absorbed it. They used some elements, added their own twist to it, and created a blend that was much easier to accept by the conquered population.

10. False. The ones with an aggressive approach were the Mixtecs. They constantly looked for new territories and went to conquer them as soon as they found one. They rarely hesitated because they believed it to be a sign of weakness.

**Timeline Answers**

1. The Mixtecs started to intermarry and take control of the Zapotec sites only around 1350 A.D., a few centuries after they settled next to the Zapotec territory.

2. The Zapotecs abandoned their capital only after the Mixtecs' arrival.

# Chapter 8: The Aztec Empire: Warriors, Temples, and the Great Tenochtitlán

With a capital larger than any other city in Mesoamerica, markets that attracted enough visitors to fill a small town, and buildings that showcased skill and grandeur, the Aztec Empire was among the most impressive in the region's history.

What made it even more remarkable is that it was built by warriors who took time to learn and gather alliances — until they could strike and take control over their own growth and the entire region's growth.

As you'll learn from this chapter, despite all these feats, the Aztecs were also known for infamous practices like human sacrifice and collecting tribute to the emperor from everyone under their control.

## Aztec Sacrificial Practices

Religion was deeply interwoven into Aztec culture — with numerous temples, statutes, plazas, and palaces built in honor of their deities. The Aztecs were devoted to gods that governed different aspects of their lives, from life to death and beyond. They would make offerings and sacrifices to the gods at these sacred places.

Offerings and rituals often included human sacrifices to honor the gods. Typically, they only sacrificed enemy warriors captured in battle, but in rare cases, they would also sacrifice women and children. This happened only when they felt the gods required a greater offering to appease or grant a wish.

Besides honoring the gods, sacrifices were also made to pay tribute to the emperor. According to the Aztecs, the emperor was a mighty man who was led to victories by the gods and to make the empire thrive. The tributes were similar to modern-day taxes as they involved giving up something (typically a product made by their state/city/region).

Bloodletting was another typical offering used by the Aztecs. During this ritual, priests and other participants would collect and offer their own blood in honor of the gods.

# Multiple Choice

1. Which god was primarily associated with the Templo Mayor in Tenochtitlan?

   a. Quetzalcoatl

   b. Huitzilopochtli

   c. Tlaloc

   d. Xipe Totec

2. How did the Aztecs call themselves?

   a. Aztlanians

   b. Mexica

   c. Texcocans

   d. Tepanec

3. When was the Aztec capital, Tenochtitlan, founded?

   a. 1325

   b. 1355

   c. 1425

   d. 1455

4. How many people lived in the Aztec-conquered territories?

   a. 1 million

   b. 2 million

   c. 6 million

   d. Half a million

5. Who is the leader known as the father of the Aztec Empire?

   a. Itzcoatl

   b. Tacloban

   c. Texcoco

   d. Moctezuma

6. Besides conquests, how did the Aztecs expand their rule?

   a. Through religion

   b. Through trade

   c. Through migration

   d. None of the above

7. Starting from the top layer, how was the society in the Aztec empire divided?

   a. Nobles, servants, workers, and enslaved individuals

   b. Leaders, priests, workers, and slaves

   c. Nobles and leaders, workers, priests, slaves

    d. Religious and political leaders, workers, and enslaved individuals

8. Who was the Aztec patron god who, according to the legends, directed the Aztecs to settle where they did, found their capital, and conquer many more territories?

    a. Tlaloc

    b. Huitzilopochtli

    c. Aztlan

    d. Tenochtitlan

9. Why was recordkeeping so fundamental for the Aztecs?

    a. It made keeping track of tributes easier

    b. It helped showcase the emperor's power

    c. It allowed for better control over the economy

    d. All of the above

10. What kind of records did the Aztecs keep?

    a. Military and trade

    b. Religious, military, and social

    c. Social and commercial

    d. Alliance and taxation

# Templo Mayor

The Templo Mayor (translated as Great Temple) was built in the center of Tenochtitlan in honor of the two most powerful Aztec deities. Each of these gods, Huitzilopochtli and Tlaloc, had a pyramid dedicated to them on the top of the temple structure. According to Aztec myths, the pyramids were the sacred mountains where the two deities were born and resided — the war god Huitzilopochtli on the Hill of Coatepec and Tlaloc on the Hill of Sustenance.

The temple was about 90 feet high, dominating the area of the capital called Sacred Precinct. Every public ritual and ceremony in the city was performed at the temple, either at one pyramid or the other. To access the pyramids, a person would have to ascend a tactically built staircase held up by two giant handrails.

On top of the temple were sculptures of human-like figures holding two posts. The Aztecs would hang the banner prepared for the current occasion between these posts. At the bottom, the staircase was guarded by carved serpent heads.

Initially, upon the founding of Tenochtitlan, the Templo Mayor was built as a small religious site dedicated to a deity. Over the next two centuries, it was expanded in several stages, displaying the extensive skill sets of the Aztec master architects.

# Fill-in-the-Blank

You may use any of the following words to fill in the blanks:

| | | |
|---|---|---|
| military | economy | channels |
| 16th | gods | ruling | water. |
| codices | Mexico | neighbors |
| lakes | agricultural | market |
| overthrow | Gulf of Mexico | Pacific |

1. Aztec sacrifices were often performed at the top of the Templo Mayor to honor the _____.

2. Soon after their arrival, the Aztecs gained _____ experience by serving in the _____ civilization's army.

3. In 1428, the Aztecs joined two of their _____ to _____ the Tepanec who ruled the region.

4. By the early _____ century, the Aztecs had conquered enough territory to span over 80,000 square miles from the _____ Ocean in the west and the _____ in the east.

5. Bringing _____ into a city through long stone _____ was a crucial Aztec innovation.

6. The biggest _____ in the Aztec capital, Tlatelolco, had 50,000 visitors on the main market days, which played a crucial role in growing the _____.

7. Tenochtitlan was built in a region made of five interconnected _____.

8. Tenochtitlan was made to thrive through a successful and productive _____ system.

9. Like the Mixtecs and the Zapotecs, the Aztecs also recorded their history and practices in _____.

10. The legacy of the great Aztec Empire as its capital, Tenochtitlan has become the capital of modern-day _____.

# What Am I?

1. I am a unique structure in the Aztec capital, Tenochtitlan, and serve as a focal point for religious ceremonies. I have several parts dedicated to different purposes. What am I?

   _____

2. I am the mythical land the Aztecs arrived from to settle in their final position in Mesoamerica. The Aztecs are named after me. What am I?

   _____

3. I am the lake near which the Aztecs first settled and established their capital. What am I?

   _____

4. I am the group that ruled over the region where the Aztecs first arrived and settled. Slowly, the Aztecs took away my power. What am I?

   _____

5. I am a unique farming system that allowed the Aztec civilization to thrive in an inland area surrounded by water and very little fertile land. What am I?

   _____

6. Besides the one built for Tlaloc, I am the only other Aztec pyramid built in honor of one major deity. What am I?

   _____

7. I am the city with the most inhabitants (around 140,000) in the entire history of Mesoamerica. I showed how powerful the Aztecs can be. What am I?

   _____

8. I am the animal the Aztecs saw and took as a sign to settle where they did in Mesoamerica in the early 14th century. I was later featured in the colonizer's art and history books. What am I?

   _____

9. I am the city that served as the capital of the civilization that governed the region before the Aztecs arrived. What am I?

   _____

10. I am one of the two surviving codices recording the tributes (taxes) paid by the individual rulers under the Aztec rule. What am I?

_____

# True or False

1. The Aztec sacrifices were purely for entertainment and had no religious significance.
   - True
   - False

2. The Aztec Empire was the last greatest civilization in Mesoamerica.
   - True
   - False

3. The Aztecs kept a joint rule with their allies after they overthrew the Tepanec.
   - True
   - False

4. The Aztecs determined how the leaders of the conquered regions would rule.
   - True
   - False

5. The human sacrifices were one of the major reasons for the fall of the Aztec Empire.
   - True
   - False

6. The nobility were exempt from serving in the military.
   - True
   - False

7. The Aztecs built only two pyramids where they offered sacrifice and honored the deities.
   - True
   - False

8. The Aztecs started their migration from the north and advanced to the south.
   - True
   - False

9. Besides valiant warriors and crafty traders, the Aztecs were also skilled builders.
   - True
   - False

10. Aztec record keeping also allowed historians to learn about earlier civilizations and all those groups the Aztecs had contact with.
    - True
    - False

# Picture-Based

1. What was the purpose of this Aztec ritual?

**Image 71**

Response:

_____

_____

_____

## 2. What do the pictures on this codex page depict?

**Image 72**

Response:

_____

_____

_____

## 3. Identify the object.

**Image 73**

Response:

_____

_____

_____

4. What's the significance of this picture?

Image 74

Response:

_____

_____

_____

5. What's shown in this picture?

**Image 75**

Response:

_____

_____

_____

## 6. What was the purpose of this Aztec ritual?

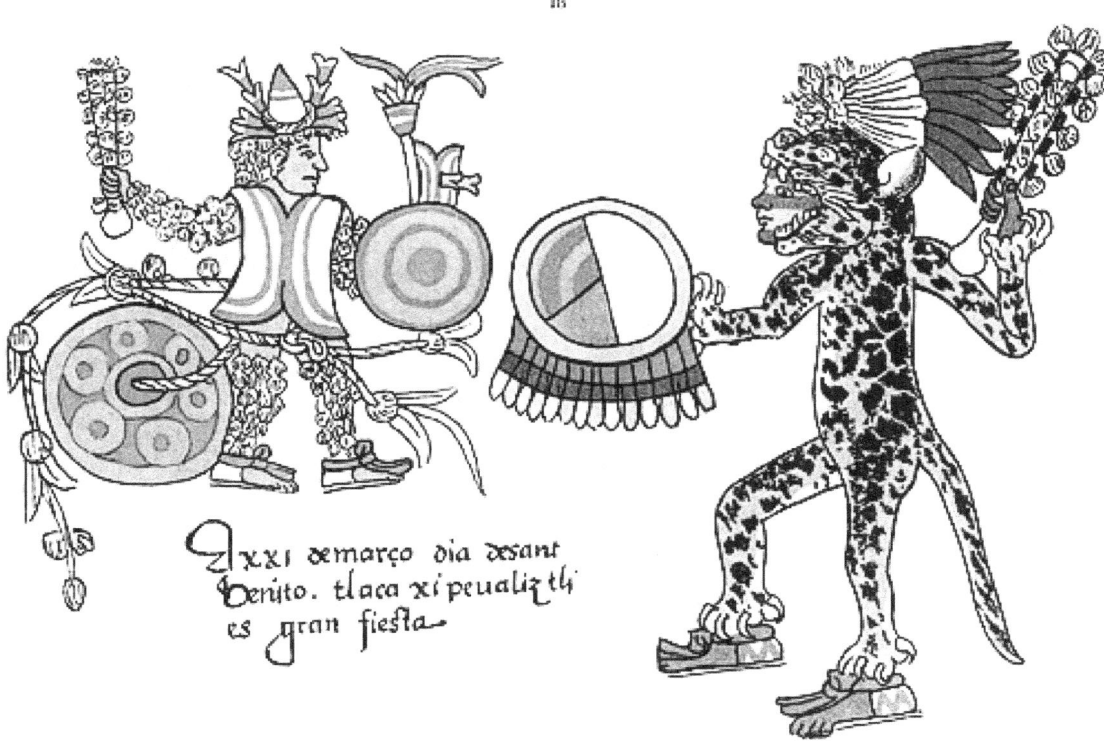

**Image 76**

Response:

_____

_____

_____

7. Identify the object.

**Image 77**

Response:

_____

_____

_____

## 8. What does this picture depict?

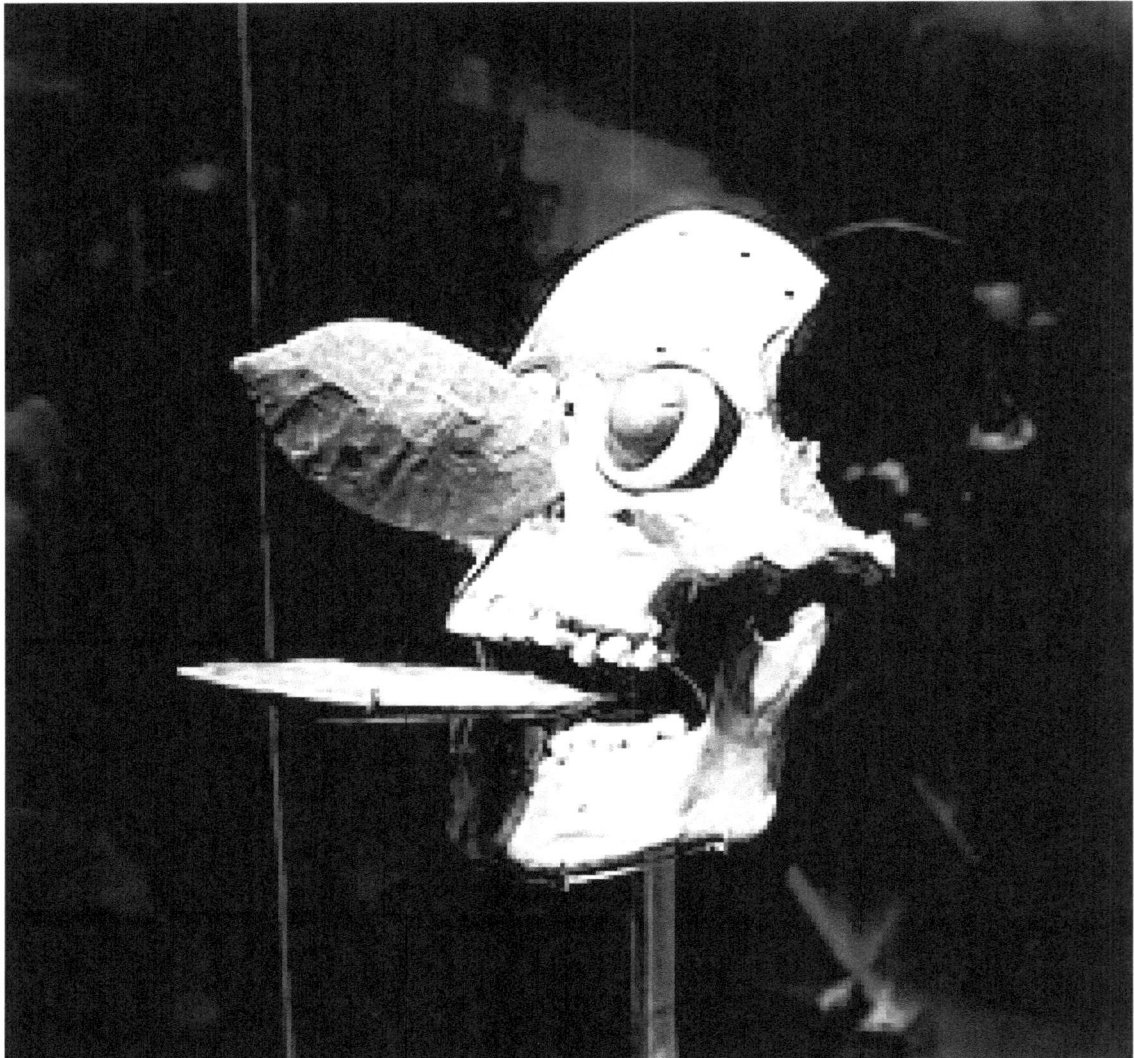

Image 78

Response:

_____

_____

_____

## 9. What does this object symbolize?

Image 79

Response:

_____

_____

_____

10. What was the purpose of these objects?

**Image 80**

Response:

_____

_____

_____

# Timeline Questions

1. Arrange the following events in chronological order:

   - The Aztecs' rival, the Tarascan civilization, began to flourish in Mesoamerica.
   - The Aztec capital, Tenochtitlan, is founded on Lake Texcoco.
   - The first recorded New Fire Ceremony is celebrated by the Aztecs.
   - The Aztecs lost a major city, Texcoco, to Tepanec forces.

2. Arrange these Aztec leaders based on when they came to rule:

   - Acamapichtli
   - Itzcoatl
   - Huitzilihuitl
   - Axayacatl
   - Ahuitzotl
   - Montezuma I
   - Montezuma II
   - Tizoc

3. Arrange these monuments based on the date they were completed:

   - The Coyolxauhqui Stone
   - The Stone of Tizoc
   - Templo Mayor
   - The Sun Stone

# Answer Key

## Multiple Choice Answers

1. C. Tlaloc. As the god of rain, Tlaloc was highly respected by the Aztecs. They believed that he gave life to them and everything in nature and helped nature's renewal and rebirth at the beginning of each year. By offering sacrifices, the Aztecs wanted to ensure Tlaloc would continue to help nurture their lands.

2. B. Mexica. Pronounced meh-SHEE-kah, Mexica is the word the Aztecs used to describe themselves in their own language. Based on this name was their land named Mexico. Historical records suggest that the Aztecs continued to refer to themselves as Mexica from when they arrived in Mesoamerica and onward — even after they were named Aztecs by other neighboring and subsequent civilizations.

3. A. 1325. The famous Aztec capital, Tenochtitlan, was founded in 1325, near the lake the Aztecs first settled a few years before. While other groups inhabited a large part of Mesoamerica, the Aztecs managed to find a large enough empty space on an island to find the city soon after their arrival.

4. C. 6 million. At the height of the empire, the number of people under the Aztec rule in Mesoamerica was estimated to be around 6 million. This included those living in the Aztec empire and the conquered territories they took possession of (including the Zapotec and Mixtec civilizations).

5. D. Moctezuma. Ruling from 1440, Moctezuma was one of the greatest warriors and became known as the father of the Aztec Empire. He was the son of Itzcoatl, the warrior who led the rebellion against the Tepanec. Like his father, Moctezuma was a fearsome leader who wanted to expand his empire and take control of the region.

6. B. Through trade. While they were fearsome warriors, the Aztecs were just as skilled at trading as they were wielding weapons on the battlefield. They established many trade routes and ensured they could transport and trade a broad range of products.

7. A. Nobles, servants, workers, and enslaved individuals. The top layer belonged to the nobility, which included all leaders (the emperor and every political and religious governor). The next layer was made up of servants and workers. At the bottom of the society were the slaves, who had the toughest lives, either being servants, warriors, or sacrifices to honor the gods.

8. B. Huitzilopochtli. As the patron god of Aztec warriors, leaders, and founders, Huitzilopochtli became legendary for directing the Aztecs to settle, conquer, and expand.

9. D. All of the above. Recordkeeping allowed the Aztecs to keep track of tributes (these were forms of taxes) made by rulers of the individual territories under the emperor's governance. It made controlling the economy easier because all trades

and transactions were recorded. Lastly, the emperor showcased his power and influence in the region by ensuring they held everything and everyone under control.

10. B. Religious, military, and social — most Aztec records fall into these three categories. These incorporated all aspects of life and culture, including connection to the ancestors, deities, and other groups through familial lines.

## Fill-in-the-Blank Answers

1. Gods.
2. Military, ruling.
3. Neighbors, overthrow.
4. 16th, Pacific, Gulf of Mexico.
5. Water, channels.
6. Market, economy.
7. Lakes.
8. Agriculture.
9. Codices.
10. Mexico.

## What Am I Answers

1. Templo Mayor.
2. Aztlan.
3. Lake Texcoco.
4. Tepanec.
5. Chinampas (or floating farm system).
6. The pyramid of Huitzilopochtli.
7. Tenochtitlan.
8. An Eagle (eating a snake on top of a cactus).
9. Azcapotzalco.
10. Codex Mendoza.

## True or False Answers

1. False. The Aztec rituals always had religious purposes, as their beliefs played crucial roles in the Aztecs' lives. Sacrifices included in rituals were often dedicated to deities or similar powers who could grant the Aztecs whatever they asked during the ritual (for example, guidance, power, a sign that they would win in a battle, etc.).

2. True. Lasting from the early 14th to the early 16th century, the Aztec Empire was the last biggest civilization in ancient Mesoamerica. The rule of the Indigenous people ended in the 16th century with the European conquests. After the Spanish colonizers arrived, they left no room for another civilization to thrive.

3. False. Soon after their allies helped them overthrow the Tepanec, the Aztecs took control over them too. From then on, they ruled a massive part of the region and set on to conquer even more of it.

4. False. The Aztecs let the leader of the conquered territories rule as they wished — with one condition. The leaders had to regularly visit and pay their tribute to the great Aztec emperor in Tenochtitlan. This included bringing gifts like cotton, gemstones, feathers, and food and drink items.

5. True. Over time, those under Aztec rule became so dissatisfied with practices like human sacrifice that they preferred to ally themselves with the Aztecs' enemies. This included the Spanish conquistadors, who eventually overtook the Aztec Empire.

6. False. Every man had to serve in the military, including the nobility. In fact, the elite men were some of the most decorated members of the Aztec military, having participated in many battles and mounted countless victories.

7. False. Besides the two major ones, the Aztecs had several more pyramids across the empire. Some served as resting places for the leaders, while others had religious purposes where the gods were worshiped through ceremonies, rituals, and sacrifice.

8. False. To arrive in Mesoamerica, the Aztecs migrated from the south to the central part of the region. From there, they started to expand in every direction, not just south or north.

9. True. The numerous religious monuments are only a fraction of what showed the Aztecs' amazing building skills. They built towns, expanded cities, roads, and more — all across the empire and within a relatively short period of time. It is enough to think of just how fast they built their capital into the largest city in the region.

10. True. Since some groups the Aztecs had contact with or learned about had no writing systems, the Aztec records proved a valuable source of information for learning about Mesoamerican history. While their records may reflect the Aztecs' opinion about these other civilizations (and not how they actually functioned), without the Aztec records, modern-day people wouldn't know much about the many groups who helped shape Mesoamerican history.

**Picture-Based Answers**

1. Protection against flooding. After their capital was flooded at the end of the 15th century, the Aztecs believed the gods were angry at them. They performed a flooding ritual to appease the deities and prevent further floodings. As the picture shows, the ritual also involved (human) sacrifice.

2. The pictures depict another Aztec ritual performed on the top of the Templo Mayor. In the first picture, the priests start the ritual with people gathered around them. On the second, a person is sacrificed on the upper front part of the pyramid/temple.

3. A drum from the Teponaztli. It was used in religious rituals and ceremonies. The Aztecs loved using drums and chanting for rites because it helped draw more attention. The more people attended, the stronger the ties in the community got.

4. Traditional headgear. The picture shows a person wearing a traditional Aztec headdress and mask. Masks with skulls and carved faces were popular in Aztec rituals and ceremonies before the Spanish conquest. They represented a connection to the ancestors and tradition.

5. A ceremonial tomb Aztecs used in burial rituals. On the top of the tomb are sculptures associated with the cycle of life — more precisely, the 52 year-cycle the Aztecs strongly believed in.

6. This was a sacrificial ritual called gladiator sacrifice. During the ritual, a person (shown on the left) had to fight against a warrior dressed as a jaguar (shown on the right).

7. An Aztec ritual stone. Given its shape, it was likely used to make sacrifices during rituals and ceremonies. This one was made around the 15th or 16th century from greenstone.

8. The picture depicts the skull of a warrior found in Templo Mayor. It was part of a decoration or headdress made in the 15th century from the skull of a defeated warrior. Adorned with sea shells, blades, and pyrite, the skull was similar to many others used in rituals honoring the dead.

9. It illustrates the use of animal shapes in Aztec art and religious symbolism. This object is shaped like a grasshopper, which is the official symbol and namesake of Chapultepec, a favorite place of retreat for the Aztec leaders,

10. Stone artifacts used for making offerings. Besides sacrifices, the Aztecs also honored their gods, ancestors, and surrounding forces by offering them symbols, gifts, food, drinks, and objects associated with them.

**Timeline Answers:**

1.

- The Aztec capital, Tenochtitlan, was founded on Lake Texcoco in 1345 A.D., marking the beginning of the rise of the Aztec Empire.
- The Aztecs' rival, the Tarascan civilization, began to flourish in Mesoamerica around 1350 A.D.
- The first recorded New Fire Ceremony was celebrated by the Aztecs in 1351 A.D.
- The Aztecs lost a major city, Texcoco, to Tepanec forces in 1418 A.D.

2.

- Acamapichtli (1375 - 1395 A.D.)
- Huitzilihuitl (1396 - 1417 A.D.)
- Itzcoatl (1427 - 1440 A.D.)

- Montezuma I (1440 - 1469 A.D.)
- Axayacatl (1469 - 1481 A.D.)
- Tizoc (1481 - 1486 A.D.)
- Ahuitzotl (1486 - 1502 A.D.)
- Montezuma II (1502 - 1520 A.D.)

3.

- The Sun Stone, showing the ages of the five suns of Aztec mythology, was built at Tenochtitlan in 1427 CE.
- The Coyolxauhqui Stone, dedicated to the Aztec goddess Coyolxauhqui, was built around 1473 A.D.
- The Stone of Tizoc, showing King Tizoc attacking warriors from the Matlatzinca was built in 1485 A.D.)
- Templo Mayor was completed and inaugurated with the sacrifice of 20,000 captives in 1487.

# Chapter 9: The Peak of the Maya: The Classic Period Enigma

Once thriving and with access to incredible skill, knowledge, technologies, and power, it's hard to imagine how the Maya civilization fell into decline. This chapter explores the possible reasons the Maya went from reaching their peak to abandoning their cities and sacred sites during the Classic Period.

Throughout the chapter, you'll find many exciting trivia questions about the Mayan decline enigma, pictures, explanations, and information about how the Maya cities were lost, along with a piece of history defined by this civilization.

## Abandoned Cities: The Maya Exodus

During its peak, the Maya society was led by rulers who were called holy lords. They demanded respect and regular tribute (donations) from their followers. However, these lords have slowly lost their power due to constant warfare. No one wanted to respect or work for them anymore. They didn't do much to help the struggling population, and the people had enough. Some began to rebel, and others left.

Besides talking about the rebellions and conflicts, archaeological evidence also suggests that people were forced to abandon the cities in many places due to food and water shortages, lack of fertile soils, and overpopulation. How much these contributed to the Mayas' downfall is still unclear. Historians are still only speculating about how the greatest Maya cities were left behind to be swallowed by the surrounding jungle.

## What Caused the Decline?

1. The decline of Maya cities is believed to be primarily due to _____ _____. Fill in the blank.

_____

_____

_____

_____

2. Tikal, one of the largest Maya cities, had likely fallen into decline because of the lack of _____ resources. Fill in the blank.

3. Besides soil erosion and lack of fertile soils, what environmental factors could have caused the decline of agriculture? Hint: it has to do with losing water due to a lack of trees.

_____

_____

_____

_____

4. How did the Maya leaders contribute to the decline? Do they cause even more problems or help their followers?

_____

_____

_____

_____

5. The constant warfare affected relationships within the society. How do you think it affected the families and communities?

_____

_____

_____

_____

6. The Mayas had extensive systems to catch and store rainfall. So why did the longer drought period cause water and food shortages?

_____

_____

_____

_____

7. Even though people could travel and secure food and water from somewhere else, they couldn't transport it to the lowlands due to the _____. Fill in the blank.

8. While initially, cities in the north have replaced cities in the south as centers of power, they, too, started to decline. Do you know why?

_____

_____

_____

_____

_____

9. Besides agriculture, the Mayas have also cut down trees for another purpose. What do you think this purpose was?

_____

_____

_____

_____

_____

10. 150 years after the southern regions, the northern lowlands have also fallen due to the collapse of _____ and _____ systems. Fill in the blanks.

# Picture-Based

1. This was one of the newest Maya capital cities, with several structures remaining. Yet it was still abandoned. Why? What could've happened here?

**Image 81**

Response:

_____

_____

_____

## 2. Name the monument.

**Image 82**

Response:

_____

_____

_____

3. Which abandoned Maya city housed this building? Why do you think it was abandoned?

**Image 83**

Response:

_____

_____

_____

4. The structures in this picture clearly belonged to a powerful city. Which city was this, and why couldn't it continue thriving?

**Image 84**

Response:

_____

_____

_____

5. While this structure is still standing, the city where it is located has long been abandoned. What's the name of the structure and the city?

**Image 85**

Response:

_____

_____

_____

6. When do you think this city was abandoned, and why?

Image 86

Response:

_____

_____

_____

## 7. Where is this structure located?

**Image 87**

Response:

_____

_____

_____

8. One of the cities on this map was the last independent Maya state. Which one?

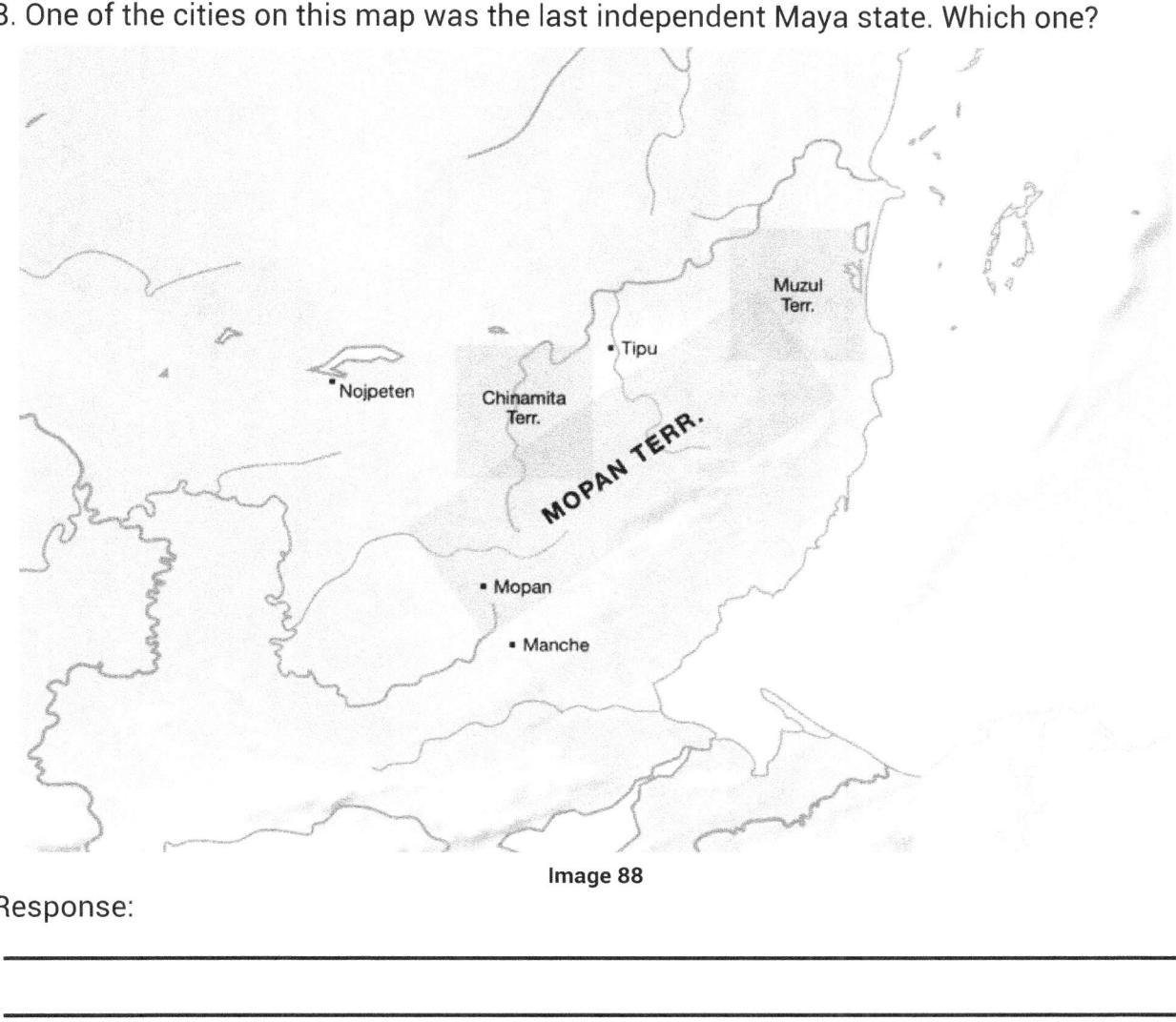

**Image 88**

Response:

_____

_____

_____

9. These are pages from one of the only remaining Maya codices. Do you know what this codex is called?

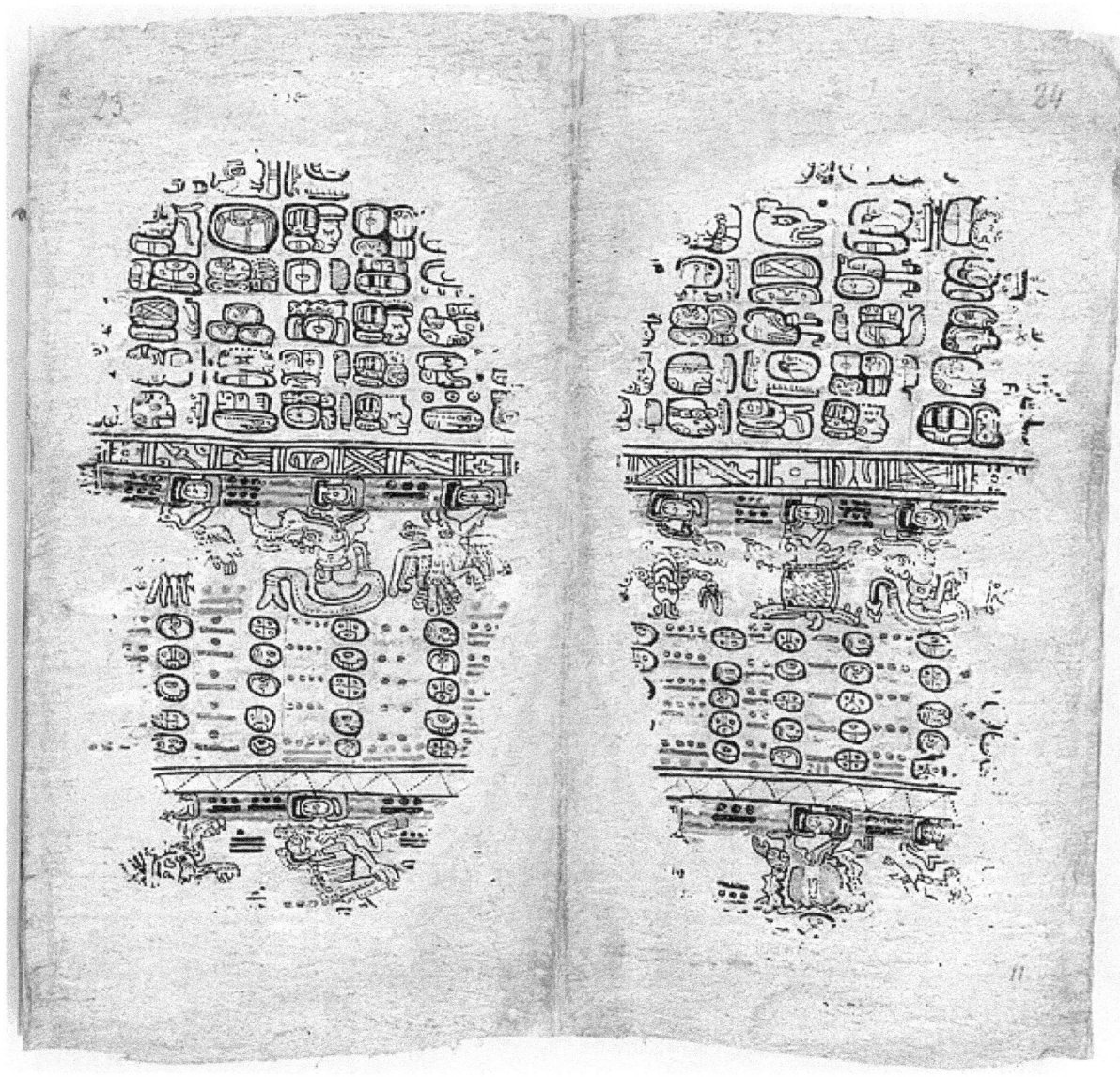

**Image 89**

Response:

_____

_____

_____

10. What's shown in this picture is one of the possible explanations for the fall of the Maya civilization. Do you know what it is?

**Image 90**

Response:

_____

_____

_____

# Multiple Choice Questions

1. Which of the following contributed to the loss of Maya codices?

    a. Theft by rival civilizations

    b. Accidental fires

    c. Destruction by Spanish conquistadors

    d. Natural disasters

2. What were some of the notable signs of the Maya collapse?

    a. Unfinished buildings and sculptures

    b. The lack of written records after 800 A.D.

    c. Evidence of personal property destruction

    d. All of the above

3. How many inhabitants did the Maya cities have during the peak of their civilization?

    a. Between 1,000 and 5,000

    b. Between 2,000 and 5,000

    c. Between 5,000 and 50,000

    d. Between 5,000 and 10,000

4. Did Mayas predict their fall?

    a. They likely did

    b. They didn't

    c. They might have

    d. They knew that their society would suffer, but not this much.

5. What major factor allowed the Mayas to reach their peak during the classic period?

    a. Wet climate

    b. Dry climate

    c. Having several rivers nearby

    d. Mountainous full of mines

6. Which region started to feel the effects of the decline first?

    a. Northern lowlands

    b. Southern lowlands

    c. Middle lowlands

    d. Southern Highlands

7. What human actions made life harder for the Mayas?

    a. Warfare

    b. Competition for work

    c. Mistrust in one another

    d. Something else

8. What characterized the Maya society?

    a. Brutality

    b. Strict hierarchy

    c. Vibrant social life

    d. All of the above

9. What were the dates in Maya codices linked to?

    a. Historical events

    b. Astrological events

    c. Rituals

    d. Community events

10. What events did the existing Maya codices cover?

    a. Events from the 12th to the 16th centuries

    b. Events from the 3rd to the 15th centuries

    c. Events from the 3rd to the 12th centuries

    d. Events from the 3rd to the 9th centuries

# Fill-in-the-Blank

You may use any of the following words to fill in the blanks:

| | | |
|---|---|---|
| trade | planners | artwork |
| cities | food | rubber |
| water | Yucatan Peninsula | chocolate |
| domino | losses | history |
| farmlands | largest | abandoned. |

1. Maya codices played a crucial role in preserving the _____ of the Maya civilization.

2. Perhaps one of the most striking effects of Maya's decline was the thousands of vibrant but unfinished _____ they left behind.

3. Whatever the primary cause of the decline was, it had an _____ effect on all the major Maya cities.

4. By 250 A.D., the Maya civilization had 40 massive _____, all of which became abandoned by 900 A.D.

5. At the peak of their civilization, Maya cities were surrounded by _____. This was crucial for supporting the city and providing it with supplies for _____ and _____.

6. The Mayas were excellent _____, yet even they couldn't plan for all the _____ they suffered over the last two centuries of the Classic Period.

7. It's unclear what happened with all the Mayas who _____ their cities. While remains were found near the _____ cities, the destiny of the majority of their population remains unknown.

8. Around the 9th century, many Maya regions experienced unexpected _____ shortages.

9. Even during their final years, the Mayas were constructing massive temples and smaller places of worship all across the _____ _____.

10. The Mayas proudly recorded their history and achievements on codices made of _____-based paper. They also made plenty of _____ and _____ during their peak.

# True or False

1. The Spanish conquistadors recognized the value of Maya codices and preserved them for future generations.
   - True
   - False

2. The decline of the Maya civilization began with the arrival of the European conquistadors.
   - True
   - False

3. When the first cities started to feel the decline, the changes were very quick.
   - True
   - False

4. The fall of the Maya civilization likely had more than one cause.
   - True
   - False

5. During the Classic Period, religion became even more important to the Maya.
   - True
   - False

6. The rapid decline in the 8th century wasn't the first the Maya suffered.
   - True
   - False

7. Some of the Maya historical records were saved because the Spanish recognized that Mayas and other indigenous groups couldn't be forced to accept the new region.
   - True
   - False

8. By understanding what caused the Maya decline, modern civilizations can help avoid similar catastrophes.
   - True
   - False

9. Experiencing difficulties, people in the biggest cities remained and tried to find solutions.
   - True
   - False

10. At its peak, the Maya society was so stable that they even recorded a 400-year period during which they thrived without decline.
    - True
    - False

# Timeline Questions

1. Arrange these important events in chronological order:

    - The beginning of the Classic Maya Period.
    - Founding of the Mayan city of Yaxchilan.
    - Founding of the Mayan city of Copán.
    - First contact with another major civilization, Teotihuacan.

2. Arrange the Maya rulers in the order they came to rule:

    - K'inich Yax K'uk Mo, ruler of Copán.
    - The governor of Uxmal in the Puuc region of Yucatán.
    - Jasaw Chan K'awiil of Tikal.
    - Pakal the Great, king of Maya Palenque.

3. Arrange these events in chronological order:

    - Yaxchilan stopped thriving.
    - Chichen Itzá reached its peak.
    - Palenque and Tikal were abandoned.
    - The Mayan city and temple complex of Chacchoben was built.

# Answer Key

## What Caused the Decline Answers

1. Environmental changes. Multiple environmental shifts happened during the Classical Period. Some were caused by Maya agriculture, while others were tied to the changing climate of the area.

2. Agricultural resources. Some evidence suggests that many Maya cities suffered food and water shortages. Even if agriculture was expanded, it couldn't have supported the cities.

3. Rising temperatures. Deforestation for agriculture meant there were fewer trees to enrich the environment (besides soil nutrition, trees are also responsible for binding water and securing rainfall). As the Mayas continued cutting down the trees, the temperatures kept rising, causing water to evaporate even faster and rainfall to become unpredictable.

4. Maya leaders wanted to maintain control the same way they did before, but this wasn't possible. Due to water and food shortages, people started to rebel against them, leading to conflicts, which was another contributing factor to the fall of the Maya civilization.

5. Like many other ancient cultures, the Mayans built their alliances on familial relationships. The neverending conflicts have likely stranded these connections, leaving people without support and access to families and communities that could've helped them when they fell on hard times.

6. Even when rain fell, it wasn't enough to last until the end of the drought period. The extensive storage systems were not helpful because there wasn't enough rain to store.

7. Roadblocks — which appeared frequently as conflicts and competition for resources intensified. The trade routes became unsafe and unreliable, causing even more strain on the cities.

8. The biggest reason for the decline in the North was the intense power struggles. Even though they continued thriving for a while, the leaders of the northern cities couldn't agree on how to rule.

9. They also needed a place to build massive monuments like temples, pyramids, palaces, and more. While they wanted a place to nurture their connection with the gods, they lost their connection with the nature that sustained them.

10. Political and economic. There weren't enough resources or people to support either, and the Maya rule had reached its final stage.

## Picture-Based Answers

1. The Maya city shown in the picture, Iximche, was decimated by an epidemic just a few years before the Spanish conquest. When the rulers surrendered to the

conquistadors, they and the remaining nobility had to go to the newly established Spanish capital, and Iximche was abandoned.

2. Located in the Maya city of Tikal, this monument is the Plaza of the Seven Temples. It is a unique temple structure created with masterful building skills the Maya were known for.

3. The structure is part of the building located at Calakmul. It was once one of the most powerful Maya cities — until it lost all its allies and started to decline due to the lack of support and trading opportunities.

4. The structure on the left is the Temple of the Sun, built in Palenque, the city that was abandoned in the late 8th century A.D. It was likely abandoned because the majority of its population migrated to other territories.

5. This is a ball court (one of the most preserved ones from the Maya period) located at Copán. Copán started to decline after the fall of its ruling dynasties, and its population decreased until there weren't enough people to maintain the city.

6. The city in this picture, Mayapán, continued thriving until the late 17th century. It became abandoned when the Spanish conquered it and led away its rulers and all those who could govern and maintain the city.

7. At Uxmal, a Maya city that, like the previous one, was well-maintained until the 17th century. From then on, it descended into a steady decline.

8. Nojpeten, the city shown on the far left, was the last Maya state to fall under the Spanish conquest in 1697. This marked the final end of the Maya civilization and the beginning of a new era for the remaining Maya people.

9. These are pages from the Paris Codex, which dates back to the postclassic period. The writer was unknown, likely a priest who recorded historical events.

10. This is the so-called slash-and-burn agriculture, the practice that involves cutting down vegetation, letting it dry, and burning it. While this provides nutrients to the soil, it also causes degradation. Since it's believed that the Maya practiced this type of agriculture their decline could have been due to the ecological collapse — they were left without an environment to grow food and sustain themselves.

## Multiple Choice Answers

1. C. Destruction by Spanish conquistadors. Very few Maya codices exist today because most of them were destroyed by the Spanish conquistadors who took over the Maya cities.

2. D. All of the above. Many unfinished sculptures and buildings look like they were abandoned mid-project, yet there are no written records of why this happened. There is also evidence that many Maya leaders and noble persons' personal properties (jewelry, sculptures, personal symbols, etc) were destroyed or discarded.

3. C. Between 5,000 and 50,000. Based on existing records, historians estimate that the largest Maya cities could have up to 50,000 inhabitants at their height. This makes their abandonment even more puzzling. How could a city with this many people fall into decline and become completely deserted?

4. D. They knew that their society would suffer, but not this much. Given the many conflicts in Mesoamerica and the attacks and shortages they suffered, the Mayas likely knew that their society would decline — but they probably didn't know that it would never rise to its former glory again.

5. A. Wet climate. Since they didn't have many rivers nearby, the Mayas relied on the wet climate to sustain their agriculture. They worked with what they had and made their society thrive using their available resources.

6. B. Southern lowlands. The first cities abandoned before or around the 9th century are located in the southern lowlands. Cities in the northern lowlands continued to thrive (some for several centuries), but eventually, they were abandoned, too.

7. A. Warfare. If the environmental challenges weren't enough, by the 9th century, wars had risen all over the Maya regions. It seemed everyone was fighting everyone, and the previously shared society was now based on shows of power through destruction.

8. D. All of the above. As vibrant as the Maya society with its urban environments settled in rainforests, it was just as brutal. Animal and human sacrifices were frequent parts of rituals made to appease the gods. Their society was also based on a strict hierarchy, ranging from the upper classes to the lowest ones.

9. B. and C. Astrological events and rituals. The remaining codices contain dates that were linked to specific Maya rituals. It's believed that these rituals aligned with certain astrological events as a deeper connection to the gods.

10. C. Events from the 3rd to the 12th centuries. Although written in the 12th century, the remaining three Maya codices cover events from the 3rd to the 12th century. The Mayas often repeated their records, so it's possible that these were the summaries of other, earlier codices.

## Fill-in-the-Blank Answers

1. History.
2. Artwork.
3. Domino.
4. Cities.
5. Farmlands, food, trade.
6. Planners, losses.
7. Abandoned, largest.
8. Water.
9. Yucatan peninsula.

10. Rubber, chocolate.

**True or False Answers**

1. False. The Spanish conquistadors ordered the destruction of Maya temples and codices because they wanted to replace the Maya culture with their own. Rather than preserving them for future generations, they burnt the codices so no one could access them.

2. False. The Maya civilization started to decline long before the arrival of the Europeans. Around 800 A.D., there were many conflicts within the Maya society and with the neighboring civilizations. Many rulers and their families were killed, and after this, the scribes stopped keeping records for the leaders, and the cities slowly became abandoned.

3. True. In many cities, large constructions began just a few years before the place was completely abandoned. The buildings and monuments were meant to have the same purpose as the ones before – to show the power and wealth of their builders. This indicates that whatever happened in the cities caused the builders to abandon their projects, likely to quickly retreat from the city.

4. True. Based on archeological evidence and scientific theories developed since the discovery of the abandoned Maya sites, many agree that it wasn't a single disaster that brought down the Mayas but rather a combination of several issues they likely faced during the two centuries before their fall.

5. True. During the Classic Period, the Mayas built numerous temples and worship sites dedicated to the gods. These were ordered by the kings who believed to be related to or led by deities. The kings felt obligated to honor their ancestors and guides. Building new worship sites also reinforced the idea that they were connected to a deity, gaining the population's trust.

6. True. During the Classic Period, around the mid-6th-mid 7th century, the Maya civilization declined slightly. They had some challenges with expanding agriculture to meet the needs of the growing population. At that time, they overcame their struggles. Later, they didn't.

7. True. While wanting to convert the Mayas as quickly as possible, the Spanish ultimately understood that using force went against their own religious values. Instead, they let the Maya keep some of their historical records and items related to their culture and slowly converted them to Christianity.

8. True. By understanding what went wrong with the thriving Maya civilization, modern societies can't avoid making the same mistakes and protect themselves against a potential downfall.

9. False. While they've likely tried to find solutions to their issues at first, many have likely realized that they must look for better opportunities (better lands, more space, fewer rivals) elsewhere.

10. True. Before the first decline, Maya society kept growing, and everything was thriving across all regions. Records show that they were especially proud of a

400-year period during which they lived in a very successful shared society across lands spanning modern-day Guatemala, Mexico, and Belize.

## Timeline Answers

1.

- The Classic Maya period began in 250 C.E.
- The Mayan city of Yaxchilan was founded in 320 C.E.
- The Mayan city of Copán was founded in 331 C.E.
- The Mayans' first contact with another major civilization, Teotihuacan, was in 378 C.E.

2.

- 426 C.E. - 437 C.E., the rule of K'inich Yax K'uk Mo in Copán.
- 615 C.E. - 683 C.E., the reign of Pakal the Great, king of Maya Palenque.
- 682 C.E. - 734 C.E., the rule of Jasaw Chan K'awiil of Tikal.
- 850 C.E. - 925 C.E., the governor of Uxmal in Puuc, Yucatán, rises to power and makes the city the capital of the region.

3.

- The Mayan city and temple complex of Chacchoben was built around 700 A.D.
- Yaxchilan stopped thriving around 800 A.D.
- Palenque and Tikal were abandoned betwwen 800 A.D. and 900 A.D.
- Chichen Itzá reached its peak between the 8th and the 12th centuries A.D.

# Chapter 10: The Spanish Conquest and the End of an Era

Concluding your journey through Mesoamerican history, this chapter will look at the end of the era brought on by the Spanish conquest. It also talks about the consequences of colonization on the native societies and the colonizers themselves. After all, the Mesoamerican culture has left its mark on the European one conquering it — along with all the other civilizations that drew and continue to draw inspiration from it.

From trivia questions and sections with interesting facts, you'll also learn how Mesoamerican culture influences the modern world and how this influence is being nurtured through different traditions.

## Mesoamerican Influence Today

The influence of Mesoamerica is clearly present in contemporary societies. From architecture trying to mimic intricate designs and simple solutions to complex problems to agriculture and food practices popular in Mesoamerica, you can see the remains of this ancient civilization nearly everywhere.

Architects continue to be inspired by the Mesoamerican structures and artists who seek to bring vibrant colors and bold shapes into their pieces. Besides geometry, many also see inspiration in sacred beliefs, like the ones that led to the creation of the Pyramid of the Sun and the Pyramid of the Moon.

Sustainability is one of the main reasons modern artists and builders seek to draw from Mesoamerican creations. The ancient people relied on sustainable and ethical resources, allowing their civilizations to thrive for centuries.

The cultural exchange that followed the Spanish invasion has left its mark not only on the former Mesoamerican territories but also on the European and later Western societies. Just as the indigenous people adopted European practices, the Europeans also gained a wealth of cultural elements from the Mesoamericans.

Thanks to the very effective Mesoamerican agricultural practices like irrigation and artificial islands, people of today can grow crops and food even in places where this wouldn't have been possible. Moreover, they get to enjoy Mesoamerican delicacies, among the world's healthiest foods.

# Mesoamerican Cultural Revival

While many communities from the former Mesoamerican territories have lost connection to the ancient traditions, they continue to uphold what customs, languages, and practices are still known to them.

In Mexico and surrounding Central American countries, you can still buy food and drinks made in the traditional, pre-Hispanic style — giving you a taste of the delicacies the Mesoamericans enjoyed every day or on special occasions. In many of these regions, you can also witness battle reenactments and rituals based on historical records and oral accounts of various Mesoamerican groups.

Traditional ceremonial dances and god worship are also frequently practiced in Central America, as these were a massive part of the Mesoamerican culture and its revival movement. Efforts to preserve indigenous languages (still numerous) have also been made in the last century or so.

Whether they have indigenous origins or are simply mesmerized by the Mesoamerican traditions, modern artists and activists from the Western world are also dedicated to reviving this ancient culture. They know that preserving their cultural heritage empowers the remaining indigenous communities and helps them proudly represent their roots and culture to the existing and coming generations.

# Multiple Choice Questions

1. Which modern-day food staple was first cultivated by Mesoamerican civilizations?

    a. Rice

    b. Wheat

    c. Corn (Maize)

    d. Potatoes

2. Whose records describe the events after the Spanish conquest?

    a. Spanish

    b. Another European colonizer

    c. Aztec

    d. Maya

3. Which culture allied themselves with the Spanish to conquer the Aztecs?

    a. Mixtec

    b. Maya

    c. Zapotec

    d. Tlaxcala

4. What important Mesoamerican concept inspired the dynamic approach to modern architecture?

    a. Spacious design

    b. Celestial bodies

    c. Intricate carvings

    d. Solid block buildings

5. What motifs appear in both Mesoamerican and modern art forms?

    a. Religious

    b. Animal

    c. Geometrical

    d. All of the above

6. After successfully defeating the Aztecs, the Spanish colonizers occupied the majority of Mesoamerica, except which region?

    a. Yucatan

    b. Northern lowlands

    c. Honduras

    d. Guatemala

7. What led to the collapse of the remaining Mesoamerican civilizations after the Spanish conquests?

   a. The power struggle between the newcomers and the Indigenous people

   b. Lack of centralized power

   c. The Fall of the Aztecs

   d. The Fall of the Maya

8. What factor caused the further decline of indigenous communities after the 16th century?

   a. Lack of education

   b. Lack of resources

   c. Inability to adapt to the Spanish culture

   d. Lack of work

9. The colonizers took away the Mesoamerican's lands by stripping them of their...

   a. Titles

   b. Rights

   c. Connections

   d. Power

10. How do contemporary indigenous communities in the former Mesoamerican territory cope with their past?

    a. With sadness over the loss

    b. By trying to preserve what's left of their culture

    c. By trying to take back power and relive their traditions

    d. All of the ab

    e. ove

# Fill-in-the-Blank

You may use any of the following words to fill in the blanks:

| | | |
|---|---|---|
| architecture | irrigation | mining |
| diseases | Spanish | gifts |
| alcohol | symbolism | Europeans |
| horses | gods | Aztecs |
| geometry | mythology. | |

1. Mesoamerican civilizations introduced the world to the concept of _____, which revolutionized agriculture.

2. Before being conquered by the Spanish, the Mesoamericans fought back valiantly, often leaving Spanish soldiers without their method of transportation — _____.

3. After the arrival of the Spanish, some Aztecs offered _____ to them because they believed they were sent by the _____.

4. The Aztecs had a law that forbade _____ consumption in certain circumstances, just like some modern laws do.

5. While detailing the events of the Spanish invasion from the _____ viewpoint, the Florentine Codex was edited by a _____ priest, so it may have been changed from its original version.

6. Inspired by Mesoamerican pyramids and temples, symmetrical _____ often appears in modern times.

7. _____ is another element of modern arts and crafts adopted from Mesoamerican art and architecture.

8. Combining _____ and modern concepts, modern artists can successfully showcase the influence of Mesoamerican artistic language in a new light.

9. Besides internal conflicts and attacks from the outside, the remaining Mesoamerican population was also decimated by _____ introduced by the _____.

10. One of the largest industries Spanish colonizers employed indigenous workers was _____.

# What/Who Am I?

1. I am a famous Mesoamerican dish made from corn dough and often filled with various ingredients. Most often, I am filled with meat. What am I?

   _____

2. I am the first city founded by the famous conquistador, Hernan Cortes, after his arrival in Mesoamerica. What am I?

   _____

3. I am the person who led the Aztecs against the Spanish in the first big battle between the two groups. I won and banished the Spaniards for a short while. Who am I?

   _____

4. Built as the most powerful city in the New World, I replaced Tenochtitlan. It was the first place where European laws and regulations were used in Mesoamerica. What am I?

   _____

5. I am an Aztec court system adopted by European and later Western societies. According to my rules, when someone is accused of the time, they must be questioned in front of a court. Only then can they be committed of a crime and receive a sentence. What am I?

   _____

6. I am a Spanish conqueror who was part of the group that captured the Aztecs. I wrote a book about my memories of the invasion of the Aztec Empire. Who am I?

   _____

7. I am an ancient Aztec weapon. Not only was I popular on the battlefield in the Aztec's time, but I am still used in Mesoamerican battle reenactments in modern times. What am I?

   _____

8. I am a 20th-century artistic movement inspired by Mesoamerican culture. I was popular in the 1920s and 1930s when I inspired many architects and artists along with Art Deco, another design concept. What am I?

   _____

9. I am one of the first European agricultural products introduced to Mesoamerica after the Spanish invasion. When lit on fire, I make smoke? What am I?

_____

10. I am a delicious chocolate drink you can drink today — but I was also used as an offering in Aztec, Mixtec, and Zapotec religious ceremonies. What am I?

_____

# True or False

1. Mesoamerican cultural revival efforts are solely focused on the preservation of ancient practices without any adaptation to modern life.

   - True
   - False

2. The Mesoamericans were frightened by the arrival of Spanish conquistadors.

   - True
   - False

3. According to some Spanish records, the Spaniards claimed to be led there by their god after their arrival in Mesoamerica.

   - True
   - False

4. Just like modern courts, the Aztec court system had different levels.

   - True
   - False

5. Not all Mesoamericans were treated equally in the early stages of Spanish colonialism.

   - True
   - False

6. Mesoamerican arts and crafts highly influence the modern approach to self-expression expression.

   - True
   - False

7. By 1550, the colonizers occupied all Mesoamerican territories, and everyone was under their rule.

   - True
   - False

8. After the Spanish invasion, the lack of power and the population decline caused the loss of traditional knowledge.

   - True
   - False

9. To integrate them into their culture, the Spanish paid good wages to the Mesoamericans who wanted to work for them.

   - True
   - False

10. The Spanish colonizers continued governing in Mesoamerica using the existing local legal systems.

- True
- False

# Picture-Based

1. From which civilization did the architects of this building borrow inspiration?

**Image 91**

Response:

_____

_____

_____

2. What does the interior of this building remind you of?

**Image 92**

Response:

_____

_____

_____

3. What inspired the facade of this building?

Image 93

Response:

_____

_____

_____

4. Several-story high, sloping design with elevated features on top. Does this design look familiar?

**Image 94**

Response:

_____

_____

_____

5. What ancient style was the artist of these pictures trying to recreate?

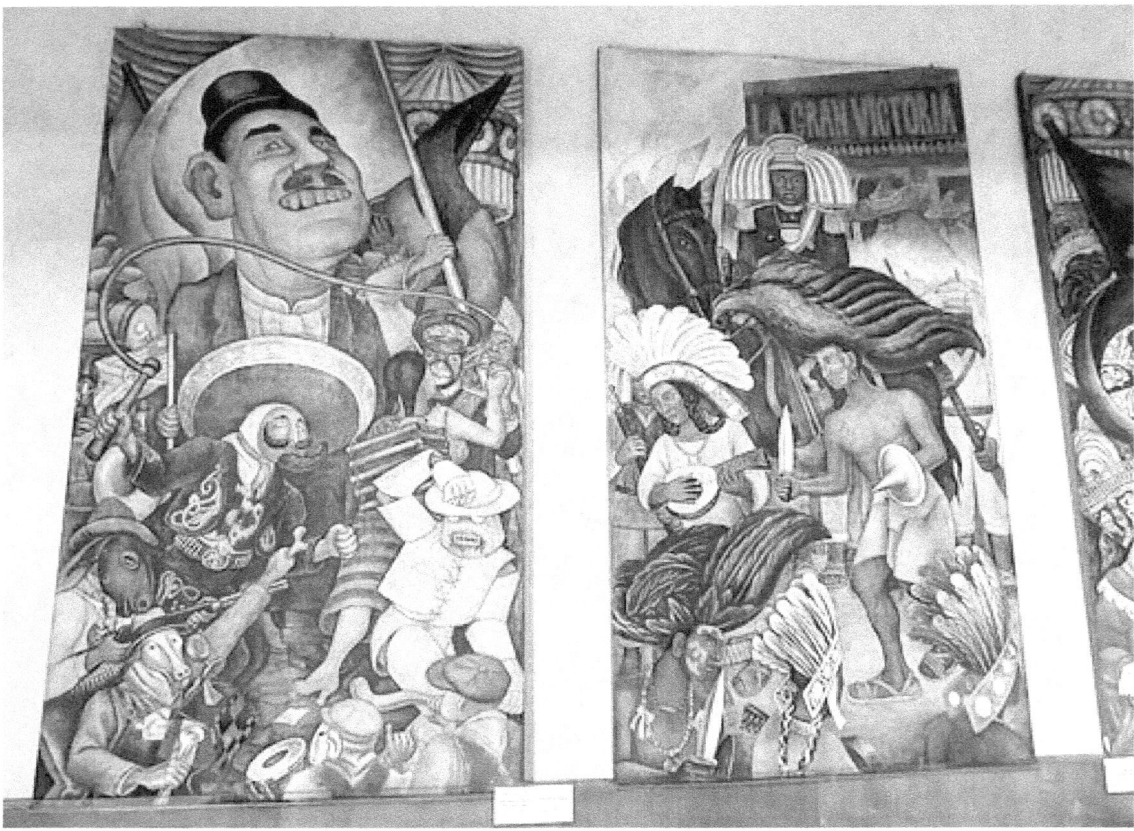

Image 95

Response:

_____

_____

_____

6. Which Mesoamerican motif inspired the creator of this design?

**Image 96**

Response:

_____

_____

_____

7. Which symbol inspired this structure?

**Image 97**

Response:

_____

_____

_____

8. What do you think people in this picture are doing?

**Image 98**

Response:

_____

_____

_____

9. What event was recorded on this codex page?

**Image 99**

Response:

_____

_____

_____

10. This picture shows a modern take on a popular Aztec solution for agricultural issues. What's its name?

**Image 100**

Response:

_____

_____

_____

# Timeline Questions

1. Arrange the events in chronological order:

   - The Battle of Utatlan
   - The Post-Classic Period
   - Rediscovery of the Mayan civilization
   - Diego de Landa burns Mayan book at Mani

2. Arrange the events in chronological order:

   - Hernan Cortés' arrival in Central America
   - The Tlaxcalteca attacked the first group of Spanish conquerors
   - The first Spanish settlements were created in Central America
   - Creation of the Triple Alliance of Tenochtitlan, Texcoco, and Tlacopan

3. Arrange these events in chronological order:

   - La Noche Triste, the Spaniards' largest defeat against the Aztecs
   - Missionaries arrived in Mexico to convert the indigenous populations to Christianity
   - Battle for Tenochtitlan
   - Cortés became captain-general of New Spain

# Answer Key

**Multiple Choice Answers**

1. C. Corn (Maize). Favorite in many cuisines across the world, corn was first cultivated and consumed in Mesoamerica. From then, it spread to the rest of the Americas, Europe, and then to the other continents as well. However, it's still the most popular in Central America and the surrounding region.

2. A. and C. Spanish and Aztec. When the Spanish colonizers first arrived in the Aztec Empire, the Aztecs wrote extensively about their experience with the newcomers. Likewise, being the conquistadors themselves, it makes sense that the Spaniards also wanted to include their conquest of Mesoamerica in their history books.

3. C. Tlaxcala. Long-term enemies and subjects of the Zapotecs, the Tlaxcala, were happy to join forces with the Spanish conquerors. They wanted to be free of the brutal Zapotec reign and believed that the Spanish would help them rule instead. They were proud of finally defeating the Zapotecs, even if the Spanish did the majority of the work. The Tlaxcala's help contributed significantly to the downfall of the Aztec Empire.

4. B. Celestial bodies. Mesoamerican buildings were often built in a way to catch the light or the shadows under a certain angle — depending on the standing of the sun and moon. Modern architecture also likes to build on the light-shadow concept, creating a dynamic view of structures based on how the light hits them.

5. D. All of the above. Religious, geometrical, and animal motifs are just as popular in modern art as they were in Mesoamerica. They have changed over time and are now represented differently (so they would fit modern ideas), but they have never been out of style.

6. A. Yucatan. Occupied by the Maya civilization, the Yucatan region was the last to be defeated. In 1525, the colonizers conquered all, but because of the strong Maya resistance, they had to wait another 20 years to take over Yucatan.

7. B. Lack of centralized power. Before the Spanish invasion, the Aztecs ruled over a massive region in Mesoamerica. When they had to surrender, the centralized power they used to rule vanished, and chaos ensued. Those under the former Aztec rule began to fight among each other, making the Spanish takeover easier and causing the collapse of the remaining Mesoamerican civilization.

8. A. Lack of education. The Spanish colonizers brought with them their education system, but this was only available to the Spaniards and the Mesoamerican elite, who willingly cooperated with them and adopted their culture. The remaining population fell behind in education, which caused them to depend on the colonizers for everything.

9. B. Rights. Slowly, the Spanish colonizers stripped the Mesoamerican natives of every right, including the right to own property. They took away their lands and any valuables they had remaining after the collapse of their civilization.

10. D. All of the above. Many indigenous communities still struggle with what happened to them after the Spanish conquest. They still fight for their rights and want to retain and revive the ancient traditions while mourning the ones that have been lost forever.

**Fill-in-the-Blank Answers**

1. Irrigation.

2. Horses.

3. Gifts, gods.

4. Alcohol.

5. Aztecs, Spanish.

6. Geometry, architecture.

7. Symbolism.

8. Mythology.

9. Diseases, Europeans.

10. Mining.

**What/Who am I Answers**

1. Tamale.

2. Veracruz.

3. Cuauhtemoc, the nephew of Montezuma.

4. Mexico City.

5. Trial by court.

6. Bernal Díaz del Castillo.

7. Macana or macuahuitl.

8. Surrealism.

9. Tobacco.

10. Tejate.

**True or False Answers**

1. False. While Mesoamerican cultural revival efforts focus on preserving ancient practices as part of a historical heritage, they don't disregard its impact on modern life either. In other words, those who want to show the elements of Mesoamerican culture often combine them with contemporary elements to make them more relatable.

2. False. By the time the Spanish arrived in the Americas, Mesoamericans were so used to the conflicts, war, and conquest in the region that they weren't too

frightened by the newcomers at first. This soon changed when the conquistadors started destroying their culture and threatening their lives.

3. True. Some Spanish accounts of the conquest talk about and show pictures of a god (or saint) standing between the Spanish and the Aztecs greeting them. In some early books, the god or saint is depicted similarly to the one who led the Aztecs to Mesoamerica — with an eagle on a cactus. This is likely an attempt to create a joint narrative between the two cultures and make converting the natives easier.

4. True. The Aztec court system had different levels. The highest one was the equivalent of the modern Supreme Court. Existing in many countries, this court structure is an adaptation of the well-organized Aztec justice system.

5. True. The elite members of the Mesoamerican societies had certain privileges under Spanish colonial rule, too — as long as they cooperated and accepted the mixing of the two belief systems.

6. True. Just like the Mesoamerican artists, modern ones think about what they want to represent and recreate it using their creative skills. And just in ancient times, no artists would represent and interpret the same idea the same way.

7. False. In some secluded territories in the interior of the region, Mesoamerican people remained independent for up to a century and a half after the first Spanish invasion.

8. True. Due to the lack of power to gain control over resources and the diseases introduced by the Europeans, the remaining Mesoamericans lost a massive workforce. There were very few people left who could continue the traditional work practices and arts and crafts. Because of this, many of these practices and traditions were lost.

9. False. While wanting to integrate the natives into their culture, the Spanish colonizers did not pay fair wages to the indigenous workers. The Mesoamerican workers were exploited (almost as if they were slaves) and even had to pay tribute (taxes) to their Spanish bosses.

10. False. The Spanish government introduced the Spanish law to Mesoamerica, along with a complex legal system that often favored the Spanish. Spanish officials were put in charge of Mesoamerican territories and governed them without any knowledge of the local judicial traditions.

## Picture-Based Answers

1. Here pictured, the Kukulkan public pavilion in Merida was inspired by the large arches and decorative elements used in Maya architecture.

2. Maya art. It likely reminded you of the colorful Maya murals that decorated many sacred buildings of the Maya civilization.

3. Aztec influence. The name of this building is Aztec Hotel — and for a good reason. The intricate Aztec writing system and art inspired the creators of its facade.

4. If it does, it's because many Mesoamerican pyramids were shaped this way. The designer of this building — the old Imperial Hotel in Tokyo — was inspired by the shapes of Mesoamerican structures in many of his works.

5. Temple Design. Diego Rivera, the author of these paintings, was trying to recreate the vivid patterns and bold shapes used by the Mesoamerican temple designers.

6. Connection to nature. Just like Mesoamericans, the architect of this structure was trying to emphasize the connection to the natural environment. The design is also simple yet intricate — just like Mesoamerican carvings and decorations.

7. The structure is very similar to the (feathered) serpents from many Mesoamerican cultures' religious symbolism.

8. They're dancing to a traditional Mexican dance that was inspired by Mesoamerican rituals. They gather in the circle, dance to the rhythm of drums, and enjoy their connection to their community and heritage.

9. The arrival of Hernan Cortes to Tenochtitlan. Despite receiving a warm welcome, Corters destroyed the city soon after his arrival.

10. It's a water channel or aqueduct. The Aztecs used it for irrigation in territories where they needed to direct water from rivers and streams to their lands.

**Timeline Answers:**

1.
- The Post Classic Period, during which most of the Mayan cities were either abandoned or fell to the conquistadors, lasted from 950 A.D. to 1524 A.D.
- The conquistador Pedro de Alvarado defeated the Maya in the Battle of Utatlan on July 1524 A.D.
- Diego de Landa burned Mayan books at Mani on July 12, 1562 A.D.
- John Lloyd Stephens and Frederick Catherwood rediscovered the Mayan civilization around 1840 A.D.

2.
- The Triple Alliance of Tenochtitlan, Texcoco, and Tlacopan against the Spaniards was formed in 1428.
- The first Spanish settlements in Central America were created in 1492, after the arrival of Columbus.
- 1504 marked Hernan Cortés' arrival in Central America.
- In 1519, the Tlaxcalteca attacked the first group of Spanish conquerors.

3.
- La Noche Triste, when 1,000 Spaniards' lost their lives largest defeat against the Aztecs, took place in 1520.
- The battle for Tenochtitlan was fought in 1521.
- Cortés was named captain-general of New Spain (Mexico or the former Aztec land) by Charles V, Holy Roman Emperor, in 1522.

- The first missionaries arrived and began their work of converting Mesoamerican natives to Christianity in 1524.

# Conclusion

Thank you for choosing and reading this trivia book, and congratulations on all the fun facts you've learned. To recap, you have seen how the Olmecs, the first builders, achieved impressive architectural marvels in their new land. Then, you've been introduced to the fascinating world of the Zapotec people and learned about their traditions and innovative expression methods like hieroglyph writing.

Another group known for their incredible scientific achievements and writing skills featured in this book was the Mayas. In the third chapter, you learned about their inventions (including their calendar), some of which still puzzle historians and scientists today. Later on, you saw how this once thriving civilization met its end in just as mysterious a way as it arose.

The fourth chapter showed a sneak peek into the life of one of the greatest and most imposing cities in Mesoamerica, Teotihuacán. You have seen how its inhabitants built and maintained it — before inexplicably abandoning it just as the Mayas did with their greatest cities.

In the fifth chapter, you've found fun facts and trivia about the Toltecs, the warriors led by a powerful and somewhat unusual deity, and the leaders it guided to victory. The Zapotecs were also artisans, just as were the subjects of the sixth chapter, the Mixtecs. While the first were known for their unique architecture, the Mixtec civilization left behind one of the most significant cultural and historical artifacts — codices or books detailing their lives, connections, victories, and more.

The seventh chapter continued to explore the lives of the Mixtecs, showing their age-old rivalry with the Zapotecs. This chapter included myths, historical facts, and lessons to be learned about the interactions of two neighboring cultures.

Towards the end of the book, you've also learned about the Aztecs, one of the two last Mesoamerican civilizations. Like the Mayans (who had fallen a few decades later), the Spanish colonizers ultimately conquered the Aztecs during the early 16th century. However, before their fall, they built an empire controlling most of the region, establishing a fearsome system.

As useful as some of the Aztec's inventions were (and still are today), this relentless rule played a crucial role in their fall. Namely, wanting to be free of the Aztec influence, smaller groups under their rule were happy to ally themselves with the European conquistadors. Together, they defeated the Aztecs, taking away their power and, eventually, their rights.

Still, as you've learned from the last chapter, the Spanish invasion has also left its mark on the Europeans — and not just the Mesoamerican natives. Their cultures have become intermingled, which you can see in the massive Mesoamerican influence on art, architecture, and gastronomy in Europe and the Western world today.

Once again, congratulations on all you've learned! We hope this book helped you on your learning journey.

# Part 2: History of Mexico

1000 Interesting Facts from Ancient Times to the Present

# Introduction

**Mexico is a nation with a captivating history, culture, and people**. It is a nation that has seen a plethora of revolutions. **This book offers an extensive exploration of the vast and tumultuous timeline of Mexico's past**, from the days of grand **pre-Columbian civilizations** to the aftermath of the 2018 election of **Andrés Manuel López Obrador**.

Beginning with the first known inhabitants in 14,000 BCE, readers will be taken on a journey through the **pre-Columbian era** and its **indigenous societies**, **the Spanish conquest** and colonization of Mexico, **the formation of Mexico's first empires**, and the impact of wars, such as **the Mexican-American War, the Reform War, and the Cristero War. Additionally**, this book will investigate the industrialization and cultural revitalization movements and the significance of **Andrés Manuel López Obrador's** election in 2018. His influence on **modern-day Mexicans** is vast, and you'll be surprised to learn the many ways he has brought—and keeps bringing—his country to the world stage.

**Who hasn't heard of Mexico's white beaches and resorts that dot its coast?** Or mariachi bands and savory dishes? On the darker side, **Mexico battles** the violence of drug wars led by powerful cartels and has suffered from a great migration of people.

Throughout **this book**, readers will gain an understanding of **the many forces that have shaped Mexico's rich culture** and **how the people of Mexico** have been resilient in the face of oppression and hardship. Gain insight into **the complex relationship between Mexico and the United States**, including **the Bracero Program, NAFTA**, and **the migration of Mexicans to the United States.**

By the end of this book**, readers will have insight into how the nation developed and an understanding of the Mexican people's creativity and resourcefulness** that have allowed them to build a strong and diverse nation. With this knowledge, readers will be well equipped to better explore the fascinating history **of this extraordinary nation**.

# Pre-Columbian Mexico
## (14,000 BCE–1519 CE)

**For centuries, the ancient people of Mexico have captivated us with their unique culture, beliefs, and practices.** From hunting and gathering to exchanging goods to playing board games like **patolli, the ancient Mexicans** have left a lasting legacy. In this chapter, we will explore the enthralling history of **the ancient Mexicans** and their remarkable accomplishments in art, science, engineering, and more.

1. **Ancient people in Mexico used stones to make tools and weapons** to help them hunt and gather food.

2. **For centuries, the people of Mexico used a system of trading** that didn't involve money. Instead, they exchanged goods like food, tools, clothing, and even cocoa beans!

3. **The ancient people of Mexico built homes out of mud bricks.**

4. Ancient Mexicans **played a game called patolli**. It was a board game that involved betting. People would bet trade goods, but sometimes, they would bet their property and even their family!

5. **Ancient Mexicans believed in many different gods and goddesses** and held ceremonies to honor them.

6. **Ancient Mexicans made very accurate readings of the sun, moon, and stars**.

7. **Ancient Mexicans were masters at engineering**, building networks of canals to help with irrigation.

8. The ancient **Mexicans were known for their skill in weaving intricate patterns into their clothing** and blankets.

9. **Ancient Mexicans wrote many of their stories and beliefs on stone tablets** and buildings.

10. **Ancient Mexicans were experts at growing and harvesting corn**, which was an important part of their diet.

11. **The ancient Mexicans used cocoa beans to make a bitter drink called xocolatl.**

12. **Ancient Mexicans traded in gold, silver, and turquoise jewelry,** which were symbols of status and wealth.

13. **Ancient Mexicans created colorful artworks from clay and stone.** Many of these artworks tell stories of their gods, goddesses, and heroes.

14. **Ancient Mexicans kept birds, turkeys, and dogs** as pets and for food.

15. **Ancient Mexicans created colorful masks and costumes to use in their ceremonies and festivals**, which is one reason colorful feathers were so valued.

16. **Ancient Mexicans celebrated the solstice** with special ceremonies and feasts.

17. **Ancient Mexicans built pyramids and temples** to honor their gods and goddesses. These pyramids are generally much different than those found in Egypt.

18. **Ancient Mexicans had a complex system of writing** that used pictures to represent different words and ideas.

19. **Ancient Mexicans believed that their ancestors could communicate with them** from the afterlife.

20. **Ancient Mexicans played musical instruments like drums, flutes,** and rattles to make music.

21. **Ancient Mexicans** held competitions to decide **who was the best at skills like running and ball playing,** with one game similar to basketball.

22. **Ancient Mexicans made colorful decorations from feathers, shells, and beads.**

23. **Ancient Mexicans**, like many people around the world, **had shamans** or what people used to call medicine men or women. These people studied the natural world for plants and other things to help in healing. They also served as a conduit between the sick and injured and the gods.

24. **Ancient Mexicans used a calendar that was based on the seasons,** the sun, and the stars.

25. **Ancient Mexicans believed that their gods and goddesses** could be found in every part of nature.

26. **Ancient Mexicans practiced religious sacrifices** by offering up valuable items like gold, food, or even people to the gods.

27. **Ancient Mexicans believed in the power of dreams** and used them to try and make sense of the future.

28. **The chief god of the Aztecs was Huitzilopochtli**. He was considered the god of the sun, war, and human sacrifice. Human sacrifices were offered to **Huitzilopochtli** to ensure his favor and protection.

29. **Ancient Mexicans built cities and trading centers** that grew to become some of the largest in the world.

30. **Ancient Mexicans built long, straight roads** to help them travel from one place to another.

# Conquest and Colonization of Mexico by the Spanish
## (1519–1821)

**In 1492, Christopher Columbus became the first European to land in the Western Hemisphere since the Vikings.** His voyage was made on behalf of **the Spanish monarchs Ferdinand II and Isabella I.** The men who followed him in the next few years were called **conquistadors** ("those who conquer"). A group of **conquistadors arrived in Mexico in 1519** with one goal in mind: establishing a Spanish empire in the new and untamed land. **The Spanish brought horses, gunpowder, a new religion, technologies, and weapons with them.** **Mexico was transformed by the Spanish**, who built new cities, roads, and bridges and established a new system of government. It is a testament to **the Spanish conquistadors'** ambition, power, and tenacity that their legacy remains in Mexico to this day.

31. Born in Medellín, Spain, in 1485, **Hernán Cortés became the leader of the Spanish conquest of the Aztec Empire.**

32. **Cortés played a significant role in the introduction of Christianity to the Americas.** He brought Catholic priests with him and established churches and monasteries throughout the newly conquered territories.

33. **The Spanish were looking to increase their trading opportunities.** However, they often seized territory and people rather than trading with the locals fairly.

34. **Spain was looking to expand its empire and gain access to new resources, such as gold and silver**, when it decided to colonize Mexico in 1519. Adding new territory would also give Spain additional power and prestige.

35. **Horses, a key component of the Spaniards' success, were introduced to Mexico by Cortés's army.**

36. **The Spanish used weapons the Aztecs had never seen before**, such as early pistols, muskets, and cannons.

37. **The Aztecs were no match for the small Spanish force of five hundred people** with their new weapons.

38. **The Spanish also practiced the policy of "divide and conquer,"** promising people who had been subject to Aztec rule more power and wealth if they helped the conquistadors. Disease also took a toll on the Aztecs and other native people.

39. **Over the next few decades, the Spanish began to colonize lands to the north and south of Mexico,** including Florida and Central America.

40. **Roman Catholicism was brought to Mexico by the Spanish**. Many native people of Mexico were forced to convert to Christianity or face death.

41. **The Spanish began to force the Aztecs and many other tribes in Mexico to learn their language.**

42. **The Spanish replaced the Aztec legal system with their own**, though both included the death penalty and other harsh penalties.

43. **The Spanish established a new taxation system in Mexico** based on the encomienda system, which meant farmers had to give a share of their crops to the Spanish.

44. **A new currency, the peso, was introduced to Mexico by the Spanish**. It was also known as "piece of eight," which is a popular term in pirate and treasure-hunting stories.

45. **The Spanish established the first universities in Mexico**.

46. **The Spanish established a new system of education in Mexico** that largely consisted of religious teaching and information about the glory of Spain and its kings and queens.

47. **The Spanish brought new forms of medicine to Mexico**, such as the cinchona tree, which was later found to contain quinine, to treat malaria. The Spanish had conquered parts of South America, and many of the people there used the plant for a variety of medical reasons.

48. **Cows, pigs, and potatoes, essential ingredients for a successful agricultural society, were introduced to Mexico by the Spanish.**

49. Even before the Spanish arrived, **the Aztecs had already developed sophisticated irrigation systems.**

50. **Many of the conquistadors were only concerned with gaining wealth,** and many searched throughout much of Mexico for El Dorado, a legendary city made of gold. Other Spanish expeditions in South America and Florida had the same goal.

51. **Baroque and Neoclassical styles of architecture**, as well as new forms of art, including painting, sculpture, and music, **were brought to Mexico by the Spanish.**

52. **New forms of literature, such as the novel and the epic poem, were introduced to Mexico by the Spanish.**

53. **Technologies, such as the printing press and the compass, were brought to Mexico by the Spanish.**

54. **Many new roads and bridges were built by Spain** to connect the cities of Mexico.

55. **The Spanish built many new cities in Mexico, including the capital, Mexico City. The great Aztec city of Tenochtitlan** had stood there since around 1325.

56. **The population of Tenochtitlan before the Spanish was about 250,000**. After the Spanish conquest, the number of native people in the area declined because of diseases brought by the Spanish.

57. **The Spanish brought diseases like smallpox to the New World**. The natives had no built-up immunity to those diseases. Millions of people died as a result.

58. **The conquistadors established the first European settlements in Mexico, including Veracruz and Mexico City. Mexico City, originally known as Tenochtitlan**, was built on the ruins of the Aztec capital.

59. **A large number of African slaves were brought to Mexico by the conquistadors**, as were natives from Cuba, another territory the Spanish had colonized.

60. **The Spanish discovered new crops in the New World, such as tobacco, cocoa, bananas, pineapples, and more**.

# Chichimeca War
## (1550–1590)

**The Chichimeca War is a pivotal yet often forgotten chapter in Mexico's history**. For nearly a century, this devastating conflict brought **Spanish colonialism** to the front door of **the Chichimeca people**. Despite their valiant efforts, **the Chichimeca were eventually defeated in 1590**. The war also marked the beginning of **the Spanish colonization of all of Mexico**, which the Spanish called **New Spain**.

61. **The Chichimeca War** (1550–1590) was a series of conflicts between **the Spanish Empire and the indigenous Chichimeca people** of central northern Mexico.

62. **The Chichimeca War was one of the longest and bloodiest wars in New Spain's history.**

63. **The Chichimeca War was a major conflict between the Spanish and the indigenous people in Mexico.** The war lasted for decades and cost the lives of tens of thousands of people.

64. **The Chichimeca weren't a tribe but a confederation of the Pames, Zacatecos, Guamares, Guachichiles, Caxcanes, Otomí, and Tecuexes.** They were all semi-nomadic hunter-gatherers who lived in the north-central region of modern-day Mexico.

65. **The Chichimeca War began when the Spanish began to make incursions into the Chichimeca territory in search of silver and gold.**

66. **The Spanish also committed widespread sexual assault on Chichimeca women,** which is what spurred the tribes to fight.

67. **The Chichimeca people fought fiercely against the Spanish by utilizing guerrilla tactics.**

68. **The Spanish used a combination of military force and missionary activity** to subdue the Chichimeca people.

69. **The Chichimeca people were known as fierce warriors and were known to use a variety of weapons,** especially bows and arrows.

70. **Chichimeca arrows were made from reeds with an obsidian head that was sharper than a razor blade**. This arrowhead could pierce Spanish armor!

71. **The Chichimeca were also renowned for their use of guerrilla tactics**, such as ambushes and raids, that often threatened Spanish food supplies.

72. **The Spanish responded to the Chichimeca guerrilla tactics by forming large groups of mounted cavalry and infantry**.

73. During the war, **the Spanish built a number of forts and settlements** to protect themselves from the many Chichimeca raids.

74. **The Chichimeca were able to successfully resist the Spanish for decades.**

75. In the 1570s, the war was not going as well for Spain as expected. **The Spanish governor-general had to write back to King Philip II for many more troops and equipment**.

76. **The Chichimeca were eventually defeated in 1590**.

77. As a result of the war, **the Spanish were able to establish a permanent foothold in central Mexico.**

78. **The Chichimeca War led to the decimation of the Chichimeca people and the destruction of their culture**.

79. **Today, very little is known about the Chichimeca people**. What we know mainly comes from the Spanish, which can be biased.

80. **The Chichimeca War is believed to have resulted in the deaths of up to eighty thousand people, mostly Chichimeca**. However, no one is certain about how many died, though most believe the total was well in excess of ten thousand.

81. **The Chichimeca War resulted in many Chichimeca people being forced to move to other regions of Mexico.**

82. **The war also led to the enslavement of thousands of Chichimeca by the Spanish.**

83. **The Aztecs regarded the Chichimeca as "uncivilized," and the name "Chichimeca" is actually an Aztec word that means "barbarian" or "uncivilized."**

84. **The Chichimeca War** had a lasting impact on the history of Mexico. It was the last great native war against the Spanish and led to a new European social, political, and economic order being imposed on the country.

85. **News traveled relatively quickly from Mexico to Spain**, considering the time and distance. Soon, many of the Spanish ruling class and a number of **important religious figures spoke out against the war** and suggested buying the Chichimeca off.

86. **The Spanish "purchased peace" with a huge sum of money**. In return, the Chichimeca promised they would not interfere with Spanish trade in their territory.

87. **The Spanish also began erecting schools and churches**. Within two generations, many of the remaining Chichimeca had become assimilated into the dominant Spanish culture.

88. **The Chichimeca War also led to the introduction of new plants and animals to new regions of Mexico**, including horses, cattle, wheat, barley, pears, apples, and figs.

89. **The Chichimeca War also led to the spread of diseases**, such as smallpox and measles, which decimated the Chichimeca population.

90. **The Chichimeca War is an important part of Mexico's history**, as it reminds us of the struggles of the indigenous people against European colonialism.

# Mexican War of Independence
## (1810–1821)

**The Mexican War of Independence was an epic struggle between the people of Mexico and the Spanish colonial government**. On September 16th, 1810, this conflict was set in motion with the cry of a **Catholic priest named Miguel Hidalgo y Costilla**. Spanning eleven years, the war was fought with a combination of conventional and guerrilla tactics and saw the introduction of various new weapons, new forms of government, and new leaders. **The Mexican War of Independence** provided the foundation for a new nation, **the United Mexican States**, and marked the beginning of a **new era for Latin America.**

91. **The Mexican War of Independence**, an epic conflict between **the people of Mexico and the Spanish colonial government,** began on September 16th, 1810.

92. **The Spanish wanted to colonize Mexico in 1519 because they believed they could find gold and silver.** They found those precious items in abundance, as well as many other resources that made Spain a wealthy nation.

93. **The struggle for independence was spearheaded by a number of Mexican revolutionaries, such as Catholic priests Miguel Hidalgo y Costilla** and **José María Morelos, Vicente Guerrero**, and **Guadalupe Victoria** (aka Manuel Félix Fernández).

94. **A number of other Latin American nations had won independence from Spain prior to the Mexican War of Independence**, including Venezuela, Paraguay, Argentina, Colombia, Peru, and Chile.

95. **The war was initiated by the cry of Miguel Hidalgo y Costilla**, a Catholic priest who made an impassioned speech at Dolores. This speech is known as **the Grito de Dolores** ("The Cry of Dolores").

96. **After Costilla's capture and execution in 1811, fellow priest José María Morelos became one of the main leaders of the revolution against the Spanish.**

97. One of the leaders of the revolution was **Josefa Ortiz de Domínguez**, also known as **La Corregidora** ("the Magistrate").

98. **Ignacio Allende**, the son of a wealthy trader, and **Mariano Matamoros**, a priest, were two others who rose to prominence during the war.

99. **Near the end of the war, former areas of Spanish Mexico became independent**. These were Guatemala, El Salvador, Honduras, Costa Rica, and Nicaragua, all of which became independent on September 15th, 1821.

100. **One of the decisive battles of the war and a Mexican victory was the Battle of Puente de Calderón** (the Battle of Calderón Bridge) in 1811.

101. **The war was fought in many parts of Mexico**, including Guanajuato, Michoacán, Oaxaca, Jalisco, and the Yucatán.

102. **The Mexican War of Independence** ended on August 24th, 1821, with the signing of **the Treaty of Córdoba**, which made Mexico an independent country.

103. **Before and after the war, Mexico was a highly stratified society**. At the top of the power pyramid were Spaniards born in Spain. Next were people of **Spanish descent born in Mexico**. The people of **"mixed" Spanish and Mexican-born Spanish heritage were the third tier**. At the bottom were the indigenous people of the country.

104. **Most of the revolutionaries were of Spanish descent who had been born in Mexico.** They were tired of being second-class citizens. **The indigenous people of Mexico remained largely without rights** or a voice in their own country.

105. **The Spanish born in Mexico were called criollos** ("creoles" in English), meaning they were of Spanish descent but born in the New World. However, the word has different meanings throughout the Western Hemisphere.

106. **The Constitution of Apatzingán was written in 1814** and was made the law of areas controlled by the revolutionaries until **it was replaced by a national constitution in 1824.**

107. **The Constitution of 1824 declared Roman Catholicism to be the state religion.** It also made guarantees about individual rights under the law. Unfortunately, there was a big difference between what was written in the constitution and reality.

108. **A new form of government gave rise to new national symbols, like the Mexican flag and the Mexican coat of arms.**

109. **The Mexican War of Independence resulted in the creation of a new nation called the United Mexican States.**

110. **Slavery was abolished in Mexico at the end of the war.**

111. The end of the war saw the emergence of political parties, namely **the Conservative Party and the Liberal Party.**

112. The war also saw the establishment of a **new capital city, Mexico City.**

113. Though it grew very slowly, **Protestantism gained new followers in Mexico** in the early 19th century. This was partly caused by exposure to Americans.

114. **This period gave birth to Mexican literature**. One of the most famous was the novel *El Periquillo Sarniento* **by José Joaquín Fernández de Lizardi**. The book, which is called *The Mangy Parrot* in English, is an allegory for Mexico's transition from colony to country.

115. **The United States recognized Mexican independence in 1822.**

116. **Agustín de Iturbide, who declared Mexico an independent nation in 1821, was one of the most prominent political figures of the war**. He was briefly called the emperor of Mexico before the new constitution was written.

117. **The Mexican Constitution of 1824** declared that the country would have three branches of government, and the executive branch would consist of three people elected by representatives.

118. **The war also resulted in the establishment of a new legal system** based on **the Napoleonic Code**, which was the dominant law code in Europe at the time.

119. The early 19th century saw the emergence of several new leaders in Latin America, such **as Simón Bolívar in Venezuela, José de San Martín in Argentina**, and **Bernardo O'Higgins in Chile.**

120. **The war also established a new national currency, the peso,** which is still used in Mexico today.

251

# First Mexican Empire
## (1822–1823)

**From its inception in 1822, the First Mexican Empire marked a dramatic shift in the trajectory of Mexico and its people**. Established as a monarchy by former royalist **general Agustín de Iturbide, the First Mexican Empire** was a brief yet influential period in Mexico's history. **Emperor Agustín I's** coronation ceremony marked the beginning of a tumultuous reign characterized by political and economic instability. Yet, despite its fragility, **the First Mexican Empire introduced reforms** that had a lasting impact on Mexico and paved the way for future generations.

121. **Agustín de Iturbide, a former general, was proclaimed emperor of Mexico** by leading military figures on May 19th, 1822.

122. **Agustín had much popular support**, although he faced opposition from representatives in Congress who wanted a republic.

123. **The First Mexican Empire only lasted a short time and was replaced by a republic in 1823.**

124. **Emperor Agustín I's lavish coronation ceremony took place in Mexico City at the Catedral Metropolitana de la Ciudad México** (the Metropolitan Cathedral of Mexico City).

125. **The fight against Spain united many Mexicans**, but after the war was over, their differences became clear.

126. **Emperor Agustín and Congress began to clash immediately because no one knew what power(s) belonged to each branch of government.**

127. **The First Mexican Empire was a monarchy**, yet the emperor held limited power. The authority of the nation was primarily held by **the Congress**, officially called **the Congress of the Union.**

128. **Congress and Emperor Agustín argued a lot**. At one point, members of Congress talked about kidnapping the emperor and his family! **Agustín responded to this threat by dismissing Congress and taking more power for himself.**

129. **In the First Mexican Empire, the Catholic Church was named the religion of the state.**

130. **Initially, the First Mexican Empire** was backed by the Catholic Church. However, that backing waned when the emperor became more authoritarian.

131. **Emperor Agustín I of Mexico implemented a policy of centralization** and vested the power of government in the emperor and his ministers.

132. **After the Mexican War of Independence, parts of the old Spanish territory of New Spain became part of Mexico.** The emperor asked these territories, which made up many of today's Central American countries, if they wanted to be part of Mexico. They refused and were let go.

133. **The First Mexican Empire passed laws restricting slavery.** The First Mexican Republic abolished it in 1829, though the practice continued in parts of the country until 1837, when it was outlawed in all regions of Mexico.

134. Mexican production, especially of its most valuable commodity, silver, dropped during **the First Mexican Empire**, leading to widespread economic hardship.

135. **Mexico had gone into considerable debt in the first years of independence** and needed to borrow more to make payments, which started a vicious cycle of borrowing, further weakening the country.

136. **The First Mexican Empire was financially fragile**, with a weak currency and hyperinflation.

137. **Agustín I was not a very good politician**, and combined with the poor state of the country, he faced growing unpopularity.

138. **Though they had mixed results, the empire period introduced economic policies focused on promoting internal trade and industrial development**. This included the encouragement of domestic production, the establishment of trade agreements with foreign countries, and the creation of a national bank to facilitate economic growth.

139. **The First Mexican Empire issued its own currency called the peso**. Some pesos were coins, while some were paper.

140. **The government began printing more and more paper money to pay its debts**, which resulted in high inflation.

141. **During the empire, opinions on education were divided**. Many wished the Catholic Church to keep its role as the main provider of education, but a growing number wished to see a secular public school system begin, which did occur after the end of the empire.

142. **The First Mexican Empire had a strong military**, including cavalry, infantry units, and a navy.

143. **The king of Spain held a lot of influence, and few nations recognized Mexico's independence. Mexico's trade suffered as a result.**

144. **Emperor Agustín I of Mexico was exiled in 1823 and replaced by a federal republic.**

145. **The First Mexican Empire** is known as a period of political and economic instability, with the peso losing its value and the government unable to pay its debts.

146. **Mexico had and still has a large indigenous population**, with many of the indigenous people living in rural areas and working as agricultural laborers.

147. **Ana María Huarte became Empress Consort** and was given the title of **Empress Ana María.** She was known for her beauty and elegance and was highly regarded in Mexican high society.

148. **After her husband's death, Ana María returned to Mexico in 1838** and dedicated herself to preserving her husband's memory.

149. **Leona Vicario** (1789–1842) was an influential journalist, activist, and poet. She supported **the Mexican independence movement** and used her writing to promote nationalist ideas. Vicario is known for her significant contributions to the Mexican press during the early 19th century.

150. **José María Heredia** (1803–1839) was a renowned **poet and writer**. He is considered one of the most important figures in Latin American Romanticism. His works often explored themes of liberty, love, and patriotism.

# First Republic of Mexico
## (1824–1835)

**The First Republic of Mexico** had a brief but transformative eleven-year history that left an indelible mark on the nation. **From recognizing the United States as a sovereign nation to abolishing slavery**, introducing the metric system, issuing paper money and coins, and establishing a bicameral legislature, this revolutionary republic sought to bring unprecedented levels of **freedom and justice to its citizens**.

151. **With its "birth" in 1824, the First Republic of Mexico broke new ground for Mexico**. Mexico became a unitary state (a united country with a powerful federal government) that sought to unite the people under **the slogan of "Union, Liberty, and Justice."**

152. **During its eleven-year history, the First Republic was led by three different** presidents who sought to bring increased levels of freedom to the people. This sometimes happened more in word than in deed.

153. **In 1835, the region of Texas declared its independence from Mexico**, sparking a struggle for power that lasted until 1826.

154. **On April 8th, 1824, this new republic enacted a new constitution that aimed to build a strong centralized government**, which was one reason the Texans later declared their independence.

155. **On December 12th, 1822, Mexico became the second nation in Latin America to recognize the United States as a sovereign nation**, the first being Colombia in June of the same year. **The United States recognized Mexico the same year**.

156. **The First Republic used the United States as a model for its structure**. Its constitution gave great autonomy to the states, much like in the US.

157. **By introducing the metric system, the First Republic of Mexico revolutionized the way people measured and understood the world**.

158. **In 1825, the First Republic of Mexico issued new paper money and coins that strengthened the nation's economy and currency**.

159. **By abolishing slavery in the early 19ᵗʰ century, the First Republic of Mexico** made a bold statement to the world about the importance of human rights and dignity.

160. The government of the republic included a bicameral legislature, **the Chamber of Deputies, and the Senate.**

161. In an effort to bring the nation together, **a national postal system was established** in 1830.

162. To ensure fairness and accuracy, **Mexico adopted a new system of weights and measures** in 1831.

163. **During the First Republic, the groundwork of the Mexican public education system was laid**, which was followed by the passage of significant laws by other Mexican regimes from 1856 to 1867.

164. **On March 28ᵗʰ, 1833, the First Republic of Mexico issued a decree that abolished the use of indigenous languages** in government, education, and church and imposed Spanish as the national language.

165. **The First Republic of Mexico constructed a series of roads** to tie the country together.

166. Railroads became an important way to move goods and people. **Mexico constructed railways throughout the country**, though many of them were controlled by rich criollo families or American and British investors.

167. **The University of Mexico is the oldest university in North Americ**a. During the First Republic, it opened its doors to more people, but it was not open to all Mexicans, especially the poor.

168. To ensure financial stability, **the First Republic of Mexico introduced a new federal tax system.** Most people ignored its regulations, and the government was too new and weak to enforce the law.

169. **In 1832, in an effort to protect writers and inventors, the First Republic of Mexico enacted a national system of copyright law.**

170. **Mexico had public hospitals since Spanish times**, both for Europeans and for indigenous people. Under the republic, the number of hospitals in Mexico increased.

171. **In 1833, the Federal Labor Law was passed**, introducing protections for workers for the first time. Compared to labor laws today, the 1833 law was simple and did not offer the same kind of protections, but it was an important beginning.

172. **The Mexican state included the territory we know as Mexico today but also Texas, Arizona, New Mexico, and a large part of California**. All of these territories were difficult to govern from Mexico City, which is one reason the Mexican government's hold on them became so weak.

173. **The Banco de Avío, an early centralized national bank**, was established in 1830.

174. The Mexican War of Independence **hero Guadalupe Victoria** was **the first president of Mexico** (1824–1829)

175. **Guadalupe Victoria was the only president of the republic who was not overthrown and replaced,** something that usually happened by the military.

176. **There were nine presidents of the First Republic**, but those nine "vacancies" were filled by only six people, as **Valentín Gómez Farías and General de Santa Anna** replaced each other frequently between 1833 and 1835.

177. Though **Antonio López de Santa Anna** was in and out of office, he dominated Mexican politics from 1833 until 1846, sometimes while he was in office and sometimes as a military dictator in all but name.

178. **The Mexican Constitution of 1824 gave the right to vote to any man over the age of eighteen,** provided they were in good standing, which meant known criminals and anyone else the people in power wished to limit.

179. **In parts of Mexico, far from the capital, indigenous people revolted against the government because of the discrimination and prejudice of authorities**. One of the biggest uprisings happened in California in 1824 when **the Chumash tribe** rose up against the government.

180. Though some important changes were made during this period, **the First Republic of Mexico was characterized by political instability and frequent changes in government**. It experienced several presidents and numerous uprisings and conflicts during its existence.

# Texas War of Independence
## (1835–1836)

**From the Battle of Gonzales to the decisive victory at the Battle of San Jacinto, the Texas War of Independence was a complex and tumultuous struggle.** The Texans, made up mostly of volunteers who were ill-prepared for battle, faced off against the large **Mexican Army led by Santa Anna**. Heroes were made, battles were fought, and a nation was born. This chapter will explore the events that led to **the Texas War of Independence**, the battles and other events of the war, and the lasting legacy of this critical piece **of Mexican and American history**.

181. **The Texas War of Independence began on October 2ⁿᵈ, 1835, with the Battle of Gonzales.**

182. **The Texas War of Independence** was fought between Mexican forces led by **General Antonio López de Santa Anna** and Texan forces led by **General Sam Houston**.

183. **Sam Houston was governor of Tennessee from 1827 to 1829 and eventually became the first president of Texas in 1836**. He would serve another term from 1841 to 1844.

184. **Many Americans headed to Texas for cheap land during the Republic of Mexico**. At first, the Mexicans welcomed this, as it brought some wealth and stability. But when more Americans came and set up their own way of running things, Mexico decided to stop selling them land, setting the stage for **the Texas War of Independence**.

185. **The Texas War of Independence was a result of the increasing tensions between Mexico and the settlers of Texas over land rights and slavery**. Most Texans were pro-slavery, whereas the Mexican government had abolished slavery years before.

186. **The Texan army was mostly made up of volunteers from the United States**, including many former American soldiers. They were poorly equipped and ill-prepared for battle when it began.

187. Many people with Mexican or **indigenous Mexican heritage decided they preferred being part of Texas instead of Mexico,** which had become a dictatorship under Santa Anna.

188. **Stephen F. Austin was known as the "Father of Texas"** and was an important leader in the Texas War of Independence.

189. **Many people believe the Texas state flag was designed by Dr. Charles B. Stewart, an important politician**, but others believe it **was designed by Peter Krag**, an artist from Austin. The flag was adopted as the national flag of Texas on January 25th, 1839.

190. **James Fannin was an American officer** who moved to Texas from Georgia in 1834. He was an early leader in the Texas War of Independence but **was executed by Mexican forces in the Goliad massacre**.

191. **The Goliad massacre was an event during the Texas War of Independence** in which over four hundred Texan prisoners of war were executed by **Colonel José Nicolás de la Portilla** because of an order issued **by Santa Anna** in which all foreigners (meaning Americans) were to be treated as bandits and executed.

192. The cannonball from the **"Come and Take It"** cannon was the first shot fired in **the Battle of Gonzales,** which began the Texas War of Independence. The local Mexican detachment demanded the Texans surrender the cannon, as it could be used against the Mexicans. The Texans refused.

193. **Davy Crockett was an adventurer and former US Congressman** from Tennessee who died defending the Alamo.

194. **The Battle of the Alamo was a thirteen-day siege**, lasting from February 23rd, 1836, to March 6th, 1836, which resulted in a Texan defeat. This is where we get the saying, "Remember the Alamo!"

195. **William B. Travis was the commander of the Texan forces** at the Battle of the Alamo and died while defending the fort.

196. **The Battle of the Alamo** is remembered as one of the most heroic stands in history, with the Texan defenders fighting against overwhelming odds.

197. **The Texan forces at the Battle of the Alamo were greatly outnumbered**, with only about two hundred men facing off against Santa Anna's army. Historians estimate that Santa Anna's force ranged between 1,500 and 6,000 men, though the lower figure is probably more accurate.

198. A famed American frontiersman, slave trader, and adventurer named **James Bowie took part in the war.** He was famous for carrying an over-sized knife, which became known as **the Bowie knife** after his death at **the Battle of the Alamo.**

199. **The victory at the Battle of Concepción** (October 28th, 1835) was the first victory for Texan forces. The Texans were led by **James Fannin and James ("Jim") Bowie**.

200. **Juan Seguin was an important Tejano leader** in the Texas War of Independence who fought for Texan independence. Tejanos are Spanish-speaking Texans.

201. **The Texian Navy was created by the Texan government** and played a small but important role in the Texas War of Independence. The navy held its own against the more modern Mexican Navy at the Battle of Campeche off the coast of the Yucatán Peninsula.

202. **The Battle of Coleto** in March 1836 was a decisive victory for Texan forces and led to the capture of Goliad, a town that had been fought over since the beginning of the war.

203. **The Texas Rangers were a paramilitary force established** in November 1835 to protect American settlers from Native American attacks. They played a significant role in key battles like the Battle of San Jacinto.

204. **The Battle of San Jacinto** was fought on April 21st, 1836, and was the final battle of **the Texas War of Independence**.

205. **The Battle of San Jacinto**, which was the pivotal battle of the Texas War of Independence, lasted eighteen minutes!

206. **Santa Anna was captured by Texan forces at the Battle of San Jacinto.**

207. Santa Anna was known as the **"Napoleon of the West"** and was the president of Mexico, although he gave up the position to lead the Mexican forces in the war.

208. **The Treaty of Velasco officially ended the Texas War of Independence** and recognized the independence of the Republic of Texas.

209. **The Texas Constitution was adopted in March 1836** and established the Republic of Texas as an independent nation.

210. **The Republic of Texas was an independent nation for nine years before being voluntarily annexed by the United States in 1845**.

# The Centralist Mexican Republic
## (1835–1846)

**In 1836, the Centralist Mexican Republic was established, marking ten years of turbulent and transformative change.** The nation saw the abolition of slavery, a new constitution, **the rise of President Antonio López de Santa Anna**, and an array of reforms that shaped Mexico's history, culture, and economy. **The Centralist Mexican Republic** was the precursor of much progress in the Western Hemisphere, foretelling many changes that would affect neighboring countries. Here are some key facts about this formidable era in **Mexico's history.**

211. **In 1835, the First Mexican Republic ended.** Bad tax collection policies, inflation, constant power struggles, and the troubles in Texas and elsewhere led to the government's collapse.

212. **The Constitution of 1824 was nullified, and a new constitution called the Seven Laws** was put in its place.

213. One man dominated this period: General (and sometimes President) **Antonio López de Santa Anna.** Many historians have likened him to a king or dictator.

214. **For ten years, the nation was divided into nineteen states and four territories**, with the military holding most of the power in the country.

215. **The Mexican-American War** wrought havoc on the political, military, and especially the economic life of Mexico, causing widespread hardship.

216. **Changes were introduced**, such as the abolition of communal landholding, **a new and centralized currency called the "real,"** and a new system of education.

217. **The president was given the authority to appoint and dismiss state governors**. He also often employed the military to silence opposition.

218. **The Seven Laws** (*Siete Leyes*) tried to create a strong national government as opposed to the Constitution of 1824, which gave more power to local and state governments.

219. **The weakness of the First Republic's government and the defeat in the war with the US led to the end of the First Republic.**

220. **Mexico was the first Latin American nation to form diplomatic relations with the United States**.

221. **European Enlightenment ideas and the Roman Catholic Church had a considerable effect on the nation's politics and laws**. Generally speaking, these two ways of thinking and looking at the world were opposed to each other.

222. **In Mexico, a split began between liberals**, who looked on Europe and the US as a model, and conservatives, who took their cue from **the Catholic Church** and monarchies in Europe.

223. **The Conservative Party dominated** the years of **the Centralist Mexican Republic.**

224. **Santa Anna gained power after commanding a unit in the Mexican War of Independence**. Military officers were not allowed to hold the presidential office, so Santa Anna "resigned" repeatedly.

225. **Santa Anna was in and out of power for years**. In 1855, he was forced into exile, which lasted until 1874. **He lived in Cuba** and, surprisingly, in the US, his former enemy, as well as Colombia and the Virgin Islands.

226. **Santa Anna tried to re-enter politics unsuccessfully** and was an unsuccessful businessman. He was buried with full military honors when he died in his homeland in 1876.

227. **Under Santa Anna, the Catholic Church was allowed to retain its privileges** and vast tracts of land in return for a monthly "donation" to the state. Some of this money made it into the hands of Santa Anna.

228. **Despite the power and influence of the Catholic Church**, Mexicans enjoyed freedom of worship during this period.

229. **The rebellion in Texas and Santa Anna's harsh treatment of captured Texans caused other parts of Mexico to rise in rebellion against centralized authority**.

230. **A rebellion in the military** against the new centralized structure of the government took place in 1838, which was defeated the next year.

231. The leader of the 1838 revolt, **General José de Urrea**, broke out of prison to join another revolt against the government, which saw fighting in the streets of Mexico City. **Santa Anna**, who had already been in and out of power twice, came back and **formed a military dictatorship in 1842.**

232. **Santa Anna ordered another constitution to be drawn up, the Bases Orgánicas, or "Organic Basis"** (of the nation), in 1843. This constitution gave even more power to the president.

233. **The Bases Orgánicas also provided for an expanded public school system, something that was important to Santa Anna.**

234. **The Centralist Mexican Republic** faced significant opposition from federalist forces and regional governments, particularly in states like **Texas, Yucatán, and Zacatecas**. These regions sought to maintain their autonomy and resisted the centralization efforts.

235. **In 1842, Santa Anna attempted to reform and recentralize the collection of federal taxes,** something that led to widespread anger and his temporary downfall.

236. **Spain finally recognized the independence of Mexico in 1836**.

237. **The Centralist Mexican Republic** formed the first true standing army of Mexico. Previously, it had relied on local militias.

238. From 1838 to 1839, **the Pastry War with France was fought over trade issues** and corruption in the Mexican government.

239. **France seized the city of Veracruz and blockaded Mexican ports until the British brokered a peace agreement between the two countries.**

240. Foreign intervention, government infighting, civil unrest, and resistance to federal rule by states and indigenous people all contributed to **the downfall of the Centralist Mexican Republic.**

# Caste War of Yucatán
## (1847–1901)

Let's look at some interesting facts surrounding **the Caste War of Yucatán. This war lasted over fifty years and saw the Maya and the Mexican government fight each other**. The Mexican government's endeavor to quell the uprising resulted in the deaths of thousands of Maya and the displacement of thousands more. **The Caste War left a lasting impact on the Yucatán region.** Let's discover why.

241. **The Caste War of Yucatán began on July 30ᵗʰ, 1847.**

242. The Caste War was **a conflict between the Maya people of the Yucatán Peninsula and the Mexican government.**

243. There were actually two revolts in **the Yucatán Peninsula** that began in the 1840s. One was **led by criollo leaders** who wanted to establish an independent state. **The other was led by the Maya,** who wanted their own independent nation, free from the Mexican government and the criollos' discrimination.

244. **The Maya army initially fought with machetes, spears, and bows and arrows since the region was poor and lacked access to modern weapons**.

245. In an effort to outwit their adversaries, **the Maya forces utilized guerrilla tactics** like ambushes in the deep forests.

246. In 1846, **some Maya rose up against the Mexican authorities**. When one of its leaders, Manuel Antonio Ay, was executed by the government, most of **the Maya people in the Yucatán rose up in revolt, starting the Caste War.**

247. **Cecilio Chí and Jacinto Pat were among the most influential leaders of the Maya forces.**

248. In the midst of the Caste War, **Maya forces proclaimed an independent nation, the Republic of Chan Santa Cruz.**

**249. The Republic of Chan Santa Cruz had a government and constitution of its own.**

250. The war was not continuous. For a time in the late 19<sup>th</sup> century, **various Mexican governments recognized that Maya Yucatán had its own government,** but changes in leadership and policy changed this in the early 20<sup>th</sup> century when a renewed government effort succeeded in absorbing **Chan Santa Cruz** back into Mexico.

251. **The Caste War** caused recurring destruction, economic hardship, and the displacement of many Maya.

252. **The Mexican government's endeavor to suppress the Maya uprising resulted in the deaths of thousands of Maya.**

253. **In 1901, Mexican forces took over the Maya people's proclaimed capital of Chan Santa Cruz and the surrounding area.** Most people knew the war was over, but it did not officially end until 1915, when the leadership of the Maya relented.

254. **After the war was over, some Maya demands were met**, like more autonomy for the region than it had before the revolt began.

255. **The Caste War was a major influence in the diminishment of the Maya population in the Yucatán region.**

256. **The Caste War** caused a loss of economic and political power for the Maya people.

257. **The Caste War caused the loss of many traditional Maya customs and beliefs.**

258. Before the war, **the Mexican government sought to incorporate the Maya people into mainstream Mexican culture using intimidation and force.** That gradually changed in the early 20<sup>th</sup> century when peaceful dialogue between the two sides developed.

259. **The Caste War is seen by many as a symbol of indigenous resistance** to oppression and exploitation and a testament to their endurance.

260. **The three most famous Maya leaders of the time—Manuel Ay, Cecilio Chí, and Jacinto Pat—all** died before the war was over. Ay was executed by the Mexican government, which was the spark that set off the war, and both **Chi and Pat were assassinated by rivals.** Still, all three are regarded as the leaders and spirit behind the Maya independence movement.

# Mexican-American War
## (1846–1848)

**The Mexican-American War** changed the course of history. In this chapter, you'll learn many new things about this conflict, including the role camels played and the **Americans who fought in Mexico who would later be leaders in the US Civil War**. The war resulted in a significant shift in the balance of power in the Southwest, with **the US gaining control of much of the region.** Let's dive in!

261. **The Mexican-American War** began in 1846 and ended two years later with **the Treaty of Guadalupe Hidalgo.**

262. **The United States and Mexico became embroiled in a conflict** due to disputes over their shared border and possession of Texas, which had become part of the US in 1845.

263. Despite having an advantage in numbers, **the Mexican Army was hampered by a lack of modern equipment and weaponry.**

264. **The US Army was led by General Zachary Taylor and General Winfield Scott.**

265. **The Mexican Army was commanded by Antonio López de Santa Anna** and was composed of professional soldiers, militia, and civilian volunteers.

266. **Santa Anna had been forced into exile in 1845 but wanted to return to his home country.** He promised the Americans that if they let him pass through their blockade, he would lead Mexico out of the war.

267. **When Santa Anna arrived in Mexico, he changed his mind, causing US forces to invade Mexico City to defeat Santa Anna and the Mexicans.**

268. The war was fought in a number of locations, including the present-day states of **California, New Mexico, Arizona, Texas, and parts of Colorado**, as well as in the deserts, mountains, and **plains of Mexico**.

269. **The Mexican Army suffered from a lack of supplies**, including food and ammunition.

270. **In Mexico, the US Army was known for its brutal tactics**, such as burning villages and crops.

271. **The US forces were aided by Seminole, Creek, and Cherokee scouts.**

272. **The US Army made use of camels for the first time** in survey and reconnaissance missions.

273. **The training base used by the "Camel Corps" was in Camp Verde, Texas.**

274. **The US Navy was able to transport troops and supplies** and shell Mexican positions and cities on the coasts.

275. **The Mexican forces used guerrilla tactics**. They employed hit-and-run tactics, such as ambushes and raids.

276. **The US Army's tactics were only a little different**, relying on a combination of siege warfare and maneuvers to outwit its opponents.

277. **The war caused the displacement of many Native American tribes from their ancestral lands,** resulting in a major shift in the balance of power in the Southwest, with the US gaining control of much of the region.

278. **At first, many Spanish-speaking people in California supported the Americans**, but the atrocities and outrageous behavior of many American volunteer units caused them to rebel. They were defeated in **the Battle of Providencia** near modern-day Los Angeles.

279. **The US Navy blockaded Mexican ports** and prohibited Mexican shipping during the war, disrupting Mexico's economy.

280. **The Mexican cavalry was made up of skilled lancers**. (A lance was a spear designed to be

used by a mounted warrior or cavalry soldier. It was used in medieval times as well.)

281. **The US cavalry was made up of dragoons armed with sabers and pistols.**

282. Many American soldiers who later became famous in the US Civil War saw action in **the Mexican-American War**. These included **Ulysses S. Grant, Robert E. Lee, and Thomas J. "Stonewall" Jackson.**

283. The president of the United States during the war was **James K. Polk**, who had promised he would only serve one term if his major goals were met. One of these goals was the conquest of Mexican territory in the west.

284. **The US Army was also aided by a large number of volunteers**, many of whom had fought in the Texas War of Independence.

285. The Tennessee Volunteers made history. **The University of Tennessee still calls its sports teams the "Vols."**

286. **Not all Americans were for the war**. Some believed it to be purely a war of conquest. One of these people was Congressman and future **President Abraham Lincoln.**

287. **The war resulted in the death of an estimated six thousand to twenty-five thousand Mexicans, including civilians.**

288. **American deaths totaled 1,733 men killed in action**. However, over eleven thousand died from disease.

289. **Many native people who had lived in California under Mexican rule were pushed out of the territory or killed when the United States took over.**

290. Estimates of **indigenous Californians killed** by white settlers and militiamen in California run between nine thousand and sixteen thousand.

291. **The Mexican-American War was the first in which the US Army used the new Colt revolver.**

292. **Winfield Scott, the overall US commander**, surrounded the Mexican coast with US ships, preventing overseas supplies from reaching Mexico.

293. **At the beginning of the US Civil War, Scott came up with the North's Anaconda Plan,** which did much the same thing to the Confederacy.

294. **The US Navy did not see any real ship-to-ship combat in the war.** Mexico's navy only existed on paper.

295. **The American victory resulted in the acquisition of over 500,000 square miles of land,** including Texas, California, Arizona, and New Mexico.

296. **After the war was won, the new treaty granted US citizens the right to acquire land in Mexico and Mexicans in the US the right to become citizens.**

297. Despite being a hero in the Mexican-American War and playing a vital role **in the Battle of Chapultepec, Ulysses Grant** later condemned the Mexican-American War and said, "To this day, (I) regard the war which resulted as one of the most unjust ever waged by a stronger against a weaker nation."

298. **US Commodore John Sloat**, who has streets, parks, and other places named for him in California, seized San Francisco from Mexico on July 9th, 1846. Other places throughout Northern California were taken over by American settlers at about the same time.

299. **The Maya in the Yucatán had closer relations with the US than they did with the Mexican government.** The US Navy used the Yucatán coast to land supplies.

300. **In the First Battle of Tabasco**, along the Mexican coast, **American naval officer Matthew C. Perry,** who would later become famous as the man that opened Japan to the outside world, was defeated when he attempted to land sailors to seize a number of towns along the coast.

# The Reform War
## (1858–1861)

**The Reform War** of the mid-19th century was a monumental turning point in **Mexican history,** ushering in a wave of social, political, and economic reforms that had far-reaching consequences. **From the introduction of a new currency to the emergence of a new type of nationalism, the Reform War gave birth to a new Mexican identity.** Let's look at some of the facts about this era!

301. **The Reform War was actually a civil war.** It was a major turning point in Mexican history, leading to the downfall of the conservative forces and the rise of the liberal forces.

302. **The war was triggered by the enactment of the Mexican Constitution of 1857**, which aimed to establish a more secular and centralized government and curtail the power of **the Catholic Church.**

303. **The liberal faction of the government, led by President Benito Juárez**, supported the new constitution and sought to implement its reforms, including **the nationalization of church properties and the separation of church and state.**

304. **The conservatives opposed the 1857 Constitution**. They were backed **by the Catholic Church and led by General Miguel Miramón.** They sought to preserve the traditional privileges and influence of the church.

305. **As a result of the Reform War, many Mexicans saw their fortunes destroyed**, leading to poverty for many.

306. **Because of corruption and mismanagement, the Mexican government found itself so strapped for cash during the Reform War** that it was forced to print paper money, which eventually became worthless.

307. **Liberals in the country wished to see the power of the military**, the Catholic Church, large landowners, and foreigners reduced in Mexico.

308. **At the start of the war, the Liberal Party and its support was located in the center of the country, including Mexico City.** Conservative support was strongest in the countryside and the north and south.

309. **The United States supported the Liberal Party** and its policies during the Reform War, while France, Spain, and Britain supported the Conservative Party.

310. **There were many issues separating Mexicans from one another.** All of their problems came to light during the fight over the contents of the 1857 Constitution. The main issue was how strong the central government was going to be in respect to the states.

311. Just before the Reform War, in 1854, a new national anthem emerged, **the Himno Nacional Mexicano,** which is the national anthem of the country today.

312. In the mid-19th century, Mexican writers began to make a name for themselves in the Spanish-speaking world, such as **Vicente Riva Palacio, Ignacio Galván**, and many others.

313. **The Reform War also saw the emergence of a new type of nationalism in Mexico**, one that was based on liberalism and "people power."

314. **The Reform War led to the reform of the Mexican Supreme Court,** which was tasked with the oversight of the judiciary system. The Supreme Court had previously been firmly under the president's control.

315. The famous (and sometimes infamous) **Federales, a police-type force** of the Mexican Army tasked with maintaining public order and protecting citizens, was established at this time. **Though the Federales are now a unique unit of the Mexican police and founded in 1999**, the term Federales was initially used by Americans to describe the original force and those that came after it.

316. **Many bloody battles took place during the Reform War**. Initially, the conservatives had the edge, but by the end of the war, conservative infighting, foreign aid, and the desire for change among many Mexicans gave the edge to the liberals, who won the conflict and set up a new government in 1860.

317. **The war lasted for four years, from 1857 to 1861**, and resulted in considerable devastation and loss of life. It caused political instability and economic hardship in Mexico, exacerbating existing social divisions.

318. **The damage done to the country's infrastructure during the war led to an economic downturn**, which gradually strengthened the conservatives, who sought support from the conservative emperor of France, Napoleon III.

319. **The Reform War witnessed significant foreign intervention. France, under Napoleon III,** took advantage of the internal conflict to invade Mexico in 1861 and establish the short-lived French-imposed regime known as the **Second Mexican Empire**.

320. The Reform War also saw the emergence of the peso again, which was designed to promote economic stability and growth. **The peso replaced the real.**

321. **Additionally, the Reform War led to the establishment of a new system of land reform,** which sought to redistribute land more equitably. Much land was taken from the Catholic Church, which had controlled not just the land but also employment on it.

322. **This conflict also saw the introduction of a new system of education,** which was designed to create a more literate population, one separate from the ideas of Catholicism. The church had dominated what education there was in Mexico until this time.

323. **The Reform War saw the emergence of a more organized and professional army in Mexico,** one that was better trained and better equipped than its predecessors.

**324. The Reform War resulted in the adoption of a new legal system** in Mexico known as the *Ley Lerdo* ("Lerdo Law"), which sought to limit the power of the Catholic Church, among other things.

**325. Benito Juárez was elected president of Mexico in 1861.** Juárez was a populist who had great appeal among the common people and loudly supported national pride, not just pride in the upper ruling classes.

**326. Juárez was the first indigenous president of Mexico and the first native person to hold power in the post-colonial era.** Most Mexicans consider **Benito Juárez** a hero today, though not all of his reforms were successful.

**327. This conflict brought about a new system of government**, which sought to limit the power of the executive and give more power to the people.

**328. At the end of the Reform War, a new type of foreign policy emerged in Mexico** that sought to distance Mexico from the European powers and instead focus on the Americas.

**329. The Reform War also led to the abolition of debt peonage,** which had been a major problem in Mexico prior to the war. Debt peonage means that people worked off debts with labor.

**330. Additionally, the Reform War saw the emergence of a new type of economy in Mexico.** This new economy was based on free trade and economic liberalization, much like more prominent Western capitalist societies of the time.

# The Second Mexican Empire
## (1864–1867)

**Another empire? Yes! The Second Mexican Empire was an attempt to restore order to a chaotic nation.** Established in 1864, **this short-lived monarchy was funded by the French government** and heavily supported by the conservative segment of the Mexican population. **Emperor Maximilian I**, the sole monarch of **the Second Mexican Empire,** initiated a series of reforms. However, his reign came to an abrupt end. Discover how, as well as **the empire's impact on Mexico.**

331. **The Second Mexican Empire** was established in 1864 and ended in 1867. Thus, it was a short period of monarchical rule.

332. **Chaos and civil war were the impetus for the Second Mexican Empire**, which was created in an attempt to restore order.

333. **Benito Juárez was forced out of the capital, but he never left the country.**

334. **Maximilian I was the only monarch of the Second Mexican Empire.**

335. **Emperor Maximilian I's reign over the Second Mexican Empire was heavily supported by the conservative elite,** who had struggled in the Reform War.

336. **The conservative Catholic Church also supported the Second Mexican Empire.**

337. As expected, **the Second Mexican Empire** was vigorously opposed by the liberal forces in Mexico.

338. **Emperor Napoleon III of France**, nephew of Napoleon Bonaparte, wanted to grow France's influence overseas. **He largely funded the effort to bring Maximilian to power.**

339. Maximilian was a member of the Habsburg family, whose members sat on the thrones of Spain and Austria.

340. **During the Second Mexican Empire, the US was involved in fighting its own civil war and was not able to prevent France's interference in Mexico.** The US continued to support the republican government, though.

341. **Empress Carlota, Maximilian's wife, was a key figure in the Second Mexican Empire.** When Maximilian was gone from the capital, he made his wife regent until he returned.

342. **Political unrest and turmoil were hallmarks of the short-lived monarchy.**

343. **A railroad from Mexico City to the important city of Veracruz was created** during the Second Mexican Empire.

344. In 1866, facing a possible war in Europe and not willing to fight the now re-united United States, **Napoleon III withdrew French troops, including the famous French Foreign Legion, and financial support from Maximilian.**

345. **Treason charges stemming from the emperor's support from France resulted in his execution,** bringing the Second Mexican Empire to a close.

346. **Empress Carlota was in Europe attempting to get more aid for the empire when her husband was killed by a firing squad.**

347. **Carlota spent the rest of her life in seclusion in Europe**. She died in 1927.

348. **The execution of Maximilian caused outrage in Europe,** leading to strained diplomatic relations between Mexico and several European countries.

349. **The Second Mexican Empire's collapse was a significant blow to European ambitions of expanding their influence in the Americas.**

350. After deposing Maximilian I, liberal forces, which favored a republic, **ended the Second Mexican Empire in 1867.**

351. **The Mexican Congress officially dissolved the Second Mexican Empire in 1867.**

352. **Mexico faced significant challenges in rebuilding and recovering from the war** and the period of foreign intervention.

353. **Maximilian and Carlota's story has inspired literature, art, and films,** contributing to their enduring place in popular culture.

354. **The events of the Second Mexican Empire had a lasting impact on Mexican nationalism and the country's sense of identity**. After this period, Mexican nationalism increased dramatically throughout the country.

355. **Despite its foreign origins, music brought by the French influenced Mexican culture to this day.** Some say mariachi music has its roots in what the French called "marriage music," when Mexican musicians were hired to play both Mexican music and European waltzes.

# Expansion of Industrialization
## (1890-1940)

**The period of industrialization between 1890 and 1940 saw Mexico undergo a drastic transformation in its infrastructure, industries, and technology.** Let's look at some key facts about this important era in **Mexico's history**, as well as explore the causes and implications of Mexico's industrial revolution.

356. **Mexico experienced significant industrialization in the period from 1890 to 1940.**

357. **In 1895, a modern railroad was built from Mexico City to Puebla.**

358. **Mexico began to focus on industrialization** to increase economic growth. It had watched the US and Europe grow their economies through industrial development.

359. **The government increased investment in infrastructure**, building improved roads and railways.

360. **Mexico passed a series of internal and external tariffs** (taxes on goods) that were partly successful.

361. **Smaller Mexican businesses were hurt by internal tariffs**, but some larger businesses, like the textile industry, benefited because foreign textile goods were taxed at a high rate.

362. **The government provided subsidies to encourage the growth of Mexican industry.**

363. **Mexican industrial growth** was hindered by a significant amount of corruption in government and business.

364. **Mexico began to produce consumer goods for other countries**, such as clothing and furniture, but most Mexicans had a hard time affording more than the necessities. This situation began to change in Mexico's biggest cities by the start of the 20th century.

365. **The number of factories in Mexico increased** significantly during the period of industrialization.

366. **Mexico's manufacturing sector was dominated by textiles, food products, and mining.**

367. During this period, **Mexico became a major producer** of petroleum and other minerals.

368. **Mexico opened its doors to foreign investment**, especially from 1876 to 1911, leading to increased economic growth.

369. **The government established a national bank in 1925** to help direct and coordinate the economy.

370. In the early 20th century, **Mexico began its own steel, cement, and other industries for construction,** which aided in the country's economic growth and lessened its dependence on other countries.

371. **Automobile production began in Mexico in 1925.**

372. **Ford opened a plant in the San Lazaro** neighborhood of Mexico City in 1925.

373. **Mexico also began to produce many kinds of chemicals and paper.**

374. The government encouraged **the development of new industries**, such as the production of electricity. It invested heavily in power plants and electrical infrastructure.

375. **The government also invested in irrigation projects to improve agricultural production,** which helped the country become a major exporter of fruits and vegetables to the US.

376. **The number of workers in the industrial sector increased** from 600,000 in 1890 to 1.2 million in 1930.

377. **The number of factories in Mexico increased** from 1,600 in 1900 to 4,000 in 1930.

378. **Mexico's industrial production increased** from 4.2 billion pesos in 1900 to 12.5 billion pesos in 1929.

379. **The number of workers in the mining sector increased** from 30,000 in 1900 to 100,000 in 1930.

380. **The number of workers in the oil industry increased** from four thousand in 1900 to seventeen thousand in 1930.

381. **The number of workers in the textile industry increased** from twenty thousand in 1900 to seventy-two thousand in 1930.

382. **Mexico's industrial output increased** by an average of 5.5 percent each year between 1890 and 1930.

383. **Mexico had the fourth-largest economy in Latin America** in 1930.

384. In 1938, **President Lazaro Cárdenas nationalized the Mexican oil industry**, which meant the government took over all oil production and sales in the country. This move also expelled the US companies that had become very influential in Mexico.

385. **The number of factories in Mexico increased** from 1,600 in 1900 to 4,000 in 1930.

386. **Copper mining grew** in importance as the number of electrical products and the use of electricity increased. Copper is an excellent conductor of electricity.

387. Despite many improvements and the growth in wealth, **most Mexicans did not see great improvements in their living and working conditions**, which led to widespread unrest in the late 19th century and early 20th century.

388. **Mexico also established a national aviation industry** in the 1920s, which helped to further facilitate trade and transportation.

389. During the industrial revolution of the 1930s, **Mexico was one of the first countries in Latin America to develop its own steel industry.**

390. **Mexico's industrialization was heavily concentrated in the northern part of the country,** particularly in the states of Chihuahua, Coahuila, and Nuevo León.

391. **Mexico's main exports were minerals and petroleum**, although the manufacturing sector also experienced significant growth.

392. **Mexico's industrialization was heavily reliant on the importation of foreign technology and capital goods,** especially from the United States.

393. **The Rockefeller family from the US was heavily invested in Mexico's industrialization** during this period.

394. **US financial involvement in Mexico** caused great resentment among the poor and Mexican nationalists, causing tension between the two countries.

395. **The period of industrialization saw the emergence of a powerful elite class** comprised of large landowners, industrialists, and financiers who controlled much of the country's wealth and resources.

# The Mexican Revolution
## (1910–1920)

**The Mexican Revolution of 1910** erupted in a blaze of fury as insurgents led by **Francisco Ignacio Madero and Emiliano Zapata** challenged the rule of **Porfirio Díaz**. As the tumult spread across the country, legendary figures were born, inspiring thousands. **The heroes of the revolution are still remembered and revered today**, and their legacies remain alive in the Mexican people's hearts.

396. **In 1910, a group of insurgents led by Francisco Ignacio Madero initiated hostilities against the Díaz administration**, launching what would become known as **the Mexican Revolution.**

397. **Francisco Ignacio Madero had run for president against Díaz** and had been jailed for a time.

398. **Díaz had been in power since the late 1870s** and had opened the country up to large foreign companies.

399. **Corruption, abuse of workers and farmers, and Díaz's refusal to abide by democratic principles led to war.**

400. The revolutionary forces were able to defeat the forces of Porfirio Díaz after a series of battles, culminating in **the Battle of Ciudad Juárez** in 1911.

401. A major player in the upheaval was **Emiliano Zapata**. He was an instrumental figure in the formation of **the Liberation Army of the South** in 1911.

402. **Pancho Villa** was another famous revolutionary. For a time, from 1914 to 1915, the US considered him **the leader of Mexico**.

403. **The US exercised significant influence during this period and launched raids into Mexico to try and catch Pancho Villa**, who had turned against the new government and launched raids into the US, partially in response to US support of **Victoriano Huerta** and interference in Mexican affairs.

404. **Huerta initially fought for Madero**, but he turned on the president during the Ten Tragic Days, the name given to Huerta's coup.

405. Two future American military heroes, **John J. Pershing**, who led the US Army in WWI, and **George Patton**, who led an army in WWII, **took part in the fight against Villa** and his men.

406. **Venustiano Carranza** had been an ally of **Porfirio Díaz** but turned against him and became an important leader of the revolution. When he became president in 1917, many believed he did not enact the reforms the revolutionaries had fought for.

407. **The Constitution of 1917 guaranteed religious freedom and gender equality for Mexicans.**

408. Women, such as **Juana Belén Gutiérrez de Mendoza and Petra Herrera**, played a notable role in the revolution, fighting side by side with their male counterparts.

409. **Peasant rebellions against wealthy landowners increased during the revolution**, though they were frequently met with harsh repression.

410. **The overthrow of Díaz created a power vacuum** that many Mexican revolutionaries attempted to fill.

411. **Madero's government was overthrown by General Huerta**, who had the support of the United States and many Mexican generals.

412. **Huerta also had the support of the German Empire**, which was just beginning to find its feet on the world stage.

413. **Huerta's coup only made the war worse**, and Huerta was forced to resign after just a year and a half in power.

414. **Huerta would flee the country**. He lived in Spain for a time but eventually moved to the US. There, he conspired with the Germans during World War I, which led to his arrest. He died in jail.

415. In the north, near the US border, **Villa's forces were able to overcome conservative forces in Ciudad Juárez.**

416. **The Battle of Zacatecas in 1914** was a crucial success for the revolutionaries, allowing them to take control of Mexico City.

417. **Newspapers increased during the Mexican Revolution**, allowing revolutionary leaders to communicate their ideas.

418. Numerous revolutionary leaders, including **Francisco Madero and Emiliano Zapata**, were assassinated during the struggle.

419. **Emiliano Zapata, a popular revolutionary, was assassinated in 1919** when he was ambushed by Mexican Army forces.

420. **The United States offered military support** to the revolutionaries, providing them with arms and ammunition.

421. After many years of fighting, assassinations, and destruction, **many of the factions fighting in the war began to negotiate an end to the fighting.**

422. The revolution culminated in the election of **Álvaro Obregón as president** in 1920.

423. The Obregón government sought to preserve the accomplishments of the revolution, including the land reforms enshrined in **the Constitution of 1917**.

424. **Obregón's government brought stability to the country** and helped to catalyze Mexico's modernization.

425. **The revolution also saw the proliferation of labor unions** that strived to improve working conditions and wages for workers.

426. **The revolution inspired a new generation of Mexican artists**, writers, and intellectuals, such as Diego Rivera (1886–1957). These thinkers sought to create a new Mexican identity.

427. **"Mexican muralism" became popular at this time,** and it still is today. Many muralists, both then and now, concern themselves with social justice issues.

428. **The corrido** (a ballad) was **a popular form of music**. It praised the heroes of the revolution, and its songs helped spread important news.

429. **Revolutionary realism**, a unique form of literature, was born from the revolution, documenting the struggles of the Mexican people.

430. **Muralism, a new form of art, emerged**, visually representing the struggles of the Mexican people.

431. **Liberalism, socialism, and anarchism were major influences in the Mexican Revolution.**

432. **The Mexican Revolution** stimulated industrialization in the country due to the government's efforts to modernize the nation.

433. Partly due to the call for change in Mexico during the revolution, **education became more available to the populace,** with the government seeking to provide educational opportunities to all citizens.

434. **Political parties proliferated, as the government sought to create a more democratic system.**

435. All of **the major revolutionary leaders were killed during the war** or not long after, sometimes by former allies.

436. **Over two million people died during the violence of the Mexican revolutionary period.**

437. **The heroes of the revolution are still revered in Mexico**, with their images present in open spaces such as parks and squares.

438. **The Mexican Revolution attracted foreign mercenaries who joined various factions in the conflict.** Notably, the Irish-born American mercenary Ambrose Bierce fought **alongside Pancho Villa's** forces for a brief period. Bierce, a renowned writer, disappeared in Mexico in 1913 under mysterious circumstances.

439. **The Mexican Revolution** witnessed the implementation of unconventional warfare tactics. One notable example is the **"Zapatista War Train,"** a mobile armored train used by **Emiliano Zapata's** forces. This train was equipped with heavy artillery and allowed for rapid movement and surprise attacks against federal troops.

440. **Many women participated as soldiers, spies, nurses, and even commanders**. Some notable examples include **Carmen Serdán**, who played a key role in **the Puebla uprising**, and **Petra Herrera**, a skilled soldier who fought while being disguised as a man.

# The Cristero War
## (1926–1929)

The changes brought about by **the Mexican Revolution Church** sparked a rebellion that would shake the foundations of the country. In this chapter, learn **how the rebels employed a variety of tactics against the forces of the Mexican government**. Also, discover the answer as to why the **Cristeros** rose up.

441. **During President Plutarco Elías Calles's regime, a faction of Mexican Catholics called Cristeros erupted into rebellion, triggering the Cristero War.**

442. During the uprising, **the Cristeros** adopted the slogan **of "Viva Cristo Rey"** ("Long Live Christ the King!").

443. **Most of the fighting and uprisings took place near Mexico City** and the center of the country, though the south and the eastern Baja coast were affected too. The northern part of Mexico remained relatively free of violence.

444. After **the Mexican Revolution**, Mexican authorities attempted to remove the influence of the clergy from government, especially local government, by passing laws restricting clergymen from holding public office.

445. **The Cristeros utilized a network of underground churches and priests to continue their services and rituals.**

446. **Calles's government attempted to create a secular government in which no religious organization held power and influence,** which is the main reason the Cristero movement began.

447. In response to the rebels, **the Mexican government** deployed its army to subdue the revolt.

448. **Wealthy landowners supplied the rebels with weapons and supplies.**

449. **The Catholic Church** offered assistance to the Cristeros by giving them funds and supplies.

450. **The Cristeros conducted successful ambushes against government troops.**

451. Atrocities occurred on both sides. For instance, a priest named **José Reyes Vega** doused **a train car with gasoline and set it on fire** because his younger brother had been killed. Fifty-one civilians died.

452. To garner public support, **the Cristeros held rallies and mass protests.**

453. Foreign powers, such as **the United States and Spain, sent aid to different sides during the war.**

454. **The Cristeros employed propaganda to spread their message** and appeal to the public.

455. As a symbol of their cause, **the Cristeros adopted a red flag with a white cross.**

456. To keep their operations a secret, **the Cristeros recruited female spies** disguised as vendors and travelers to gather information and smuggle guns and ammunition.

457. Many **Mexican Catholics**, as well as some **non-Catholics, provided support to the Cristeros and their cause.**

458. **The Mexican government employed various tactics to defeat the Cristeros,** such as burning villages and executing suspected rebels.

459. **The Mexican government resorted to harsh tactics, such as torture and public executions,** to try and intimidate the Cristeros into surrendering.

460. **To defeat the Cristeros, the Mexican government utilized air power to bomb the Cristero strongholds.** The pilots were reportedly American WWI veterans.

461. **In 1929, the Cristeros were defeated by the Mexican government.**

462. As a consequence of their defeat, **the Cristero War's leaders were either imprisoned or executed.**

463. **In the end, an estimated ninety thousand people perished in the Cristeros War.**

464. Following the Cristeros' defeat, **the Mexican government continued to monitor the Catholic Church** to prevent it from wielding political power.

465. Though most of **the Cristeros were motivated by religious reasons**, many others who joined the rebellion were poorer farmers and people of mixed Spanish and native backgrounds. These people fought for land reform, which came slowly and is still an issue in the country.

# Institutional Revolutionary Party Era
## (1929–2000)

For over seven decades, **Mexico experienced a period of authoritarian rule under the** *Partido Revolucionario Institucional* **(PRI)**. A lot happened during this era, such as the monopolization of the media, economic expansion, and a high degree of patronage and corruption. Let's dive in to discover more about this influential period!

466. **During this prolonged period of authoritarian rule, the Mexican government monopolized the media, broadcasting only approved messages.**

467. A formidable **political machine based on patronage and bribes was established.**

468. **Patronage was utilized to ensure loyalty among public servants.**

469. While economic expansion in the form of large industries like oil and steel occurred, the majority of **the wealth was disproportionately allocated to a small group of elites.**

470. **The PRI maintained its control of power for over seven decades**, partly through electoral manipulation.

471. **Notorious for their opulence, PRI leaders were known to lead lives of luxury and host grandiose celebrations.**

472. **Mexico was heavily reliant upon external investment and loans from the United States** during this time period.

473. **Powerful drug cartels were formed during the rule of the PRI.** Many PRI officials were "on the take."

474. **Corruption and favoritism within the government were rampant.**

475. The emergence of **the Mexican labor movement,** which was committed to the defense of worker rights and social justice, happened during the PRI era.

476. **Some social and economic reforms were introduced to improve the quality of life for Mexicans.**

477. **The military was utilized to oppress political opponents.**

478. **Land reforms were implemented** to redistribute wealth to the poorest citizens, but they were few and far between. Corruption also weakened their effect.

479. **Censorship and propaganda were employed to manage public opinion.**

480. **The Catholic Church** reemerged as a powerful entity.

481. **Unions and political parties sought to eliminate the PRI's monopoly,** but they developed slowly.

482. **The Mexican border was militarized to deter illegal immigration.**

483. During the reign of the PRI, a powerful intelligence agency called the "**Dirección Federal de Seguridad,**" the "**Federal Security Directorate,**" or "**DFS,**" was created to monitor dissident groups.

484. **Political factions intended to challenge government control arose during the PRI era.**

485. **Indigenous rights groups**, hoping to oppose government policies, gained traction during this era.

486. **Highly influential business interests impacted much of Mexico's social, economic, and political life.** Businesses engaged in corruption, intimidation, and bribery.

487. In the 1980s, **Mexican drug cartels** served as conduits for the huge South American cocaine trade.

488. **Most of the leading PRI officials were from the criollo or Caucasian minority,** adding ethnic tension to Mexican social and political life.

489. **The use of torture and human rights abuses against political dissidents was commonplace.**

490. Though the Mexican government worked to keep its distance from US policies in Latin America and often opposed them, it did occasionally support US efforts in the region. For instance, **Mexico supported the US-led invasion of Panama in 1989**.

491. **Women's rights groups challenged traditional gender roles in this period**. It took time for these groups to achieve substantial progress.

492. Student organizations sought to oppose government policies. One protest in particular, **the deadly Tlatelolco massacre**, marked the beginning of the PRI's slow decline.

493. **Environmental organizations striving to protect the environment were founded** in the PRI Era.

494. **Peasant organizations dedicated to the betterment of rural Mexicans were established** during this period, but the period of PRI rule is known for the party's favoritism toward the rich and powerful.

495. **Economic nationalism** was employed to protect domestic industries during this era.

496. **Trade unions that were committed to improving wages and working conditions developed.** Most unions were secretly monitored by the government.

497. **Electoral fraud was a big problem in PRI Mexico**, drawing condemnation from the US and others.

498. **In the 1970s, the Mexican economy went through many crises**, lowering the standard of living for most Mexicans. The decline of the PRI slowly began during this decade.

499. **A clandestine network of prisons was maintained to detain political dissidents.**

500. From the 1960s to the 1980s, successive PRI governments waged what is called the **"Mexican Dirty War"** on anyone who opposed them. The main target of the PRI were peasants and other reformers who were believed to be influenced by communism.

# Mexican Oil Expropriation
## (1938)

**When President Lázaro Cárdenas declared the Mexican oil expropriation of 1938, it sent shockwaves throughout the energy production industry** and was met with vehement opposition from foreign oil companies. Undeterred by the backlash, **the Mexican government pursued the nationalization of natural resources** and embarked on a journey to create a financially independent nation. Let's uncover the controversy behind such a decision.

501. **In 1938, the Mexican government sent shockwaves throughout the world, especially the United States, when it nationalized oil and mineral production in the country.**

502. **The Mexican government** kicked out many foreign, mostly **American, oil companies that had invested millions in Mexico.**

503. **President Lázaro Cárdenas was undeterred by the backlash and vigorously pursued the nationalization of natural resources**, prompting boycotts and economic sanctions from other countries.

504. One definition of expropriation is **"the act of dispossessing an owner, either wholly or to a limited extent, of his property or proprietary rights."** Despite the international pressure, the Mexican government remained committed to expropriation and strove to create a financially independent nation.

505. **The Mexican oil expropriation of 1938 actually led to an increase in foreign investment** since countries were eager to invest in the newly nationalized oil industry.

506. To ensure the legality of the expropriation, **the Mexican government had to negotiate settlements with the displaced foreign oil companies**, which was a lengthy and complex endeavor.

507. Before WWII broke out, **negotiations between Mexico and foreign oil companies** led to Mexico compensating them for its takeover.

508. For the policy to be successful, **the government had to invest** significantly in the construction and operation of pipelines, refineries, storage facilities, and the new national oil company, **Petróleos Mexicanos** (Pemex).

509. **The expropriation of oil was a catalyst for economic growth and exports** but also led to criticism that the government was squandering the nation's resources and disregarding oil quality and the environment in pursuit of quantity.

510. Furthermore, **the expropriation of oil has been accused of being politically motivated** and of exacerbating inequality, leading to a debate that has surrounded it for decades.

511. For its new energy policies to reach their full potential, **the Mexican government had to pour in a great amount of investment for the development and maintenance of newly built infrastructure.** This money came from other programs, including help for the lower classes in Mexico.

512. **The United States worried that the Mexican nationalization of the oil industry** might be a first step to socialism or even communism.

513. In 1952, the Mexican government commissioned the statue and fountain called **the Fountain of Mexican Petroleum,** which was erected on a main boulevard in Mexico City.

514. When the policy was implemented, **Mexico witnessed a period of economic success and prosperity**, with oil exports becoming a major source of the government's revenue.

515. Still, **the oil industry was highly regulated by the government**, with production quotas, prices, and taxes all managed by the state.

516. **The Mexican government kept gas prices in Mexico low**, which was popular with the people.

517. In 2022, **Mexico ranked twelfth in oil production**, pumping 1.7 million barrels a day.

518. The president of Mexico during the expropriation was **Lázaro Cárdenas del Rio**, who was in office from 1934 to 1940.

519. **The expropriation of 1938 remains an iconic moment in Mexico's history**, especially since the United States was against it and interfered in Mexican politics to prevent or change the policy through boycotts, bribery, and other forms of intimidation.

520. **The oil expropriation also initiated a wave of nationalization in Mexico**, with the government taking control of other industries, such as electricity, telecommunications, banking, and railways.

521. Initially, **the United States, Great Britain, and the Netherlands boycotted all other Mexican goods as a reaction to the loss of their interests in Mexico**. The boycott ended with negotiations when WWII started.

522. **The nationalization of oil** that occurred in 1938 has been credited with providing a spark of inspiration to other Latin American countries, consequently leading to the rise of similar policies.

523. **Despite the success of oil expropriation**, the policy was and is considered highly controversial by some, with arguments questioning whether the government should have allowed foreign companies to continue to carry out operations in the country.

524. **The oil expropriation of 1938 has been credited with increasing national wealth** and helping to reduce inequality to a small degree.

525. Its detractors contend that it stifled competition and created an inefficient, **state-run oil industry.**

526. **The oil expropriation also increased government control** of the most important resource in the country.

527. The policy has also been accused of allowing **the government to become too reliant on oil revenues** to the detriment of other areas of the economy, resulting in economic stagnation and dependence on energy exports.

528. **The environmental impact of the oil expropriation has been subject to criticism**, with the production and development of the industry being blamed for pollution and the destruction of natural resources.

529. Furthermore, **many criticized the PRI for the move**, which they believed was politically motivated. The government was accused of using it to gain popular support and consolidate its power.

530. Despite its successes, **the oil expropriation of 1938 has been derided for its lack of transparency and its failure to benefit the population**, serving as a reminder that the power of nationalization should be carefully considered and applied.

# Bracero Program
## (1942–1964)

**What began as an effort to meet the labor needs of American farmers during World War II, the Bracero (meaning "manual laborer")** Program quickly spiraled into a complex web of labor rights violations, wage theft, and unjust treatment. **The Bracero Program had a long-term impact on the Mexican economy,** labor market, and demographics, resulting in **the permanent migration of millions of Mexicans to the United States**. Let's take a look at several important facts about this program.

531. **The Bracero Program was a series of bilateral labor agreements between the United States and Mexico.**

532. Contrary to popular belief, **the Bracero Program** was not originally intended to be a long-term arrangement.

533. **The Bracero Program was established in 1942 to meet the labor needs of American farmers** who were fighting in World War II.

534. **Mexican citizens were recruited to work in US fields**, primarily in California, Arizona, and Texas.

535. **Braceros were required to sign a contract**.

536. **They were supposed to be supplied with transportation, medical care, and housing**, although this did not always happen.

537. **The contracts were often written in English and Spanish**, with the Spanish versions often containing fewer rights than the English versions. Thus, many non-English speaking workers were not aware of their rights in the US.

538. **Penalties for contract violations included deportation and fines.**

539. **Deportations and fines** could also result from unscrupulous and/or racist farm owners.

540. **Brutal working conditions, low wages, and inadequate housing** were common for Braceros.

541. **The Bracero Program ended in 1964** and was plagued by labor rights violations and other issues.

542. According to the Pew Research Center, **the Bracero Program issued over 4.6 million contracts to Mexican workers** over its 22-year run.

543. **The US government estimated that Braceros earned an average of one dollar per hour,** which was below the federal minimum wage (which began in 1938).

544. **It is estimated that between $500 million and $1.5 billion of Bracero wages were never paid.**

545. In 1998, a settlement was agreed upon that allowed many **surviving Braceros to be paid lost wages.** In 2019, there were still thirty-six thousand Braceros awaiting payment of the settlement money.

546. **The settlement only applied to those Braceros who lived in the United States.**

547. In 2001, **several former Braceros filed a class-action suit in a federal court against the governments of the United States and Mexico**, three Mexican banks, and Wells Fargo Bank. The federal judge dismissed the lawsuit in 2002, citing expired statutes of limitations and sovereign immunity.

548. In some cases, **Braceros were forced to pay kickbacks** (bribes) to hire agents to secure employment.

549. Upon the program's termination, **many Braceros were deported** and unable to access the wages they had earned.

550. **The Bracero Program had a long-term impact on the Mexican economy** and labor market. For instance, Mexico sought to benefit from Braceros sending money back home to relatives. They also hoped that new agricultural techniques from the US would be learned.

551. **The program had a significant impact on the demography of the US-Mexico border region.**

552. It is estimated that **the Bracero Program resulted in the permanent migration** of many Mexicans to the United States.

553. According to the Migration Policy Institute, **the Bracero Program led to a decrease in the number of unauthorized Mexican immigrants in the US** since the program provided a legal and regulated way for Mexicans to enter the US.

554. **Many Mexican workers came to the US illegally** to avoid the bribes that were often necessary to enroll in the program in Mexico.

555. **The program's termination in 1964 led to a dramatic decrease in wages and working conditions for Mexican farm workers in the United States.** This was one of the main issues that led to the United Farm Workers of America, a union that was founded in the 1960s.

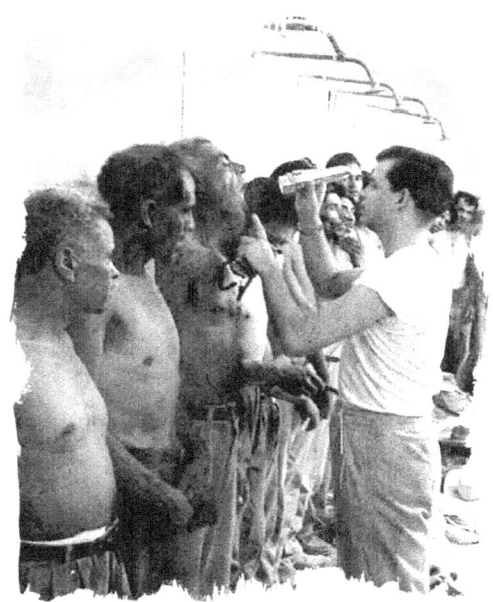

556. **The termination of the Bracero Program** had a limited impact on the flow of undocumented migrants crossing the US-Mexico border since the number of unauthorized immigrants had already been declining prior to the program's end in 1964.

557. **The legacy of the Bracero Program** continues to shape the debate over immigration reform in the United States.

558. **The US took 10 percent of Braceros' pay, sending it to Mexico** to be held for them when they returned, but most of them were never repaid.

559. **Many Braceros were checked for venereal diseases** when they entered the United States, which most found demeaning in the extreme.

560. The program is credited with forging stronger cultural and **economic ties between the United States and Mexico.**

561. **The Bracero Program led to the emergence of a new generation of Mexican-American families.**

562. **The program also created a new class of legal immigrants** known as legal aliens or non-citizens.

563. **The Bracero Program had a profound impact** on the lives of millions of people in the United States and Mexico.

564. **The program led to the creation of an extensive network of recruiters, labor contractors, and brokers** who continue to operate in the US and Mexico today.

565. **The Bracero Program** expanded the scope of immigration enforcement in the United States, leading to the development of more stringent immigration laws.

566. **The program led to the development of a new type of employer-sanctioned immigration,** whereby employers were able to hire foreign workers on a temporary basis.

567. **The Bracero Program** also had an effect on the language spoken in **the US-Mexico border region,** leading to the emergence of a new hybrid Spanish-English language.

568. In 1954, a major labor dispute known as **the Bracero Strike occurred in California.** Thousands of Braceros went on strike to protest against low wages and poor treatment, demanding better conditions and higher pay.

569. **The program was criticized by various civil rights organizations,** labor unions, and activists who argued that it exploited and marginalized Mexican workers and undercut wages and job opportunities for American workers.

570. **The Bracero Program officially ended on December 31st, 1964**, after years of controversy and criticism. However, its legacy continues to shape discussions on immigration, labor rights, and the relationship between the United States and Mexico.

# Student Movement of 1968

On October 2nd, 1968, a significant event in Mexican history was set in motion. **A group of student activists organized a demonstration of thousands of people from all walks of life.** They were determined to challenge the oppressive rule of the Mexican government and **promote social and economic reform**. What happened during this **momentous protest**? Discover what happened to the students and why the movement is remembered as a pivotal moment in **Mexican history**.

**571. The protest known as the Mexican Student Movement or the Movement of 1968 was planned by a group of student activists.**

**572. In the months leading up to the October 2nd march in Mexico City,** clandestine meetings between **students and teachers occurred to plan the demonstration.**

**573. The march on October 2nd was planned to coincide with the start of the 1968 Olympic festivities in Mexico City** and drew international attention to Mexico.

**574. The student movement** was seen as a catalyst for a broader movement of social change in the country.

**575. The student movement led to the formation of the National Strike Council**, a coalition of student, labor, and peasant organizations.

**576. The event was sparked by the government's decision to increase fees and enforce stricter regulations on student organizations.**

**577. Pamphlets were distributed throughout Mexico City** prior to the protest to gain backing and publicize the cause.

**578. On October 2nd, 1968, the culmination of the protest was reached, with thousands of students congregating on the Zócalo, the main square in Mexico City,** and then marching through downtown Mexico City.

579. **Other demonstrations took place in cities around the country at the same time.**

580. **An estimated half a million people filled the streets** of Mexico City for the protests.

581. **The Mexican government's response to the protests** was a heavy-handed one, sending in the military to quell the demonstrations and arresting participants.

582. **The protest at Tlatelolco Plaza in Mexico City** was met with fierce police and military response.

583. **More than seven hundred people were killed**, and thousands were detained during and after the protest.

584. **The protest consisted primarily of peaceful strategies, including sit-ins and marches**, but there had been violence between rival groups of students. The government used this fact to endorse a violent crackdown supposedly on crime and communists.

585. **The government heavily censored the news**, preventing any coverage of the event. Still, word got out. Despite this, the Olympic Games were still held in Mexico City.

586. **The Mexican government used extreme measures**, such as beatings, torture, and imprisonment, to suppress protests throughout the country, although these measures were mainly used in Mexico City.

587. **The government's severe reaction to the protests resulted in public outrage**, but fear of the government and police kept many people silent.

588. **In the aftermath of the movement, the government passed laws that increased the power of the military and police in Mexico.**

589. **The movement had an influence on the 1968 Summer Olympics in Mexico City**, with the government imposing a curfew on the entire city.

**590. After the protest, some students were expelled.** Some were arrested and imprisoned.

**591. In the aftermath of the protest, many in Mexico,** including students in Mexico City and elsewhere, demanded the release of those arrested on October 2nd. Most of them were released.

**592. The protests of 1968 brought no immediate change to the Mexican government,** but the legacy of October 2nd inspired later student and civic movements, which helped break the PRI's hold on power many years later.

**593. The Student Movement of 1968 inspired other student protests globally** in a year that saw protests almost every day on a variety of issues, from human rights to the war in Vietnam.

**594. The movement gained significance as a symbol of resistance to the government's oppressive rule in Mexican history.**

**595. Mexican youths were heavily influenced by the student movements in France and the US,** which were reaching their peak at this time.

**596. The Mexico City Movement** of 1968 is regarded as the first organized student movement in Mexico.

**597. Although the protest failed to bring about its political aims, the event had a lasting impact on Mexican society,** with many of the participants later becoming influential figures in politics and business.

**598. Octavio Paz, Nobel Prize-winning author and ambassador to India, was one of many Mexican intellectuals who supported the Student Movement of 1968.**

599. The legacy of the movement is still carried on today by organizations like **the National Union of Students.**

600. Increased public awareness of the need for **a more democratic Mexico was one of the outcomes of the protests,** eventually leading to the formation of new political parties and movements.

# Mexican Debt Crisis
## (1982–1988)

**In 1982, Mexico's foreign debt dramatically increased, sparking a crisis of extraordinary proportions.** Let's explore the consequences of **the Mexican debt crisis** and the steps the Mexican government took to address it. You may find yourself surprised by many of the following facts!

601. **In 1982, Mexico's foreign debt dramatically increased from $80 billion to $107 billion!**

602. **This crisis was exacerbated by over-borrowing**, skyrocketing inflation, and a weakened peso.

603. **In response, the IMF and World Bank provided Mexico with loans to stave off a total financial disaster.**

604. **Austerity plans were created by the government to help**. Reducing spending and raising taxes were the plans' main components.

605. **The Mexican debt crisis kept rising, culminating in a 1985** moratorium on repayment of foreign debt and the introduction of the nuevo peso at half the value of the old peso, which only increased inflation.

606. **The currency reform initially stabilized the economy** but caused a drastic devaluation of the peso in the global market.

607. **The peso was devalued by a staggering 80 percent!**

608. **The president of Mexico** throughout the crisis was **Miguel de la Madrid.**

609. **In 1985, a huge earthquake struck the country, further damaging the economy.** The president was booed almost everywhere he went because of his slow response to these crises.

610. **Countries like the US and Japan provided financial aid to Mexico during the crisis.**

611. This crisis was part of **the larger Latin American debt crisis,** which impacted many countries during the 1980s.

612. **The US response was lukewarm, mainly because Mexico had a history of defaulting on debt**. The US was wary of committing funds to a potentially bad investment.

613. **The crisis caused a massive capital flight from Mexico,** with foreign investment in the country declining by nearly 90 percent between 1982 and 1988.

614. **The crisis had a devastating effect on the Mexican economy**, leading to a decrease in economic growth and investment.

615. **The crisis also reduced the power and influence of the PRI** (Institutional Revolutionary Party), which was held responsible for the crisis.

616. To address the crisis, **the Mexican government introduced a series of reforms,** including the liberalization of the economy and the privatization of many state-owned companies. Pemex, the largest company in Mexico, would not become privatized.

617. To reduce its debt burden, **Mexico also implemented debt consolidation and payment rescheduling.**

618. **The overvaluation of the peso made it difficult for Mexico to export goods,** exacerbating the crisis.

619. In 1988, **Mexico was able to renegotiate its debt and obtain new loans** from international lenders, finally overcoming the crisis.

620. **Despite the crisis, Mexico still maintained a positive trade balance**, with exports rising by 35.5 percent between 1982 and 1988.

621. In 1988, **Mexico completed an agreement with its foreign debtors** that allowed it to reschedule its debt and reduce its payments by more than 70 percent.

622. In 1989, **Mexico initiated a debt-reduction program**, allowing the country to decrease its debt by $10 billion over four years.

623. **The crisis had a long-lasting effect on the Mexican economy**, with the country's GDP dropping by almost 8 percent between 1982 and 1988.

624. **The crisis had a major effect on Mexico's international relations**, straining the country's relationship with the US and other major creditors.

625. Because of the crisis, **Mexico adopted a more independent stance from the US** and other major creditors.

626. **Mass protests and strikes occurred in Mexico during this crisis**. Many people believed the end of PRI rule was coming, though it took about another twenty years for the party to lose control of the federal government completely.

627. To improve fiscal management, **the Mexican government adopted fiscal reforms**, such as the fiscal responsibility law, which, among other things, called for a balanced national budget. This did not happen, at least not in the way the law had planned.

628. **The crisis brought about significant changes to the Mexican financial sector**, making it more competitive and efficient.

629. **The crisis also had a negative impact on the country's balance of payments**, leading to an account deficit in 1986.

630. By 1989, **Mexico and the US were talking about a free trade agreement between them to stabilize the Mexican economy** and reduce illegal immigration to the US.

# Cultural Revitalization Movement
## (1980–Present)

Since the 1980s, **Mexico has been undergoing cultural revitalization, a movement that has been embraced by President López Obrador**. With an investment of more than $1.6 billion, **this movement aims to preserve and promote Mexico's indigenous languages, cultures, and traditions.** So far, efforts have resulted in tremendous changes in Mexican culture. Let's find out more about these changes in this chapter.

631. **Mexico's cultural revitalization movement began in the 1980s.**

632. The main goal of this movement is to **preserve and promote the country's indigenous languages, cultures, and traditions** after centuries of neglect or suppression.

633. Today, **over twenty-three million people in Mexico identify as indigenous**. That is almost 20 percent of the population!

634. **The foundation of the National Institute of Indigenous Languages** (INALI) in 2003 has contributed greatly to a sense of nationalism and unity in Mexico.

635. **The Mexican Secretariat of Culture** was founded in 1988 as the National Council for Culture and Arts to promote and protect Mexican art and museums.

636. In the later years of the 20th century, the works **of Mexican artists like Diego Rivera** (1886–1957) and **Frida Kahlo** (1907–1954) began to garner international attention.

637. **Cultural revitalization has led to the creation of over one hundred community radio stations around the country.** These stations are dedicated to broadcasting in the many indigenous languages of Mexico.

638. **Mexico is now home to over twelve million speakers of indigenous languages**, with a majority speaking Nahuatl, the language of the Aztecs (sometimes known as the Mexica), who dominated central Mexico during the pre-Columbian era.

639. **Spanish is the Mexican government's official language**. However, it recognizes sixty-eight languages, sixty-three of which are indigenous languages.

640. **The National Language** Plan created by **the Mexican government** implemented several initiatives to protect and promote the country's **indigenous languages.**

641. **The movement also encourages the development of educational materials in indigenous languages,** including textbooks, dictionaries, and audio-visual materials.

642. **The movement has seen the revival of traditional cultural practices**, such as the **Maya ball game**, which was banned by the Spanish in the 16<sup>th</sup> century. **Reenactors and enthusiasts often play a game** thought to be very similar to what the ancient Maya played.

643. **The movement has also seen the emergence of new cultural forms**, such as rap and hip-hop, which are performed in indigenous languages and in the majority language, Spanish.

644. It has also led to the creation of numerous indigenous-led organizations, such as **the National Indigenous Congress and the National Commission for the Development of Indigenous Peoples.**

645. **The movement gradually led to an increase in political participation by indigenous people,** with the election of several indigenous representatives to municipal and state posts and a smaller number of federal posts.

646. Many several successful films, such as *Roma* (directed by **Alfonso Cuarón**), explore **the struggles of indigenous people in Mexico.**

647. In recent years, numerous museums and cultural centers have become dedicated to preserving the country's indigenous heritage, such as **the Wixárika Cultural Center in Jalisco.**

648. **There has also been a revival of traditional crafts, such as weaving, pottery, and wood carving,** which are sold in markets and galleries around the world.

649. **Indigenous movements have not always been peaceful, such as the Zapatista Army of National Liberation,** which is dedicated to preserving the rights of indigenous people.

650. **The Zapatistas, a leftist organization, have been fighting a guerrilla war against the Mexican government since 1994**. They seek indigenous control over local resources, especially land.

651. **The movement has also seen the revival of traditional musical forms, such as mariachi and son jarocho**, which are now performed in public spaces around the country.

652. The movement led to the establishment of numerous festivals and events, such as **the Festival de la Primavera Indígena, which celebrates indigenous cultures.**

653. Literary works, such as **the novels of Elena Poniatowska** (who was wounded in the Tlatelolco Massacre), explore the lives of indigenous people in Mexico.

654. The movement saw the creation of **the National Network of Indigenous Women**, which is dedicated to defending the rights of women.

655. A new generation of filmmakers has emerged. People like **Natalia Beristáin** are dedicated to telling the stories of **indigenous people in Mexico.**

656. Numerous indigenous-controlled schools, such as **the Escuela de la Tierra**, have been established and are dedicated to **teaching students indigenous languages.**

657. Mexico has also seen the emergence of new political movements, such as **the Indigenous Rights Movement,** which is dedicated to protecting the rights of indigenous people.

658. The movement influenced education policies, leading to the inclusion of indigenous history and culture in school curricula. **Efforts were made to promote cultural diversity and respect for indigenous knowledge systems** within educational institutions.

659. **Traditional indigenous arts and crafts experienced a resurgence during the cultural revitalization movement**. Artists and artisans sought to revive traditional techniques and motifs, creating a market for indigenous artwork within Mexico and internationally.

660. **Indigenous dances and music were revitalized and incorporated into public celebrations and cultural events.** Traditional ceremonies, such as **the Day of the Dead** and other **pre-Hispanic rituals**, gained renewed popularity and became **important elements of Mexican cultural identity**.

# Mexico City Earthquake
## (1985)

**In 1985, an 8.0 magnitude earthquake struck Mexico City**. The giant tremor resulted in a large death toll and billions of dollars in destruction and struck fear in the hearts of the city's inhabitants. **Learn how this terrible tragedy affected the global economy and how Mexico rebuilt itself** from the rubble of this history-changing event.

661. On **September 19th, 1985**, a seismic event of unprecedented magnitude, estimated at **8.0, wreaked havoc on Mexico City.**

662. **The earthquake caused a death toll of five thousand to ten thousand.**

663. **The earthquake caused an estimated $5 billion in destruction.**

664. **The quake's epicenter** was located nearly two hundred miles southwest of the city.

665. **The tremor's reverberations spread across the Pacific Ocean.**

666. **The capital's** dense population and inadequate building code contributed to the number of fatalities.

667. **In the city itself, nearly four thousand structures were either destroyed or heavily damaged.**

668. The force of the quake was so strong that it **was felt as far away as Houston and Los Angeles!**

669. **After the main quake, numerous aftershocks**, some as powerful as 7.0, were felt.

670. **The disaster had ramifications in other Mexican cities**, including Guadalajara, Monterrey, and Puebla.

671. **In the capital, many government structures were either totally or partially demolished.**

672. **The quake caused serious harm to Mexico City's** public transportation system.

673. In the northern part of the city, **two huge apartment complexes were almost completely destroyed.**

674. Altogether, **Mexico City lost thirty thousand living spaces**, resulting in widespread homelessness.

675. Calculations suggest that **more than twenty thousand individuals were injured** because of the earthquake.

676. In certain parts of Mexico City, **the power blackout lasted a few days.**

677. Initially, about **two thousand soldiers and militiamen were sent into the streets** of the city to prevent looting and search for victims.

678. **Several ancient Aztec ruins were damaged by the tremor**.

679. **In the suburb of San Angel**, the seismic activity set off a massive fire injuring six hundred people.

680. In response, **Mexico City's government created a fund to provide aid to earthquake victims.**

681. **Numerous gas leaks and explosions were reported** in the aftermath of the disaster.

682. **The rupture of several major pipelines resulted in serious environmental damage.**

683. In the wake of the calamity, **the Mexican government proclaimed a state of emergency.**

684. **The tremor led to the displacement of over 100,000 people.**

685. Landslides triggered by **the earthquake obstructed roads** and caused additional destruction.

686. **Rebuilding was slowed due to the widespread corruption in government** and businesses.

687. As a result of **the government's slow response to the earthquake, many people formed civic organizations,** some of which later led to new political parties.

688. **The tremors were so powerful** that they caused the ground to sink up to one meter in some parts of Mexico City.

689. To help with reconstruction, **the Mexican government provided $4 billion in financial aid,** though the ruling PRI was heavily criticized for the slowness of their response and their initial refusal to accept foreign aid, which might have cost hundreds of lives.

690. **Foreign aid arrived** when the government admitted it could not handle the rescue and rebuilding efforts. **The United States and Israel were of significant help.**

691. Many of **the city's hospitals were damaged** beyond repair due to the quake, leading to the loss of hundreds of lives.

692. **The earthquake had a significant economic impact**, with estimates indicating that the global economy was affected to the tune of $6 billion.

693. **The seismic waves of the quake** were visible on seismographs in Washington, DC.

694. **The Mexican government declared three days of national mourning** in the wake of the disaster.

695. **The earthquake was the result** of the subduction of the Cocos Plate beneath the North American plate along the Middle America Trench.

696. In the aftermath of the quake, **over thirty thousand people were made destitute.**

697. **The quake caused the water level** of the city's main lake, Texcoco, **to drop by more than three feet.**

698. In some places near Mexico City, **the earth shook for more than five minutes!** This is an extraordinarily long time for an earthquake.

699. **The tremors caused a number of landslides**, resulting in the collapse of several mountainsides and hillsides.

700. **Exactly thirty-seven years later, on September 19th, 2022, a series of earthquakes hit Mexico and Mexico City.** Though the death toll was only two people, many buildings were damaged. Many people who had lived through the 1985 earthquake thought another "big one" might be coming.

# North American Free Trade Agreement (NAFTA)
## (1994)

**The North American Free Trade Agreement** (NAFTA) was signed in 1992 and enacted two years later. **The purpose of the deal was to reduce trade barriers between the countries,** and it certainly achieved that goal. However, **NAFTA has also been denounced for possibly causing the displacement of workers** in specific industries and infringing upon labor rights and ecological regulations. Let's dig into this historic agreement!

701. At the time **the North American Free Trade Agreement** (NAFTA) was signed in 1992, **it was the biggest free trade agreement in the world.**

702. **NAFTA involved Canada, the US, and Mexico.**

703. **The agreement included** provisions for environmental and labor regulations.

704. The principal purpose of NAFTA was **to diminish tariffs and other trade impediments between the countries.**

705. Subsequently, **the amount of trade between the three nations** skyrocketed to more than $1.2 trillion in 2018 from $297 billion in 1993.

706. **In Mexico and Canada, NAFTA has been credited with promoting productivity,** job creation, and higher wages, thereby leading to improved living standards.

707. **The treaty abolished most taxes on goods traded between the countries** and ended non-tariff barriers, such as quotas.

708. **The agreement also set up methods for resolving disputes** between the signatories.

709. In addition, **NAFTA created the North American Development Bank**, which gives grants and loans for economic and social development projects in Mexico and the US.

710. **NAFTA has also been denounced for possibly causing the displacement of workers** in certain industries and infringing upon individual national labor rights and ecological regulations.

711. **Due to the structure of NAFTA**, which took years to negotiate and pass, there were very few ways to enforce violations of the agreement.

712. Despite this, **NAFTA has been credited with pulling Mexico from economic stagnation and many Mexicans from poverty**, creating millions of jobs in the US, Mexico, and Canada, as well as diminishing the cost of consumer goods in all three countries.

713. The agreement also gave birth to **the North American Leaders' Summit**, which meets yearly to address economic and security matters. This meeting of the leaders of Mexico, the US, and Canada is often referred to as **the "Three Amigos Summit"** in the press.

714. **NAFTA contributed to improved relations between the US and Mexico.**

715. **NAFTA was the first free trade agreement to feature a dispute resolution** mechanism, allowing signatories to settle disagreements without going to court.

716. It was also credited with **reducing poverty and inequality in Mexico and raising the quality of goods produced** in all three nations.

717. **It has been criticized for its lack of provisions for the protection of intellectual property rights and labor rights.**

718. Although **President Bill Clinton is often credited with the creation of NAFTA**, negotiations began during the Reagan administration.

719. **NAFTA brought about enhanced efficiency and cost savings** in the production of many goods, such as automobiles.

720. **It has also been credited with decreasing the expense of cross-border investments.**

**721. The agreement is said to have assisted in decreasing Mexico's reliance on oil exports** and making the country more competitive in manufacturing and service industries.

**722. NAFTA has been credited with improving access to markets in all three countries** and lowering corruption in some parts of the Mexican economy.

**723. It also leveled the playing field for small- and medium-sized businesses** in all three countries.

**724. The agreement is believed to have helped create a more unified North American energy market**, leading to greater efficiency and savings.

**725. Small-scale farms in Mexico benefited more from NAFTA** than large-scale ones. Farming was popular among many of the indigenous people of the country.

**726. NAFTA was the first free trade agreement that included provisions** for the protection of intellectual property rights.

727. Once NAFTA was implemented, the amount of **foreign direct investment in Mexico increased** greatly compared to before its introduction.

728. **The treaty has been responsible for the creation of over fourteen million jobs** in all three countries combined.

729. **NAFTA became a bone of contention in the 1994 US presidential election**. Republican candidate **Bob Dole** and independent candidate **Ross Perot** claimed NAFTA would cost the US more jobs than it created. This was somewhat true in the automobile industry.

730. Most moderate and progressive economists agree that **NAFTA was a positive for the US, Mexico, and Canada.**

731. One positive for Mexico was that despite some ups and downs, **NAFTA helped the agricultural and beef sectors** of its economy.

732. **Changes in income have led to a fundamental shift in the Mexican diet.** With a higher per capita income, the Mexican diet has begun to include more beef and less vegetables.

733. **The middle class in Mexico has grown** since the implementation of NAFTA.

734. With an exception during **the Great Recession of 2008/09,** unemployment in Mexico has trended downward since the passage of NAFTA.

735. In 2018, **NAFTA was renegotiated and replaced with the United States-Mexico-Canada Agreement** (USMCA), which began in 2020.

# Formation of the Party of the Democratic Revolution (PRD) (1989)

Since its inception in 1989, **the Party of the Democratic Revolution (PRD) has been a strong voice and major force in Mexican politics**. Walk with us as we learn about **Cuauhtémoc Cárdenas's** journey and how it marked the beginning of an unprecedented period of political turmoil in Mexico. **Let's look at how the PRD has been an important voice in Mexico's** struggle for democracy, freedom, and social justice.

736. **The PRD was founded in 1989 by Cuauhtémoc Cárdenas, the son of former President Lázaro Cárdenas** (1934–1940), and other left-wing intellectuals and activists.

737. **The party was created in response to the lack of electoral choice in Mexico** and aimed to represent a "third way" between the ruling **Institutional Revolutionary Party** (PRI) and the right-wing **National Action Party** (PAN).

738. **The PRD, which included a number of former PRI members**, was the first party to challenge the PRI's decades-long domination of Mexican politics.

739. **The PRD's founders included** academics, intellectuals, and activists, such as **Ricardo Lagos, Marcela Lombardo, and Emilio Álvarez Icaza.**

740. **The party's political platform** was based on the values of democracy, freedom, and social justice.

741. **Cárdenas was the leader of the PRD** and was elected head of government of Mexico City, a powerful position that gave the PRD a very public platform.

742. **Cárdenas was elected to the Senate in 1976** and became governor of the state of Michoacán in 1980.

743. **In 1997, the PRD had the second-largest percentage of seats in the Chamber of Deputies,** which was a remarkable rise, considering the PRI waged a campaign of intimidation, violence, and assassination against the PRD.

**744. The PRD's rise to power led to a period of intense political turmoil in Mexico** since there was an intense battle for control of the government. Many PRD supporters were jailed, killed, or "disappeared" during this time.

**745. During this time, the PRD was active in advocating for electoral reforms**, including the introduction of proportional representation, the abolition of the single-member district system, and the introduction of direct presidential elections.

**746. The PRD's influence waned in the early 2000s**, as the party became increasingly divided and was unable to agree on a unified strategy.

**747. A number of PRD officials were caught receiving bribes.**

**748.** In 2006, the PRD candidate **Andrés Manuel López Obrador** narrowly lost the presidential election to **Felipe Calderón of the PAN.**

**749. In 2012, the PRD again backed López Obrador**, but he lost the election to a resurgent and "changed" PRI, whose candidate was Enrique Peña Nieto.

**750. The PRD also had success at the local level,** winning numerous mayoral and state races in Mexico City and the states of Michoacán, Chiapas, Puebla, and Veracruz.

**751.** Though **the PRD's influence waned in the early 2000s**, it was critical in creating change in the Mexican political landscape by giving the people a reasonable alternative to the PRI.

**752. The PRD is a member of the Socialist International** and has close ties to the Mexican Workers' Party, the Ecologist Green Party of Mexico, and other leftist political organizations.

**753. The PRD was one of the first Mexican political parties to support the legalization of same-sex marriage** and the adoption of other progressive policies on social issues.

754. **The PRD has faced numerous legal challenges** over the years, including accusations of electoral fraud and misappropriation of public funds.

755. **PRD members have also been accused of corruption** and involvement in organized crime.

756. **The party has been accused of using patronage and favoritism** to build its political base, particularly in the state of Michoacán.

757. **Corruption and financial irregularities have decreased the popularity of the PRD in recent years.**

758. **The PRD has close ties to labor unions and other social movements**. It has been active in advocating for improved labor rights for Mexican workers.

759. In recent years, **the PRD has been criticized for its perceived lack of internal democracy,** with party leaders accused of stifling debate and restricting the involvement of rank-and-file members.

760. **The party has been accused of being too closely aligned with President López Obrador** (elected in 2018), who splintered off from the PRD and created **the Morena Party** in 2018. Critics claim the party has become too "presidentialist" in its approach to politics. In other words, they believe there is too much power in the executive branch.

761. **The PRD's success has inspired the formation of numerous other parties in Mexico**, including **the Citizens' Movement, the Morena Party, and the Social Encounter Party.**

762. Since 2020, the PRD has been part of a multi-party coalition in Mexico called **"Va por Mexico,"** meaning "It's for Mexico."

763. **The party has taken steps to improve its internal organization,** introducing new rules and regulations to ensure greater transparency and accountability.

764. More recently, **the PRD has been active in the international arena**, advocating for indigenous rights and taking part in international conferences.

765. **The PRD has been a major force in Mexican politics** for more than three decades and continues to influence Mexican politics.

# Zapatista Uprising
## (1994)

On the morning of January 1st, 1994, **Subcomandante Marcos**, known to many of his supporters as **the Masked Angel of Revolt**, became the "face" of **the Zapatista Uprising**. Let's look at this revolutionary movement and the indelible marks it left on the world.

766. **Subcomandante Marcos became the "face" of the Zapatista Uprising.** Marcos had been a brilliant student and professor of philosophy and literature at the Autonomous Metropolitan University in the 1980s before adopting revolutionary politics and moving to Chiapas in 1984.

767. **On the same day the North American Free Trade Agreement was inked, the Zapatista Uprising began.**

768. **The Zapatista Uprising was a movement to battle the exploitation of indigenous people in Mexico**, especially in rural Chiapas.

769. **The Zapatista Uprising** was one of the first political revolts covered on the internet.

770. In 1994, **the Zapatistas called for an armed uprising against the Mexican government,** but they did not garner the countrywide support they had hoped for.

771. **On the day of the protest, civic centers were attacked**, indigenous prisoners were released, and land records were destroyed.

772. **The police and army were sent to put down the uprising**. Around three hundred people were killed.

773. **The Zapatistas waged their "war" in the media** and by word of mouth, telling the world about the abuses and discrimination **indigenous people in Chiapas** and all of Mexico experienced.

774. **Though the Zapatista Uprising did not accomplish its aims**, other indigenous groups in Latin America were inspired by it.

775. Well-known people like **director Michael Moore** and philosopher and scientist **Noam Chomsky** lent their support to the Zapatista Uprising.

776. **The Zapatista Uprising played a significant role in the emergence of the "anti-globalization" movement.**

777. Films, books, and other media have chronicled **the Zapatista Uprising**, such as the movie *Zapatista* released in 1999.

778. **The movement was named in honor of Emiliano Zapata**, one of the leaders of the 1910 revolution.

779. **The Zapatistas called for land reform and less globalization**, which they saw as causing greater poverty in Chiapas and among many indigenous groups in Latin America.

780. Today, **areas of Chiapas are recognized**, even if it's unofficially, as being autonomous parts of Mexico.

781. **The Zapatista Uprising was successful in garnering international attention** for the problems of indigenous people in Mexico.

782. **Subcomandante Marcos's real name is Rafael Sebastian Guillen Vicente**, and he is still a prominent figure in Chiapas almost thirty years after the uprising began.

783. **There are a number of political parties that reflect many of the Zapatistas' core beliefs.**

784. **The Zapatistas** gained a great deal of support overseas.

785. Though **the Zapatistas** did not achieve their immediate goals, the Mexican government's failure to stop it signaled to much of Mexico that the PRI was not as strong as it had been.

786. **The Zapatista Uprising** is believed to have given rise to autonomous indigenous communities in Mexico.

787. **The Zapatista Uprising has been credited with inspiring the Intercontinental Network of Indigenous Peoples and Nations.**

788. Before the uprising, **the Zapatistas organized a group of women** that wrote what is known as **the Zapatista Women's Revolutionary Law**, which helped women participate in the movement and gain equality in decision-making.

789. In 1997, **forty-five members of a religious group associated with the Zapatistas were massacred by a right-wing paramilitary group in Acteal, a small village in Chiapas.**

790. In 2020, **the Mexican government released information linking the Secretariat of Home Affairs**, a government agency, to the massacre.

# Migration to the United States
## (1970s–present)

**For decades, the influx of Mexican immigrants to the United States has been a source of controversy and political complexity**. Learn how the influx of **Mexican immigrants and immigrants from other Latin American countries** crossing the border has affected the US and Mexico. Discover how **the Trump administration stepped up immigration enforcement efforts,** and explore some facts about **Mexican immigration** under the Biden administration.

791. **In the 1970s, the estimated number of Mexican immigrants annually moving to the United States exceeded a million,** though most of those people either returned to Mexico permanently or traveled between both countries, mostly illegally.

792. **In the 1970s, Mexican immigrants were often excluded from government programs** meant to aid other immigrant groups.

793. **Most Mexican migrant workers engaged in agricultural, construction, and service** vocations in the United States from the 1970s to the 2020s.

794. In the 1970s, **the majority of Mexican immigrants living in the United States were young men** searching for work opportunities.

795. During the 1990s, **more than half of Mexican immigrants to the United States were below the age of twenty-five.**

796. The number of **Mexican immigrants to the United States** saw a growth in the 1980s and 1990s, reaching over seven million in 2000.

797. By 2017, the total number of **Mexican immigrants to the United States** had grown to about 10.5 million.

798. The estimation of **undocumented Mexican immigrants in the United States yearly is over ten million since 2000.** This number includes immigrants who become permanent or semi-permanent residents and those who migrate between the two countries.

799. Since 2000, the number of **Mexican immigrants to the United States** has grown at a slower rate than other immigrant groups from Latin America.

800. In the 2010s, **the United States experienced a downturn in Mexican immigrants** for the first time since the 1970s.

801. From 2011 to 2017, the number of **Mexican immigrants to the United States declined** by 8.4 percent.

802. **Today, most of the migrants coming to the US from Latin America are not Mexican,** but they use Mexican territory to get to US shores, which is a problem for both governments.

803. **In 2015, Mexicans made up about 55 percent of the illegal immigrant population in the US.** In that year, there were around twelve million illegal immigrants.

804. The number of **Mexican immigrants removed from the United States** in 2017 was the highest amount since 2012.

805. **The Trump administration** sought to curb legal **immigration from Mexico** through the implementation of the Remain in Mexico policy.

806. **Donald Trump's campaign promise to make Mexico pay for his planned wall** on the US-Mexico border was met with both derision and hostility in Mexico.

807. Since 2020, **the US government** has sought to reduce the number of asylum seekers from Mexico.

808. In 2021, **the Biden administration instituted policies meant to protect the rights of Mexican immigrants in the United States.**

809. **In 2021, the United States observed a substantial expansion in the number of Mexican immigrants entering the country**, with a calculated 100,000 entering from January to March. Part of the reason for this was the need for workers in the US during the 2020 pandemic.

810. In 2021, **the Biden administration aimed to expand access to legal immigration for Mexican immigrants** and to reunite families separated by deportation.

811. Despite **the U.S.-Mexico border wall's** use of the latest in fencing and surveillance technology, it is still regularly breached by criminals and migrants. The wall does not run along the entire border.

812. **As of January 2020, the wall had cost over eleven billion dollars**, and most of what was supposed to be built was not. The Biden administration halted building the wall, saying it was costly and ineffective.

813. **The border wall is divided into three sections with different types of barriers**. The **first section is a physical barrier** made of steel posts that are eighteen to thirty feet tall. **The second section is a virtual wall** made up of sensors, cameras, and radar systems. The **third section is a "virtual fence"** that uses drones, helicopters, and other aircraft to monitor the border.

814. **The construction of the wall has been met with significant opposition from Native American groups and environmentalists.**

815. **The wall has caused significant economic disruption in border towns**, including reduced tourism and disruption of traditional farming methods.

816. **The US government has used eminent domain to take land from private citizens** for the construction of the wall.

817. **The wall has caused considerable social tension**, as it divides families and communities along the border.

818. While **the wall did not reduce the number of immigrants from Latin America** to any great degree, it has changed the manner in which many people cross the border, including some very dangerous methods.

819. **The wall has been a source of political tension between the US and Mexico**, with the latter accusing the former of violating its sovereignty.

820. In addition to facing discrimination and more in **the US, immigrants from Latin America and Mexico are regularly abused and taken advantage of by drug cartels and "coyotes,"** people who specialize in beating the US Border Patrol for a large price.

# National Action Party (PAN) Era
## (2000–2012)

**The PAN (Partido Acción Nacional) era was a transformative period in Mexico**, as the country embraced unprecedented gains in technology, trade, and improvements to standards of living. Its infrastructure also saw massive investment, resulting in a wide variety of new national programs. **It is no surprise that the PAN era is remembered as a period of tremendous progress and innovation for Mexico.**

821. **In 2000, PAN leader Vicente Fox was the first non-PRI member elected president in seventy years.**

822. **The economy of Mexico grew** by an average of 3 percent annually during the PAN era.

823. **During the PAN era, Mexico began using biometric technology** to issue national identification cards to curb crime, drug smuggling, terrorism, and illegal immigration.

824. **Under PAN, Mexico signed free trade agreements with the United States, Canada, and other countries** that have proved largely beneficial.

825. **Vicente Fox proposed Plan Puebla Panama in 2001**, a joint strategy with other Central American countries to provide new superhighways along the Pacific and Gulf coasts, as well as other improvements and political agreements.

826. **PAN oversaw the completion of the Trans-Isthmus of Tehuantepec Railway, connecting the Pacific and Atlantic coasts of Mexico.** The railway is known today as the Ferrocarril Transístmico.

827. **The G20 Summit, an important meeting of the world's largest economies, was hosted by Mexico in 2012 during the Enrique Peña Nieto administration.**

828. **Under PAN, Mexico made significant progress** in reducing poverty.

829. **The party believes in minimal interference from the government in private enterprise,** concerning some in Mexico who believe corruption is still rife in the country.

830. **Despite his personal popularity, Vicente Fox** had difficulty governing because he was elected when **PAN only controlled a minority of seats in Congress.**

831. **Under PAN, Mexico launched the Program for the Strengthening of Local Governments,** giving greater autonomy to the country's municipalities.

832. During the PAN era, **many Mexicans began to form environmental protection groups.**

833. As a response to **the Zapatista** movement, **PAN encouraged and sponsored a number of indigenous peoples' groups.**

834. Under **PAN, Mexico made strides in modernizing its energy sector**, developing renewable energy sources and reducing dependence on fossil fuels.

835. **Despite opposition from PAN, abortion became legal in Mexico in 2000.**

836. **During the PAN era, Mexico made significant advances in the fight against drug trafficking and organized crime**, but there is still much work to be done.

837. **Since it lost power in 2012, PAN has been plagued with much infighting between factions.**

838. **There are two main factions within PAN today**: moderates and conservatives.

839. Some Mexicans are uncomfortable with the **close relationship between PAN and the Roman Catholic Church in Mexico.**

840. **Mexican presidents serve one six-year term**. In the 2018 presidential election, PAN came in a distant second to **the Morena Party**, with **López Obrador becoming president.**

# Election of Andrés Manuel López Obrador (AMLO)
## (2018)

**Andrés Manuel López Obrador, commonly known as AMLO, has been a significant force in Mexican politics in recent years**. From his earlier years in the student movement to his victorious campaign and election to the Mexican presidency in 2018, **AMLO has been a dedicated advocate for social welfare, democracy, and anti-corruption.** He is the leader of many firsts during his term as president. Let's look at how he has brought a new level of success to his country.

841. **Andrés Manuel López Obrador**, commonly known as **AMLO**, was born in 1953 in the Mexican state of Tabasco.

842. **He is the youngest of seven children and was raised in the small town of Macuspana.**

843. **He has been active in politics since the 1970s.**

844. **AMLO held local, state, and federal posts** before becoming president.

845. He was a founding member of **the Mexican Democratic Party** (now defunct) and has been involved in many political campaigns.

846. **From 2000 to 2005, AMLO served as the head of government (mayor) of Mexico City.**

847. While **mayor of Mexico City**, he implemented a range of social welfare projects, including **free public transportation for students and the elderly.**

848. In the early 2000s, **AMLO became a vegetarian.**

849. **He does not consume alcohol**; he has been candid about his dislike of drinking.

850. After unsuccessfully running for president twice (2006 and 2012), **he was elected in 2018 with a landslide victory.**

851. **He was the first president since 1988 to win an outright majority**. He carried thirty-one of Mexico's thirty-two states!

852. **He is known for his anti-corruption stance.**

853. **AMLO is the first president from Morena**, a left-wing political party that was founded in 2012 and focuses on advancing social welfare and promoting democracy.

854. **He is the first president in Mexican history not to come from the two major parties; for decades,** the two major parties, the PRI and PAN, held a monopoly on the Mexican presidency.

855. **AMLO is the first leftist president in Mexico in over seventy years.** The last leftist president in Mexico was Lázaro Cárdenas, who was in office from 1934 to 1940.

856. **AMLO's administration has been focused on providing social welfare programs.** He has sought to reduce inequality and increase access to services such as healthcare, education, and housing.

857. **He has instituted many policies and measures to increase his government's transparency and accountability**, though his implementation of a new transparency policy has been criticized as being "not transparent enough."

858. **His administration has implemented a number of initiatives to increase wages and reduce educational inequality,** such as raising the minimum wage and providing free tuition for public universities.

859. **He has implemented a universal pension program for the elderly**, providing a basic pension to all elderly people over the age of sixty-five, regardless of whether they were formally employed or not.

860. **He has lowered the salaries for high-ranking public officials** and instituted salary caps for these positions.

861. **He has called for a moratorium on oil drilling in the Gulf of Mexico**, taking a stand against reckless oil drilling.

862. **He has reduced tax exemptions for the wealthy and added a luxury tax on high-end items.**

863. **AMLO has increased subsidies for small farmers and rural communities**, seeking to reduce poverty in rural areas by providing subsidies for small farmers he believes have been hurt by NAFTA.

864. **He has focused on improving infrastructure throughout Mexico**, including new budgets for building new roads, bridges, and public transportation systems.

865. **His administration has been a major proponent of renewable energy sources** and has encouraged the development of solar and wind power.

866. **He has implemented a series of initiatives to reduce poverty by providing subsidies for food, housing, and education.**

867. He has increased **the focus on protecting Mexico's environment**, taking steps to reduce pollution, conserve water, and protect endangered species.

868. **He has attempted to reduce the power of drug cartels in Mexico,** taking a hard stance against organized crime and implementing measures to combat drug trafficking, but it's a tough battle that continues today.

869. **AMLO has increased public spending on healthcare** and created policies to reduce the cost of prescription drugs.

870. **López Obrador has reduced income taxes for middle- and lower-income earners** to reduce inequality.

871. **Access to clean water and sanitation**, particularly in rural areas, has been a priority.

872. **He has sought to increase access to the internet and technology for all Mexicans.**

873. **Increased access to justice and legal services** for all Mexicans is on AMLO's agenda.

874. **He has sought to protect Mexico's cultural heritage and identity**, increasing funding for cultural programs and initiatives. He has also taken steps to preserve indigenous languages and traditions.

875. **AMLO has been more focused on domestic affairs instead of foreign relations** since becoming president.

# War on Drugs
## (2006–present)

**Mexico's war on drugs is a conflict shrouded in violence and tragedy.** To combat the spread of organized crime, **the Mexican government has taken many steps**, as you'll learn below. Since this situation involves the US as well, we will also take a look at **how America has provided extensive support to the Mexican government** and extradited hundreds of drug traffickers for prosecution. As **the war on drugs continues**, learn how Mexico is increasingly relying on cutting-edge technology to bring the conflict to an end.

876. **The drug wars in Mexico** have resulted in the deaths of over seventy thousand people since the 1980s, perhaps more.

877. **Exacerbated by corruption, hundreds of police officers and politicians have been arrested or convicted for their involvement in the drug trade.**

878. **The US has offered financial, logistical, and intelligence support to the Mexican government** in its fight against organized crime. Hundreds of drug traffickers have been extradited to the US for prosecution.

879. **The Sinaloa Cartel and the Jalisco New Generation Cartel** are two of the most powerful drug cartels active in Mexico today.

880. **Hundreds of thousands of Mexican troops and police have waged a war on drugs** and drug cartels in the last few decades.

881. In addition to cocaine and other drugs, **Mexico struggles with the import, production, and trafficking of the deadly drug fentanyl.**

882. The use of **private security companies to protect businesses** and wealthy individuals from the violence of **the drug wars has become commonplace in Mexico.**

883. Despite the Mexican government's massive effort to end the drug wars, **Mexico has met widespread criticism for its failure to significantly reduce the power of drug cartels** and the skyrocketing increase in violent crime.

884. **Disappearances have risen sharply in recent years,** with many believed to be connected to organized crime and drug trafficking.

885. **The Mexican government has sought to strengthen border security** and increase the number of drug interdiction operations.

886. In 2008, **Mexican President Felipe Calderón declared a "war on drugs"** and launched a nationwide campaign against drug cartels.

887. **The US and Mexico signed a joint declaration to fight drug trafficking** and organized crime in 2011.

888. **The Mexican Navy has played an integral role in the war on drugs,** conducting several high-profile operations against drug traffickers.

889. **Mexico has established several specialized police forces to combat drug trafficking and organized crime.** These units have been chosen and carefully screened for corrupt activity, but no program is perfect.

890. **The Mexican government launched a new strategy to combat drug trafficking** in 2012, emphasizing reducing violence, increasing intelligence gathering and sharing, and strengthening international cooperation.

891. In 2014, **the US and Mexico signed a new border security agreement** that included increased information sharing and increased security along the border.

892. In 2015, **Mexico launched a new campaign to combat drug trafficking,** prioritizing the prevention of violence and the protection of human rights.

893. **Mexico embarked on a new anti-drug strategy** centered on prevention, enforcement, and alternative development programs in 2016.

894. In 2021, **Mexico legalized the recreational use of marijuana**, partly to free up police for the fight against other drugs.

895. **The Mexican government has started a number of social programs** to reduce poverty and improve public safety in areas affected by drug trafficking.

896. **Mexico has taken a hardline stance against drug traffickers,** including the use of asset forfeiture and the extradition of suspects to the US.

897. Like the DEA (**Drug Enforcement Agency**) in the US, **special law enforcement units have been created by Mexican** authorities to investigate money laundering and financial crimes related to drug trafficking.

898. In 2017, **the Mexican government launched a new strategy focusing on the disruption of drug supply networks,** improved intelligence sharing, and increased international cooperation.

899. **The Mexican government has taken steps to reduce the demand for drugs,** such as launching public awareness campaigns and implementing public health programs.

900. **Mexico has also sought to strengthen the law and reduce impunity by prosecuting high-level drug traffickers.**

901. **Mexico has deployed military forces to protect a number of key infrastructure projects,** such as oil pipelines, from drug-trafficking activities.

902. **Drug gangs essentially run many towns and cities,** especially near the US border, and have used money from the drug trade to branch out into other areas. Some of these other activities are legal, but most are illegal.

903. **Mexico has sought to increase public confidence** in the rule of law by creating an independent police oversight agency and launching an anti-corruption reform effort.

904. **Many drug dealers have been extradited to the US,** not only because of American pressure but also because **the Mexican judiciary has been affected by corruption and intimidation by the cartels.**

905. **Mexican authorities have increasingly relied on technology to combat drug trafficking,** such as drones, facial recognition software, and biometric identification systems.

# Increase in Gang Violence
## (2010–present)

**An alarming surge in gang-related violence has struck Mexico, a problem that is affecting much of the world**. While this topic is difficult to discuss, it is important to understand how this kind of violence disrupts daily life. Though the **Mexican government has responded with a number of initiatives**, experts believe more needs to be done to **tackle the root causes of the violence**. Let's consider some of the important facts surrounding this **alarming trend and the war aimed at decimating it.**

906. **Mexico has seen periods of alarming growth and occasional declines in its murder rate** since 2005. In 2020, the homicide rate was around twenty-eight people per every thousand. The US murder rate in 2020 was half that.

907. **The Mexican government estimates that there are currently over 100,000 drug gang members in Mexico**, with many more involved in other criminal activities.

908. **The majority of those gang members are under the age of twenty-five.**

909. **Drug trafficking is the main source of income for gangs in Mexico**, with the drug trade estimated to generate $19 to $29 billion annually.

910. **The two largest gangs in Mexico are the Sinaloa Cartel and the Juarez Cartel**, each concentrating on drug trafficking.

911. Other gangs **include the Gulf Cartel, the Tijuana Cartel, the Knights Templar, and the Zetas,** although some of them are no longer active.

912. **Gang members are increasingly using more deadly weapons**, such as **AK-47s** and **grenades**, to conduct their activities.

913. **Gang violence has become so severe that some Mexican cities are among the most dangerous in the world.**

914. **The border cities of Tijuana, Ciudad Juarez, and Nuevo Laredo are particularly affected by gang violence.**

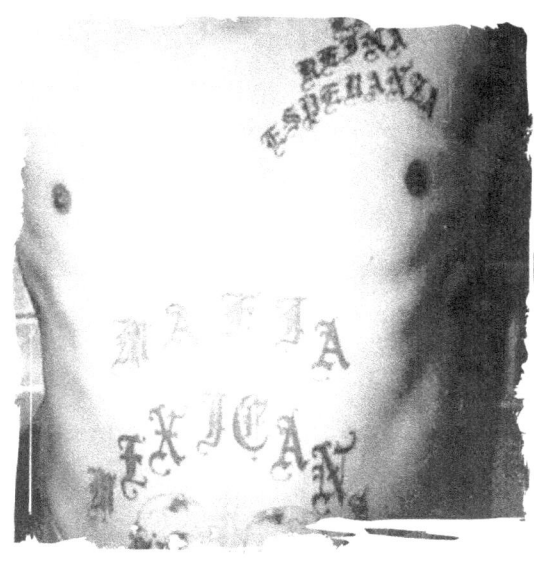

915. **The Mexican government has responded to the rising violence by deploying the army** to help local police forces.

916. **The government has implemented a variety of social programs** to try to address the root causes of gang violence.

917. **The government has also tried to combat the gangs by offering rewards for information** leading to the arrest of gang leaders.

918. **The US government has been actively involved in helping Mexico fight the gangs,** providing training, equipment, and intelligence to the Mexican police and military.

919. **The Mexican government has recently begun collecting data on gang-related homicides,** but the data is incomplete and often unreliable. Not all gang violence is public. Much of it goes on behind the scenes, and most witnesses are threatened to keep quiet.

920. **The lack of reliable data on gang violence makes it difficult to measure the effectiveness of the government's efforts to combat it.**

921. **Corruption is another major problem in Mexico,** as gangs often use bribery and intimidation to avoid prosecution.

922. **Mexico's weak justice system is another factor** that has enabled gangs to operate with impunity.

923. **Poverty and inequality have been identified as major factors** driving the growth of gangs in Mexico.

924. **Gangs have been able to exploit the lack of economic opportunities in Mexico's** poorer districts and have used violence to control local markets.

925. **The violence of Mexico's gangs has had a devastating impact on the country's economy,** with some estimates suggesting that the cost of gang violence could be as high as $50 billion a year.

926. **Gangs have also been linked to the proliferation of weapons**, as they often use violence to acquire and protect their illegal arms caches.

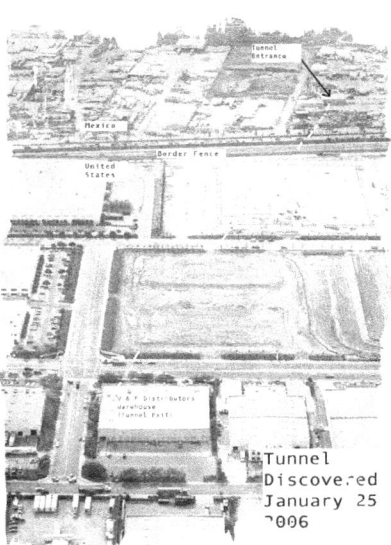

927. **The violence has led to a dramatic increase in the number of people fleeing the country,** with more than 600,000 people leaving Mexico in 2017 alone.

928. **Gang violence has had a devastating impact on Mexico's education system**, with many teachers and students fleeing the country or being forced to stay away from school due to fear of violence.

929. **The gangs have been linked to the trafficking of women and children**, as they often use them as sexual slaves or to smuggle drugs.

930. **The gangs have also been linked to the illegal mining of gold and other minerals**, as they often use violence and intimidation to control mining operations in remote areas of the country. In recent years, there have been concerns that they are taking control of the logging and fishing industries.

931. **Many fear that if the violence continues, the Mexican government could swing very right** and see the re-emergence of right-wing "death squads," which were part of the Mexican political scene in the 1970s.

932. **The government has recently implemented a number of measures aimed at tackling gang violence**, including the creation of a **National Council for Security** and a new anti-gang program.

933. **The government has implemented a series of measures aimed at improving the functioning of the justice system**, including the creation of a new federal police force and the establishment of a specialized anti-gang unit.

934. **Top secret anti-corruption units have been tasked** with rooting out bribery and intimidation by the drug cartels within the legal system and other parts of the government.

935. **Many Mexican gangs have members operating in the United States and Mexico.**

# Sports in Mexico

**Mexico has produced a remarkable number of sports icons** who have left an indelible mark on the world stage. **From football fields to golf courses and boxing rings to racquetball courts,** these extraordinary individuals have captured the hearts of fans and exemplified the grit, talent, and determination that define **Mexican sporting** prowess.

In this section, we delve into **the fascinating world of Mexican sports icons**, uncovering thirty-two unique facts that showcase their remarkable achievements, contributions, and enduring legacies.

936. **Hugo Sánchez, known as "Hugol," is the only Mexican football** (called soccer in the US) player to have won **the Pichichi Trophy as the top scorer in La Liga.**

937. **Footballer Cuauhtémoc Blanco** was renowned for his skillful dribbling and unique playing style.

938. **Ana Gabriela Guevara won a silver medal** in the 400-meter race at the 2004 Summer Olympics in Athens.

939. **Julio César Chávez is considered by many to be one of the greatest boxers** who ever lived.

940. **Paolo Longoria has the most wins in International Racquetball Federation history.** She was the first Mexican woman to win the number ranking **on the Ladies Professional Racquetball Tour.**

941. **Taekwondo athlete María Espinoza** won gold at the 2008 Olympics.

942. **Footballer Rafael Márquez** captained the Mexican national team in five World Cups and enjoyed a successful career in Europe.

943. **Fernando Valenzuela, a Mexican baseball pitcher**, enjoyed tremendous success in the US Major Leagues. He achieved the rare feat of winning both the Cy Young Award and the Rookie of the Year Award in the same season in 1981.

944. **Football goalkeeper Jorge Campos** revolutionized the position with his colorful and innovative playing style.

945. **Germán Villa Castañeda** was on two Mexican World Cup teams and is considered one of **the best Mexican footballers** of recent years.

946. **Saul "Canelo" Álvarez from Guadalajara** has been ranked as the best or one of **the best boxers in the world** for the last few years and is a superstar in Mexico today.

947. **Paola Espinosa** has won multiple Olympic medals and is considered one **of Mexico's greatest divers.** She represented Mexico at three Olympic Games: 2004, 2008, and 2012.

948. **Javier "Chicharito" Hernández, a popular football striker**, has represented Mexico in multiple World Cups and achieved success in European and American leagues. In the summer of 2023, he suffered a massive knee injury that may end his career.

949. At the Sydney 2000 Olympic Games, **Soraya Jiménez, a weightlifter**, became the first female Mexican athlete to win a gold medal.

950. **Football goalie Antonio Carbajal** holds the record for being the only player to have appeared in five consecutive World Cups (1950–1966). Carbajal passed in 2023 at the age of ninety-three.

951. **Joaquín Capilla, a diver, won four Olympic medals**, including a gold at the 1956 Melbourne Olympic Games.

952. **Salvador Sánchez, a celebrated boxer,** held the WBC (World Boxing Council) featherweight championship and had a formidable boxing record. He was killed in a car crash at the age of twenty-four in 1982.

953. **Ana María Torres, a professional boxer**, became a world champion in the super flyweight division and inspired female boxers in Mexico.

954. **Sául Hernández won first place in the 1500-meter wheelchair race** at the 2000 Olympic Games. He has won six medals in the Paralympic Games, with his career lasting from 1988 to 2008.

955. **Diver Fernando Platas won silver at the 2000 Olympics** and represented Mexico in four consecutive Olympic Games.

956. **Football coach Salvador Reyes** led the Mexican national team to victory in the 1999 FIFA Confederations Cup.

957. **Juan Manuel Márquez, a boxing sensation**, achieved multiple world championships and engaged in thrilling battles with Philippine boxing legend Manny Pacquiao.

958. **Mexico is known for bull riding and bullfighting**. It is one of the few countries that still allow bulls to be fought in the traditional way, where bulls are raised to die by a matador's sword.

959. **Salvador Cabañas, a football forward**, enjoyed success in Mexico and abroad and played a pivotal role in Paraguay's national team.

960. **Middle-distance runner Ana Fidelia Quirot** won numerous medals and set records in international competitions.

961. **Sergio "Checo" Pérez, a Formula 1 driver**, has achieved multiple podium finishes and became the first Mexican to win a Grand Prix race.

962. **Renowned golfer Lorena Ochoa** held the top spot in the Women's World Golf Rankings for over three years.

963. **Fighter Mariana Juárez won multiple world titles in the flyweight division** and was known for her tenacity in the ring.

964. **Judoka Nabor Castillo was the first Mexican to win a medal at a World Judo Grand Prix event.**

965. **Ricardo del Real, a taekwondo athlete**, won the 1997 World Cup Taekwondo Championship.

966. **Marco Antonio Barrera is a retired boxer** who held the world title in three weight classes and who fought some of the great bouts of the early 21st century.

967. **Football goalkeeper José Salvador Carmona** played a key role in Mexico's success in the 1999 FIFA Confederations Cup.

# Mexican Actors, Musicians, and Celebrities

In this section, you'll learn about thirty-three of **the most famous Mexican actors, singers, and musicians.** Like the United States, **Mexico is a celebrity culture**, and online papers and social media carry stories about them daily. **Each name on this list represents a story of talent, passion, and dedication**, and their contributions have enriched the artistic landscape of Mexico and beyond. **From award-winning actors and visionary filmmakers to chart-topping musicians and influential artists**, this compilation celebrates the diversity and **creativity that Mexico has brought** to the global stage.

968. **Actor and producer Gael García Bernal** is known throughout the world. He began his career as a child actor and recently co-founded the production company Canana Films.

969. **Director Diego Luna made the critically acclaimed film *Cesar Chavez*,** which is about the struggles of the famous Mexican-American labor leader. Diego Luna is also known for appearing as Cassian Andor in the *Star Wars* universe.

970. **Alfonso Cuarón won two Academy Awards for Best Director for *Gravity*** (2013) and *Roma* (2018).

971. Making hits since the 1960s, **Carlos Santana is known for his signature guitar sound called "Santana sound"** and is in the Rock and Roll Hall of Fame.

972. **Popular singer Thalía is known as the Queen of Latin Pop** and has sold fifty million records worldwide.

973. **Eugenio Derbez is one of Mexico's most successful comedians** and has appeared in several Hollywood films.

974. **Artist and pop culture icon Frida Kahlo** was renowned for her unique self-portraits and is considered one of Mexico's greatest artists.

975. **Alejandro González Iñárritu was the first Mexican filmmaker** to be nominated for an Academy Award as a director and producer. He has also won an Oscar for Best Picture and Best Screenplay.

976. **Vicente Fernández was a legendary Mexican ranchera singer** and actor known as **El Rey de la Música Ranchera** ("The King of Ranchera Music"). His most famous song is "Guadalajara."

977. **Pedro Infante is considered one of the greatest actors and singers** of the golden age of Mexican cinema (1936–1959).

978. **Singer Luis Miguel is often referred to as El Sol de México** ("The Sun of Mexico") and is one of the most successful Latin American artists of all time. He was born in Puerto Rico but has lived most of his life in Mexico.

979. **Kate del Castillo** gained international attention for her role as **Teresa Mendoza** in the hit **TV series** *La Reina del Sur* (*Queen of the South*).

980. **Ricardo Montalbán played the iconic character Mr. Roarke** in the television series *Fantasy Island*. He also played Khan in *Star Trek II: Wrath of Khan*.

981. **Ana de la Reguera starred in the critically acclaimed film *Nacho Libre*** alongside **Jack Black.** She has also starred in telenovelas and HBO shows.

982. **Juan Gabriel was a prolific singer-songwriter** and is considered one of the greatest Mexican musicians of all time.

983. **Diego Rivera was an internationally renowned painter** and muralist and was married to Frida Kahlo.

984. **Dolores del Río was one of the first Mexican actresses** to achieve international recognition and success in Hollywood.

985. **Mario Moreno "Cantinflas" was a beloved comedian** and actor known for his quick wit and humorous social commentary.

986. **Carlos Slim is one of the wealthiest individuals in the world** and has made significant philanthropic contributions in Mexico. He owns several businesses, but most of his money comes from telecommunications. He is working to bring Mexican sports to more US television networks.

987. **Chavela Vargas was an influential ranchera singer** and a symbol of Mexican LGBTQ+ culture. She was born in Costa Rica but lived in Mexico for over seventy years.

**988. Emilio Azcárraga Jean is the CEO of Grupo Televisa**, one of the largest media companies in the Spanish-speaking world.

**989. Salma Hayek is an international movie star** who got her start in Mexican telenovelas (soap operas).

**990. Lupe Vélez was one of the first successful Mexican actresses in Hollywood.** She appeared as Carmelita Fuentes in eight Mexican Spitfire films.

**991. Diego Boneta gained international fame for his portrayal of Luis Miguel** in the TV series *Luis Miguel: The Series*.

**992. Belinda began her career as a child actress** and has transitioned into a successful singer and actress.

**993. Paulina Rubio is a pop icon** and has sold over twenty million records worldwide. She is often credited with bringing interest back to Latin music in the 1990s.

**994. Benny Ibarra is a singer, songwriter, and actor** known for his solo career and as a member of the band Timbiriche.

**995. Lucero has been a prominent figure in Mexican entertainment** since childhood and is known for her successful singing and acting career.

**996. Kuno Becker is an actor and singer** who gained popularity for his role as Santiago Muñez in the film *Goal!*

**997. Kalimba is a singer, songwriter**, and actor known for his soulful voice and charismatic performances.

**998. Natalia Lafourcade is a Grammy-winning singer-songwriter** known for her fusion of Latin American folk and pop music.

**999. Grupo Firme is a Mexican musical group** known for their energetic performances and unique blend of regional Mexican music styles. The group was formed in 2013 by their lead vocalist and founder, Eduin Caz, in Tijuana, Baja California, Mexico.

**1000. Guillermo del Toro has won Academy Awards** for Best Picture, Best Director, and Best Animated Feature. He has worked on multiple blockbusters, including ***Hellboy*** and ***Pacific Rim***.

# Conclusion

**Mexican history** is a tapestry woven with ancient civilizations, colonization, revolutions, and cultural richness. **From the pre-Columbian era to the present day, Mexico's history** has shaped its identity as a nation that embraces its **indigenous heritage** while navigating complex challenges and forging its path toward progress.

**Today, Mexico is a modern, vibrant country** with a much more stable political structure than before. However, it still **struggles with corruption, immigration** issues, and a tremendous amount of **gang violence** caused by the immense profits from the sale and trafficking of illegal drugs. Although it is facing more than its fair share of problems, **people recognize Mexico as a cultural powerhouse.**

# Check out another book in the series

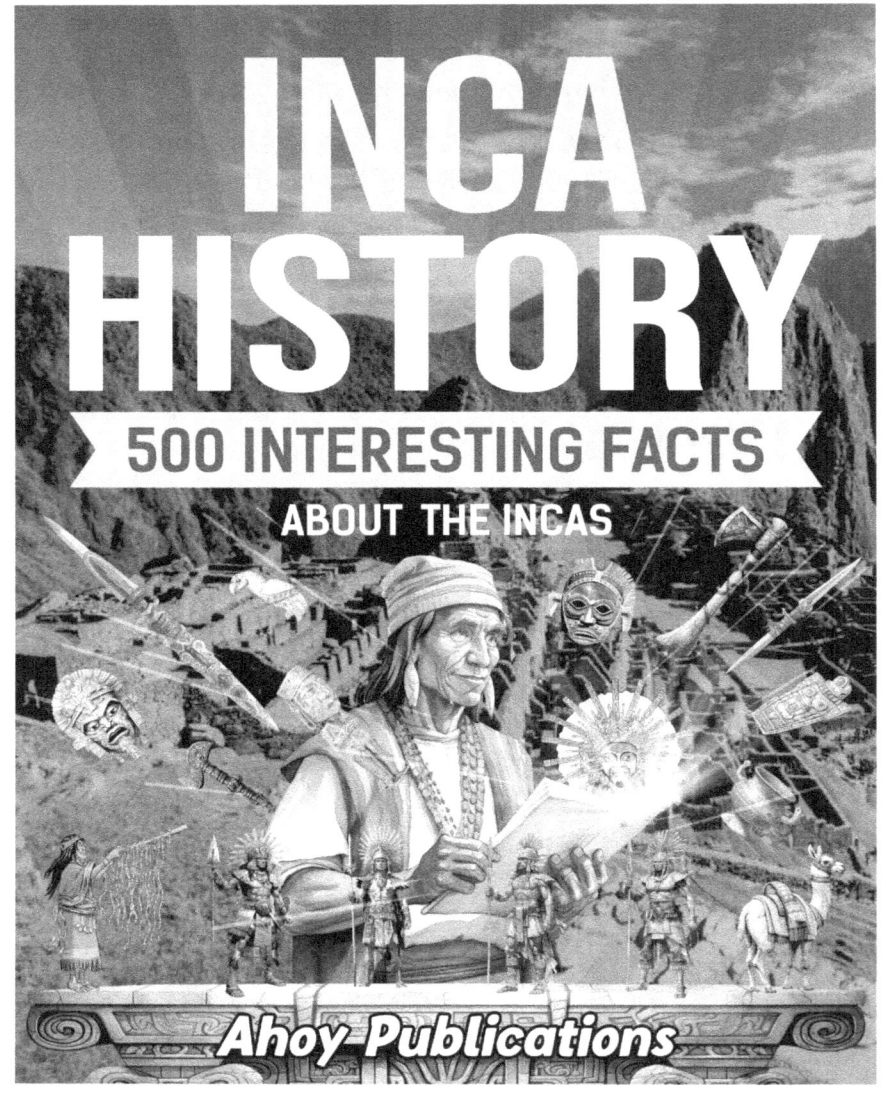

# Welcome Aboard, Check Out This Limited-Time Free Bonus!

Ahoy, reader! Welcome to the Ahoy Publications family, and thanks for snagging a copy of this book! Since you've chosen to join us on this journey, we'd like to offer you something special.

Check out the link below for a FREE e-book filled with delightful facts about American History.

But that's not all - you'll also have access to our exclusive email list with even more free e-books and insider knowledge. Well, what are ye waiting for? Click the link below to join and set sail toward exciting adventures in American History.

Access your bonus here: https://ahoypublications.com/

Or, Scan the QR code!

# References

**Part 1**

Abdou-Fitton, D. (2022a, August 29). onisi-paris. ÓNÍSÌ PARIS. https://onisi-paris.com/en/jewelry-from-the-world/what-defines-mexican-jewelry/

Barrios, A. (2023, August 10). What really caused the collapse of the Maya civilization? Premium. https://www.nationalgeographic.com/premium/article/mayan-empire-collapse-mystery

BBC - A History of the World - Object: Olmec stone mask. (2014a). Bbc.co.uk. https://www.bbc.co.uk/ahistoryoftheworld/objects/rxxK1FgBQNSsipmXhCIAXQ

Beginning and End of the Maya Classic Period (c. 250 CE–900 CE). (n.d.). Climate in Arts and History. https://www.science.smith.edu/climatelit/beginning-and-end-of-the-maya-classic-period/

Bruton, J. M. (2022, May 31). The Puma Mural Historical Marker. Hmdb.org. https://www.hmdb.org/m.asp?m=105734

Cartwright, M. (2018, April 27). Toltec Civilization. World History Encyclopedia. https://www.worldhistory.org/Toltec_Civilization/

Cartwright, M. (2021, January 22). Mesoamerican Civilizations. World History Encyclopedia. https://www.worldhistory.org/collection/109/mesoamerican-civilizations/

Cecil, J. (2011, February 17). BBC - History - Ancient History in depth: The Fall of the Mayan Civilisation. Www.bbc.co.uk. https://www.bbc.co.uk/history/ancient/cultures/maya_01.shtml

ContentKeeper Content Filtering. (2024). Mesoamericancivilizations.com. https://mesoamericancivilizations.com/mayan-language-and-cultural-revival/

drcegme. (2023). A Look at the Mixtec Semasiographic Writing System. Ufdatastudio.com. https://ufdatastudio.com/posts/2023-08-29-mixtec-blog/

Editorial. (2024, March 6). Exploring the Intricacies of Mixtec Codices and Writing - Mesoamerican Civilizations. The Insurance Universe. https://mesoamericancivilizations.com/mixtec-codices-and-writing/#Structure_and_Components_of_Mixtec_Codices

Editors, H. com. (2009, October 29). Maya. HISTORY. https://www.history.com/topics/ancient-americas/maya#mayan-pyramids-of-the-classic-maya-a-d-250-900

Exploring the Influence of Mexico's Pre-Columbian Architecture on Modern Art. (2024). Mexicohistorico.com. https://www.mexicohistorico.com/paginas/Exploring-the-Influence-of-Mexico---s-Pre-Columbian-Architecture-on-Modern-Art.html#google_vignette

Fery, G. (2020, October 23). Popular Archeology - Burning the Maya Books: The 1562 Tragedy at Mani. Popular Archeology. https://popular-archaeology.com/article/burning-the-maya-books-the-1562-tragedy-at-mani/

Geographic, N. (2023a, October 19). Olmec Civilization | National Geographic Society. Education.nationalgeographic.org. https://education.nationalgeographic.org/resource/olmec-civilization/

Gracht, C. R. van der. (2021, November 22). Teotihuacán, the enigmatic city at the center of the universe. Yucatán Magazine. https://yucatanmagazine.com/teotihuacan-the-enigmatic-city-at-the-center-of-the-universe/

GUGGENHEIM. (2004). The Aztec Empire. The Guggenheim Museums and Foundation. https://www.guggenheim.org/publication/the-aztec-empire

Hearn, K. (2017, January 1). Who Built the Great City of Teotihuacan? | National Geographic. History. https://www.nationalgeographic.com/history/article/teotihuacan

Heyworth, R. (2014, November 12). Teotihuacan: Temple of the Feathered-Serpent | Uncovered History. Uncovered History. https://uncoveredhistory.com/mexico/teotihuacan/teotihuacan-temple-of-the-feathered-serpent/

History Skills. (2014). Teotihuacan: The mysterious ancient city that continues to puzzle archaeologists. History Skills. https://www.historyskills.com/classroom/year-8/teotihuacan/?srsltid=AfmBOoqBvudGcho7_MQvwxS8pgMeW-cMPOjuyvChRMp8egb5da_h0Cdb

History.com Editors. (2009, October 27). Aztecs. History; A&E Television Networks. https://www.history.com/topics/ancient-americas/aztecs

King, H. (2019). Tenochtitlan: Templo Mayor. Metmuseum.org. https://www.metmuseum.org/toah/hd/teno_2/hd_teno_2.htm

Lambert, A. F. (2012). Olmec Ferox: Ritual Human Sacrifice IN THE ROCK ART OF CHALCATZINGO, MORELOS. Olmec Ferox: Ritual Human Sacrifice.

Legend of Quetzalcoatl Learn Spanish. (n.d.). Spanish School.uninter.edu.mx. https://spanishschool.uninter.edu.mx/Anniversary/Mexican-Culture/Legend-of-Quetzalcoatl

Maestri, N. (2019, July 3). Who Were the Ancient Warriors and Artisans Known as the Mixtecs? ThoughtCo. https://www.thoughtco.com/the-mixtec-culture-171769

Malones, L. (2021, April 30). 8 Pre-Hispanic Drinks To Sip In Mexico — Salt & Wind Travel. Salt & Wind Travel. https://saltandwind.com/pre-hispanic-drinks-sip-your-next-trip-mexico/

Meaney, M. T. (2022, May 1). The Aztecs: A Society with Great Influence on Modern Culture. Talk Diplomacy. https://www.talkdiplomacy.com/post/the-aztecs-a-society-with-great-influence-on-modern-culture

Mixtec and Zapotec. (2024). Blogspot.com. https://epicworldhistory.blogspot.com/2012/10/mixtec-and-zapotec.html

Mixtec Jewelry: Symbols of Power, Religion, and Status. (2024). Mexicohistorico.com. https://www.mexicohistorico.com/paginas/Mixtec-Jewelry--Symbols-of-Power--Religion--and-Status.html

Mixtec Mythology: Stories of the Gods and Heroes. (2024). Mexicohistorico.com. https://www.mexicohistorico.com/paginas/Mixtec-Mythology--Stories-of-the-Gods-and-Heroes.html

Mixtec: Codex Zouche-Nuttall (article) | Khan Academy. (n.d.). Khan Academy. https://www.khanacademy.org/humanities/art-americas/early-cultures/mixtec/a/mixtec-codex-zouche-nuttall

National Geographic Society. (2023, October 19). Aztec Civilization. Education.nationalgeographic.org; National Geographic. https://education.nationalgeographic.org/resource/aztec-civilization/

National Geographic. (n.d.). Mesoamerica. Education.nationalgeographic.org. https://education.nationalgeographic.org/resource/resource-library-mesoamerica/

Olmecs and the Civilizations of the Gulf of Mexico. (2024a). Pacmusee.qc.ca. https://pacmusee.qc.ca/en/press-room/press-releases/press-release-ol-mecs-mexico/

Peterson, L., & Haug, G. (2017, February 6). Climate and the Collapse of Maya Civilization. American Scientist. https://www.americanscientist.org/article/climate-and-the-collapse-of-maya-civilization

Pre-Hispanic Mixtec Codices. (n.d.). Www.mexicolore.co.uk. https://www.mexicolore.co.uk/aztecs/writing/introduction-to-mixtec-codices

Schmal, J. (2019). The Mixtecs and Zapotecs: Two Enduring Cultures of Oaxaca. Indigenous Mexico. https://www.indigenousmexico.org/articles/the-mixtecs-and-zapotecs-two-enduring-cultures-of-oaxaca

Schwerin, von. (2011). THE SACRED MOUNTAIN IN SOCIAL CONTEXT. SYMBOLISM AND HISTORY IN MAYA ARCHITECTURE: TEMPLE 22 AT COPAN, HONDURAS. Ancient Mesoamerica, 22(2), 271–300. http://www.jstor.org/stable/26309376

Spanish Invasion | Mesoamerican Cultures and their Histories. (n.d.). Blogs.uoregon.edu. https://blogs.uoregon.edu/mesoinstitute/about/curriculum-unit-development/spanish-conquest/

The Aftermath of the Spanish Conquest on Mesoamerican Civilization. (2024). Mexicohistorico.com. https://www.mexicohistorico.com/paginas/The-Aftermath-of-the-Spanish-Conquest-on-Mesoamerican-Civilization.html

The Artistic Legacy of the Toltecs in Mesoamerica. (2024). Mexicohistorico.com. https://www.mexicohistorico.com/paginas/The-Artistic-Legacy-of-the-Toltecs-in-Mesoamerica.html

The Influence of the Zapotecs on the Mixtecs. (2024). Mexicohistorico.com. https://www.mexicohistorico.com/paginas/The-Influence-of-the-Zapotecs-on-the-Mixtecs.html

The Met. (2022). Teotihuacan: Mural Painting. Metmuseum.org. https://www.metmuseum.org/toah/hd/teot4/hd_teot4.htm

The Met. (n.d.). Teotihuacan-Style Hollow Figurine with Removable Chest Plate | Escuintla. The Metropolitan Museum of Art. Retrieved November 4, 2024, from https://www.metmuseum.org/art/collection/search/684338

The Mixtec Influence on the Zapotec Civilization. (2024). Mexicohistorico.com. https://www.mexicohistorico.com/paginas/The-Mixtec-Influence-on-the-Zapotec-Civilization.html

The Olmec Gods and Goddesses: Unveiling the Ancient Deities of Mesoamerica - Old World Gods. (2023a, November 21). Oldworldgods.com. https://oldworldgods.com/other/the-olmec-gods-and-goddesses/

The Toltecs | World Civilization. (n.d.). Courses.lumenlearning.com. https://courses.lumenlearning.com/suny-hccc-worldcivilization/chapter/the-toltecs/

Toltec Civilization | History Timeline. (2019). History Timelines. https://historytimelines.co/timeline/toltec-civilization

Toltec Writing Systems: Glyphs and Symbols in Temples and Art. (2024). Mexicohistorico.com. https://www.mexicohistorico.com/paginas/Toltec-Writing-Systems--Glyphs-and-Symbols-in-Temples-and-Art.html#google_vignette

USA-NC. (2020, December 9). The Rise and Fall of Mayan Civilization. New Acropolis Library. https://library.acropolis.org/the-rise-and-fall-of-mayan-civilization/

Van Dop Dejesus, J. (2023, February 21). Aztec civilization. History. https://kids.nationalgeographic.com/history/article/aztec-civilization

Zapotec Mythology: Stories of the Gods and Creation. (2024). Mexicohistorico.com. https://www.mexicohistorico.com/paginas/Zapotec-Mythology--Stories-of-the-Gods-and-Creation.html

Zorich, Z. (2024, October 3). The Maya Sense of Time - The Maya Codices - Archaeology Magazine - November/December 2012. Archaeology Magazine. https://archaeology.org/issues/november-december-2012/collection/groiler-dresden-codex/the-maya-sense-of-time/

**Part 2**

Captivating History. *History of Mexico*. 2020.

Jaffary, Nora. *Mexican History: A Primary Source Reader*. 2009.

O'Neill, Bill. *The Great Book of Mexico: Interesting Stories, Mexican History & Random Facts About Mexico*. 2020.

Shawcross, Edward. *The Last Great Emperor of Mexico*. 2021.

Sherman, William. *The Course of Mexican History*. 1979.

Smith, Benjamin. *The Dope: The Real History of the Mexican Drug Trade*. 2021.

# Image References

1  Gary Todd, CC0, via Wikimedia Commons. https://commons.wikimedia.org/wiki/File:Olmec_Green_Stone_Mask_with_Traces_of_Cinnabar.jpg

2  Mariordo (Mario Roberto Durán Ortiz), CC BY-SA 4.0 <https://creativecommons.org/licenses/by-sa/4.0>, via Wikimedia Commons. https://commons.wikimedia.org/wiki/File:Garra_Alada_Olmeca_Museo_de_Jade_INS_CRI_01_2020_4282.jpg

3  Madman2001, CC BY-SA 3.0 <https://creativecommons.org/licenses/by-sa/3.0>, via Wikimedia Commons. https://commons.wikimedia.org/wiki/File:Small_Olmec_Figurines_(Met).jpg.

4  andrésmh, CC BY-SA 2.0 <https://creativecommons.org/licenses/by-sa/2.0>, via Wikimedia Commos. https://commons.wikimedia.org/wiki/File:Olmec_woman.jpg

5  Gary Todd, CC0, via Wikimedia Commons. https://commons.wikimedia.org/wiki/File:Olmec_Stone_%22Wrestler,%22_Veracruz,_Protoclassic,_600-100_BC,_66cm.jpg

6  https://www.flickr.com/photos/rosemania/, CC BY 2.0 <https://creativecommons.org/licenses/by/2.0>, via Wikimedia Commons. https://commons.wikimedia.org/wiki/File:Seated_Olmec_Jaguar_from_San_Lorenzo,_Veracruz.jpg

7  Wikipedia Loves Art participant "artifacts," CC BY 2.5 <https://creativecommons.org/licenses/by/2.5>, via Wikimedia Commons. https://commons.wikimedia.org/wiki/File:WLA_lacma_Olmec_jadeite_pendants.jpg

8  Gary Todd, CC0, via Wikimedia Commons. https://commons.wikimedia.org/wiki/File:Olmec_Monument_19,_La_Venta,_1300-400_BC.jpg

9  Madman2001, CC BY-SA 3.0 <https://creativecommons.org/licenses/by-sa/3.0>, via Wikimedia Commons. https://commons.wikimedia.org/wiki/File:Olmec_bloodletting_spoon.jpg

10 Simon Burchell, CC BY-SA 3.0 <https://creativecommons.org/licenses/by-sa/3.0>, via Wikimedia Commons. https://commons.wikimedia.org/wiki/File:Olmec_bird-man_head,_Museo_de_Am%C3%A9rica.jpg

11 Interfase, Public domain, via Wikimedia Commons. https://commons.wikimedia.org/wiki/File:Bat_god.jpg

12 Siren-Com, CC BY-SA 3.0 <https://creativecommons.org/licenses/by-sa/3.0>, via Wikimedia Commons. https://commons.wikimedia.org/wiki/File:Vase_effigie_Zapot%C3%A8que_2.jpg

13 Wolfgang Sauber, CC BY-SA 3.0 <https://creativecommons.org/licenses/by-sa/3.0>, via Wikimedia Commons. https://commons.wikimedia.org/wiki/File:Monte_Alb%C3%A1n_-_Priesterfigur.jpg

14 © José Luiz Bernardes Ribeiro. https://commons.wikimedia.org/wiki/File:Statue_of_Zapotec_god_Pitao_Cozobi_from_Tututepec_(200-500_BCE)_-_Oaxaca_-_National_Museum_of_Antropology_-_Mexico_2024.jpg

15 Walters Art Museum, Public domain, via Wikimedia Commons. https://commons.wikimedia.org/wiki/File:Zapotec_-_Vessel_of_a_Bat_Foot_with_Claws_-_Walters_2006153_-_Three_Quarter.jpg

16 Walters Art Museum, Public domain, via Wikimedia Commons. https://commons.wikimedia.org/wiki/File:Zapotec_-_Figural_Urn_of_a_Masked_Deity_-_Walters_2006158_-_Three_Quarter.jpg

17 Cleveland Museum of Art, CC0, via Wikimedia Commons. https://commons.wikimedia.org/wiki/File:Mexico,_Oaxaca,_Zapotec,_6th-8th_Century_-_Pendant_Plaque_-_1948.358_-_Cleveland_Museum_of_Art.tif

18 Cleveland Museum of Art, CC0, via Wikimedia Commons. https://commons.wikimedia.org/wiki/File:Mexico,_Oaxaca,_Zapotec_-_Urn_Figure_Head_Fragment_-_1990.275_-_Cleveland_Museum_of_Art.tif

19 Daderot, CC0, via Wikimedia Commons. https://commons.wikimedia.org/wiki/File:Snake_creature_-_Monte_Alban_pottery_-_Ethnological_Museum,_Berlin_-_DSC00894.JPG

20 Walters Art Museum, Public domain, via Wikimedia Commons. https://commons.wikimedia.org/wiki/File:Zapotec_-_Effigy_Urn_of_Cocijo_-_Walters_482788_-_Three_Quarter.jpg

21 Simon Burchell, CC BY-SA 4.0 <https://creativecommons.org/licenses/by-sa/4.0>, via Wikimedia Commons.
https://commons.wikimedia.org/wiki/File:Jaguar_paddler_god,_Ixlu_Stela_2.jpg

22 Walters Art Museum, Public domain, via Wikimedia Commons.
https://commons.wikimedia.org/wiki/File:Mayan_-_Dwarf_Figurine_-_Walters_20092036_-_View_A.jpg

23 Walters Art Museum, Public domain, via Wikimedia Commons.
https://commons.wikimedia.org/wiki/File:Mayan_-_Face_Pendant_-_Walters_2009208_-_View_A.jpg

24 Adam Jones, CC BY-SA 2.0 <https://creativecommons.org/licenses/by-sa/2.0>, via Wikimedia Commons.
https://commons.wikimedia.org/wiki/File:Original_Mayan_Calendar_Stone_-_El_Cedral_-_Cozumel_-_Mexico.jpg

25 Zde, CC BY-SA 4.0 <https://creativecommons.org/licenses/by-sa/4.0>, via Wikimedia Commons.
https://commons.wikimedia.org/wiki/File:Mayan_woman,_ceramic_sculpture,_Classic_period_of_Mayan,_NM_Prague,_191512.jpg

26 Metropolitan Museum of Art, CC0, via Wikimedia Commons.
https://commons.wikimedia.org/wiki/File:Earflare_Set_MET_VS1994_35_591.jpeg

27 Walters Art Museum, Public domain, via Wikimedia Commons.
https://commons.wikimedia.org/wiki/File:Mayan_-_Warrior_Figurine_-_Walters_20092038.jpg

28 Jebulon, CC BY-SA 4.0 <https://creativecommons.org/licenses/by-sa/4.0>, via Wikimedia Commons.
https://commons.wikimedia.org/wiki/File:Disque_Chichen_Itza_Mayas_cropped.jpg

29 Gary Todd, CC0, via Wikimedia Commons.
https://commons.wikimedia.org/wiki/File:Maya_Jade_Artifacts.jpg

30 amanderson2, CC BY 2.0 <https://creativecommons.org/licenses/by/2.0>, via Wikimedia Commons. https://commons.wikimedia.org/wiki/File:Jade_Mask_660-750_AD_found_in_tomb_of_Ruler_laying_by_him_when_excavated_in_1984.jpg

31 Vhlafuente at English Wikipedia, CC BY 3.0 <https://creativecommons.org/licenses/by/3.0>, via Wikimedia Commons
https://commons.wikimedia.org/wiki/File:Jaguar_Mural,_Teotihuacán.jpg

32 Daniel Case, CC BY-SA 3.0 <https://creativecommons.org/licenses/by-sa/3.0>, via Wikimedia Commons
https://commons.wikimedia.org/wiki/File:Pyramid_of_the_Moon_from_Pyramid_of_the_Sun,_Teotihuacán,_in_sunlight.jpg

33 NASA/METI/AIST/Japan Space Systems, and U.S./Japan ASTER Science Team, Public domain, via Wikimedia Commons
https://commons.wikimedia.org/wiki/File:Teotihuacán,_Mexico_(ASTER).jpg

34 Rene Trohs, CC BY-SA 4.0 <https://creativecommons.org/licenses/by-sa/4.0>, via Wikimedia Commons
https://commons.wikimedia.org/wiki/File:Panoramic_view_of_Teotihuacán.jpg

35 HighVibrationStation, CC BY-SA 4.0 <https://creativecommons.org/licenses/by-sa/4.0>, via Wikimedia Commons
https://commons.wikimedia.org/wiki/File:Teotihuacán_serpent.jpg

36 Eric Polk, CC BY-SA 4.0 <https://creativecommons.org/licenses/by-sa/4.0>, via Wikimedia Commons
https://commons.wikimedia.org/wiki/File:Teotihuacán_old_man_fire_god_censer_NHMLA.png

37 Juan Carlos Fonseca Mata, CC BY-SA 4.0 <https://creativecommons.org/licenses/by-sa/4.0>, via Wikimedia Commons
https://commons.wikimedia.org/wiki/File:Gran_Diosa_de_Teotihuacán_-_Mural_del_Tlalocan_de_Tepantitla.jpg

38 Mary Harrsch, CC BY-SA 4.0 <https://creativecommons.org/licenses/by-sa/4.0>, via Wikimedia Commons
https://commons.wikimedia.org/wiki/File:Ceramic_Crouching_Dog_Effigy_Vessel_from_Teotihuacán_300-600_CE_at_the_Penn_Museum.jpg

39 © José Luiz Bernardes Ribeiro
https://commons.wikimedia.org/wiki/File:Teotihuac%C3%A1n_-_Temple_of_Quetzalcoatl_(replica)_-_National_Museum_of_Antropology_-_Mexico_2024.jpg

40 Eric Polk, CC BY-SA 4.0 <https://creativecommons.org/licenses/by-sa/4.0>, via Wikimedia Commons
https://commons.wikimedia.org/wiki/File:Teotihuac%C3%A1n_open_chest_figure_NHMLA.png

41 Eric Polk, CC BY-SA 4.0 <https://creativecommons.org/licenses/by-sa/4.0>, via Wikimedia Commons

https://commons.wikimedia.org/wiki/File:Toltec_block_with_glyphs_front_NHMLA.png

42 CarlosL96, CC BY-SA 4.0 <https://creativecommons.org/licenses/by-sa/4.0>, via Wikimedia Commons https://commons.wikimedia.org/wiki/File:Toltec_Head.jpg

43 AlejandroLinaresGarcia, CC BY-SA 3.0 <https://creativecommons.org/licenses/by-sa/3.0>, via Wikimedia Commons https://commons.wikimedia.org/wiki/File:TulaSite21.JPG

44 https://commons.wikimedia.org/w/index.php?curid=30843098

45 Sailko, CC BY 3.0 <https://creativecommons.org/licenses/by/3.0>, via Wikimedia Commons https://commons.wikimedia.org/wiki/File:Messico,_toltechi-aztechi,_ornamenti_del_serpente_piumato,_XI-XV_sec,_oro_sbalzato.JPG

46 Gary Todd, CC0, via Wikimedia Commons https://commons.wikimedia.org/wiki/File:Toltec_Stone_Throne,_Early_Postclassic,_900-1250_AD.jpg

47 Mabarlabin, CC BY-SA 3.0 <https://creativecommons.org/licenses/by-sa/3.0>, via Wikimedia Commons https://commons.wikimedia.org/wiki/File:Toltec_influence.jpg

48 See page for author, CC BY 4.0 <https://creativecommons.org/licenses/by/4.0>, via Wikimedia Commons https://commons.wikimedia.org/wiki/File:Mexican_pottery_figure_representing_Ocelot,_Toltec_period_Wellcome_M0012360.jpg

49 Musée du quai Branly, CC BY-SA 2.0 FR <https://creativecommons.org/licenses/by-sa/2.0/fr/deed.en>, via Wikimedia Commons https://commons.wikimedia.org/wiki/File:Quetzalcoatl-71.1878.1.59-DSC00065-white.jpg

50 See page for author, Public domain, via Wikimedia Commons https://commons.wikimedia.org/wiki/File:Quetzalc%C3%B3atl_como_la_serpiente_emplumada_y_el_dios_del_viento_Eh%C3%A9catl,_en_el_folio_19.jpg

51 An author from the Mixteca region c.1500, CC BY-SA 4.0 <https://creativecommons.org/licenses/by-sa/4.0>, via Wikimedia Commons https://commons.wikimedia.org/wiki/File:Codex_Zouche-Nuttall_-_Lord_12_Rain_%27Coyote%27_(from_Guaxolotitlan)_pays_hommage.png

52 Walters Art Museum, Public domain, via Wikimedia Commons https://commons.wikimedia.org/wiki/File:Mixtec_-

_Polychrome_Standing_Figure_with_Raised_Hand_-_Walters_482812_-_Three_Quarter.jpg

53 hiart, CC0, via Wikimedia Commons
https://commons.wikimedia.org/wiki/File:Slate_mask_of_Tlaloc_(the_rain_god),_Mixtec_people,_Valley_of_Oaxaca,_c._900-1200_CE.JPG

54 Michel Wal, CC BY-SA 3.0 <https://creativecommons.org/licenses/by-sa/3.0>, via Wikimedia Commons https://commons.wikimedia.org/wiki/File:Mixtec_shield.jpg

55 Gary Todd, CC0, via Wikimedia Commons
https://commons.wikimedia.org/wiki/File:Mixtec_Ceramic_Censer.jpg

56 Daderot, CC0, via Wikimedia Commons
https://commons.wikimedia.org/wiki/File:Ceremonial_knife,_Mexico,_Alta_Highlands,_Mixtec,_c._1200-1500_AD,_obsidian,_turquoise,_spondylus_shell,_resin_-_De_Young_Museum_-_DSC00408.JPG

57 Gary Todd, CC0, via Wikimedia Commons
https://commons.wikimedia.org/wiki/File:Mixtec_Ceremonial_Vessel_(Xantile)_Lid_Combining_Aspects_of_Gods_Xochipilli_%26_Xiuhtecuhtli.jpg

58 Metropolitan Museum of Art, CC0, via Wikimedia Commons
https://commons.wikimedia.org/wiki/File:Pendant_MET_DP216447.jpg

59 Thelmadatter, CC BY-SA 3.0 <https://creativecommons.org/licenses/by-sa/3.0>, via Wikimedia Commons
https://commons.wikimedia.org/wiki/File:MixtecPlaqueCuilapam.JPG

60 ArbyBB, CC BY-SA 4.0 <https://creativecommons.org/licenses/by-sa/4.0>, via Wikimedia Commons
https://commons.wikimedia.org/wiki/File:Top_of_mixtec_tree_of_life.jpg

61 By Anónimo, probablemente del 1566. - Códice Selden, Public Domain,
https://commons.wikimedia.org/w/index.php?curid=41724346

62 An author from the Mixtec region, CC BY-SA 4.0
<https://creativecommons.org/licenses/by-sa/4.0>, via Wikimedia Commons
https://commons.wikimedia.org/wiki/File:Codex_Bodley_-_Lord_8_Grass_king_of_Tlaxiaco_and_1st_wife_Lady_9_Deer.png

63 An author from the Mixteca region c.1500, CC BY-SA 4.0
<https://creativecommons.org/licenses/by-sa/4.0>, via Wikimedia Commons
https://commons.wikimedia.org/wiki/File:Codex_Zouche-Nuttall_-_8_Deer_Jaguar_Claw.png

64 A mixtec author from the 16th century, CC BY-SA 4.0
<https://creativecommons.org/licenses/by-sa/4.0>, via Wikimedia Commons
https://commons.wikimedia.org/wiki/File:Codex_Selden_-_Lord_9_Lizard_king_of_Jaltepec.png

65 An author from the Mixteca region c.1500, CC BY-SA 4.0
<https://creativecommons.org/licenses/by-sa/4.0>, via Wikimedia Commons
https://commons.wikimedia.org/wiki/File:Codex_Zouche-Nuttall_-_Lady_12_Flower_queen_of_Tilantongo.png

66 An author from the Mixtec region, CC BY-SA 4.0
<https://creativecommons.org/licenses/by-sa/4.0>, via Wikimedia Commons
https://commons.wikimedia.org/wiki/File:Codex_Bodley_-_Lord_8_Deer_of_Tlaxiaco_king_of_Zaachila.png

67 Lienzo de Guevea, Public domain, via Wikimedia Commons
https://commons.wikimedia.org/wiki/File:Cosiiopii_II.png

68 An author from the Mixteca region c.1500, CC BY-SA 4.0
<https://creativecommons.org/licenses/by-sa/4.0>, via Wikimedia Commons
https://commons.wikimedia.org/wiki/File:Codex_Zouche-Nuttall_-_Lord_5_Reed_king_of_Zaachila.png

69 Noah Edits, CC BY-SA 4.0 <https://creativecommons.org/licenses/by-sa/4.0>, via Wikimedia Commons
https://commons.wikimedia.org/wiki/File:Zapotec_in_Oaxaca.svg

70 Gary Todd, CC0, via Wikimedia Commons
https://commons.wikimedia.org/wiki/File:Zapotec_Ceramic_Jaguar-shaped_Urn,_Monte_Alban_III.jpg

71 Diego Duran, Public domain, via Wikimedia Commons
https://commons.wikimedia.org/wiki/File:Aztec_ritual_for_flooding.jpg

72 Gary Francisco Keller, artwork created under the supervision of Bernardino de Sahagún between 1540 and 1585. CC BY 3.0
<https://creativecommons.org/licenses/by/3.0>, via Wikimedia Commons
https://commons.wikimedia.org/wiki/File:The_Florentine_Codex-_Aztec_Rituals.tiff

73 Musée du quai Branly, CC BY-SA 2.0 FR <https://creativecommons.org/licenses/by-sa/2.0/fr/deed.en>, via Wikimedia Commons
https://commons.wikimedia.org/wiki/File:Teponaztli_ritual_drum-71.1952.71.1-DSC00055.JPG

74 DanielElisalde1, CC BY-SA 4.0 <https://creativecommons.org/licenses/by-sa/4.0>, via Wikimedia Commons
https://commons.wikimedia.org/wiki/File:Aztec_ritual_interpretation.jpg

75 Gary Todd, CC0, via Wikimedia Commons
https://commons.wikimedia.org/wiki/File:Aztec_Ceremonial_Tomb_to_Bury_Ritual_Sculptures_Which_Symbolize_52-Year_Cycle_(Like_Our_Century).jpg

76 See page for author, Public domain, via Wikimedia Commons
https://commons.wikimedia.org/wiki/File:Codex_Magliabechiano_(folio_30).jpg

77 Metropolitan Museum of Art, CC0, via Wikimedia Commons
https://commons.wikimedia.org/wiki/File:Ritual_Stone_(pulidor)_MET_1989.314.6.jpg

78 Arjuno3, CC BY-SA 4.0 <https://creativecommons.org/licenses/by-sa/4.0>, via Wikimedia Commons
https://commons.wikimedia.org/wiki/File:Aztec_Skull_Mask_from_Templo_Mayor,_Tenochtitlan_(DSC08002a).jpg

79 Gary Todd, CC0, via Wikimedia Commons
https://commons.wikimedia.org/wiki/File:Aztec_Chapulin_(Grasshopper),_Symbol_of_Chapultepec.jpg

80 Arjuno3, CC BY-SA 4.0 <https://creativecommons.org/licenses/by-sa/4.0>, via Wikimedia Commons
https://commons.wikimedia.org/wiki/File:Aztec_offerings_(DSC08010b).jpg

81 Colocho, Public domain, via Wikimedia Commons
https://commons.wikimedia.org/wiki/File:Iximch%C3%A9.JPG

82 Simon Burchell, CC BY-SA 4.0 <https://creativecommons.org/licenses/by-sa/4.0>, via Wikimedia Commons
https://commons.wikimedia.org/wiki/File:Plaza_of_the_Seven_Temples,_Tikal_22.jpg

83 Arian Zwegers from Brussels, Belgium, CC BY 2.0 <https://creativecommons.org/licenses/by/2.0>, via Wikimedia Commons
https://commons.wikimedia.org/wiki/File:Calakmul,_Structure_II_(14386305393).jpg

84 Bernard DUPONT, CC BY-SA 2.0 <https://creativecommons.org/licenses/by-sa/2.0>, via Wikimedia Commons
https://commons.wikimedia.org/wiki/File:Temple_of_the_Sun_(left),_Temple_XIV_and_the_Palace_(right)_from_the_top_of_Temple_of_the_Cross_-_Palenque_Maya_Site,_Feb_2020.jpg

85 Adalberto Hernandez Vega from Copan Ruinas, Honduras, CC BY 2.0 <https://creativecommons.org/licenses/by/2.0>, via Wikimedia Commons https://commons.wikimedia.org/wiki/File:Cop%C3%A1n_Ballcourt.jpg

86 Joeldesalvatierra, CC BY-SA 3.0 <https://creativecommons.org/licenses/by-sa/3.0>, via Wikimedia Commons https://commons.wikimedia.org/wiki/File:Mayapan_perspectiva_1.jpg

87 Infrogmation, CC BY-SA 4.0 <https://creativecommons.org/licenses/by-sa/4.0>, via Wikimedia Commons https://commons.wikimedia.org/wiki/File:Uxmal_Adivino_3.jpg

88 Asdfjrjjj, CC BY-SA 4.0 <https://creativecommons.org/licenses/by-sa/4.0>, via Wikimedia Commons https://commons.wikimedia.org/wiki/File:Mopan_Territory_map.png

89 Unknown Maya scribe(s), Public domain, via Wikimedia Commons https://commons.wikimedia.org/wiki/File:Paris_Codex,_pages_23-24.jpg

90 Matt Zimmerman, CC BY 2.0 <https://creativecommons.org/licenses/by/2.0>, via Wikimedia Commons https://commons.wikimedia.org/wiki/File:Amazon_slash_and_burn_agriculture_Colombia_South_America.jpg

91 Photo by Infrogmation of New Orleans or one of his parents, CC BY-SA 3.0 <https://creativecommons.org/licenses/by-sa/3.0>, via Wikimedia Commons https://commons.wikimedia.org/wiki/File:Merida75ParqueAmericasKukulkanob.jpg

92 Dig Downtown Detroit, CC BY 2.0 <https://creativecommons.org/licenses/by/2.0>, via Wikimedia Commons https://commons.wikimedia.org/wiki/File:Fisher_Building_Lobby_(4634810509).jpg

93 Flickr user Living in Monrovia, CC BY-SA 2.0 <https://creativecommons.org/licenses/by-sa/2.0>, via Wikimedia Commons https://commons.wikimedia.org/wiki/File:Aztec_Hotel

94 Postcard, Public domain, via Wikimedia Commons https://commons.wikimedia.org/wiki/File:Imperial_Hotel_Tky.jpg

95 Luis Alvaz, CC BY-SA 4.0 <https://creativecommons.org/licenses/by-sa/4.0>, via Wikimedia Commons https://commons.wikimedia.org/wiki/File:Carnaval_de_la_vida_mexicana,_pol%C3%ADptico_de_Diego_Rivera_en_el_Palacio_de_Bellas_Artes_01.jpg

96 Marrovi, CC BY-SA 4.0 <https://creativecommons.org/licenses/by-sa/4.0>, via Wikimedia Commons
https://commons.wikimedia.org/wiki/File:Culiac%C3%A1n_(32).jpg

97 Gary Todd from Xinzheng, China, CC0, via Wikimedia Commons
https://commons.wikimedia.org/wiki/File:Bronze_Surrealist_Sculpture_of_Crocodile_by_Leonora_Carrington_(9779062745).jpg

98 Muzammil, CC BY-SA 4.0 <https://creativecommons.org/licenses/by-sa/4.0>, via Wikimedia Commons
https://commons.wikimedia.org/wiki/File:Mexican_Traditional_Dance1.JPG

99 Diego Durán, Public domain, via Wikimedia Commons
https://commons.wikimedia.org/wiki/File:Hern%C3%A1n_Cort%C3%A9s_and_La_Malinche_1576_Dur%C3%A1n_Codex.jpg

100 John Ferguson / Aqueduct https://commons.wikimedia.org/wiki/File:Aqueduct_-_geograph.org.uk_-_1176814.jpg